T0381447

Fate

What ever is meant for you

John Glass

authorHOUSE®

AuthorHouse™ UK
1663 Liberty Drive
Bloomington, IN 47403 USA
www.authorhouse.co.uk
Phone: UK TFN: 0800 0148641 (Toll Free inside the UK)
*   UK Local: (02) 0369 56322 (+44 20 3695 6322 from outside the UK)*

Published by AuthorHouse 11/26/2024

ISBN: 979-8-8230-9083-4 (sc)
ISBN: 979-8-8230-9084-1 (e)

Library of Congress Control Number: 2024924445

Print information available on the last page.

Contents

Chapter 1

The Letter

One morning in June 2018, Dave was sitting in his garden enjoying the warmth from the early morning sun, a letter arrived and was passed to him by his wife. On the envelope in bold print his old address where he had lived back in 1964. This was scored out and his present address penned along the bottom. Gazing at the envelope, his eye was caught by the faint postmark; it was dated two months earlier and posted in Nottingham, England. Dave mused, *'now here's a letter that's been desperate to reach me.'* As he carefully opened the envelope, he pondered what mysterious news would surprise him from within.

Removing the letter, it started.

'Hello David,

I hope you don't mind me calling you David, as that was the only name my mother used when she spoke of you.'

Of the first few words, he didn't recognize the writing style of anyone he knew. As he read on, in the back of his mind the feeling increased that there was a similarity to handwriting he hadn't seen in a long, long time.

'*I'm sure you won't remember me for I was only eighteen-months old when you first knew me. My married name now is Victoria Langdon, but my name then was Victoria Hingham. My mother's name was Lynne.*'

Lynne, he contemplated with great affection, *now that is a name that I remember.* He sat pondering over the name, memories from the past flooded back, filling his thoughts of the times he had spent with her family when out in Malaya, all those years ago.

Victoria's letter went on to say that Lynne had died after being fatally injured in a car crash. Those words of her death although only on paper, gave him a jolt and a tear formed in his eyes as a pang of sadness swept over him. Victoria's words went on to say that she herself had been forty-five years old when the accident happened.

His hand holding the letter dropped, and it slipped from his grasp as the sadness in his heart grew stronger for someone special, whom he had cared for a long, long time ago.

As Dave endeavoured to control his emotion, he raised his head and stared at the clear blue sky as though searching for something, what, he knew not. Shaking his head in dismay, he was surprised at how strong his feelings were at that moment. After a few minutes had past, he settled and the memories of good times swept through him and momentarily his world stood still as a picture of Lynne's face, came into his thoughts. Her face that morning was as vivid to him then, as it had been when they first met all those years ago. These thoughts filled him, and he recalled all the laughter and tender moments stolen, and of how these times had kept him alive with hope when he could not perceive any future after his National Service time was up.

It was then that he remembered her parting words to him

when their lives went different paths. 'Be happy, and remember I love you.'

Picking up the letter, Victoria's words went on to tell all about their life with Lynne after her separation from Mike their dad. She also wrote of her mum's subsequent trials of courtship with other men whom she never found happiness with.

It was what she wrote next that shook him,

'As my brother Mike and I grew older, mother told us of a young National Service soldier called David that she had met when out in Malaya. Mother said that he had befriended her at a time when she was desperately in need of a friend. It was not until just before mother's accident that we learned the full truth when she showed us a photo of you, and that you were that soldier, and about how much you had meant to her.

As the words flowed from her pen, what she wrote next, filled his heart with a warm feeling.

Mother told me that she never again found the same kind of affection, that both she and you had had for one another during that brief time you were together. She also told me, if anything happened to her, I was to let you know how she felt about you and to thank you for sharing that time with her.

She concluded with an apology for not having sent a letter sooner, as it had only been lately that she had come across his old address.

Even as he sat reminiscing, he felt he wasn't alone, for in his memories he could sense her fragrance all around him, and as the tears that had formed started to cloud his eyes, he mused, *'after all those years, she had remembered me as I still do her at this moment in time, with fondness.'*

3

Victoria's letter started him thinking of Lynne in a way he had not done for a long time, and he felt once more a depth of sadness at the news of her death. Sitting back letting his memories engulf him, releasing thoughts that had been deeply stored away in the back of his mind and never spoken of since meeting his wife. However, the news of Lynne's death had stirred up those long-forgotten memories and he found himself, being drawn back in time as he relived the days when out in Malaya, and of his own narrow escape with death.

Chapter 2

Malaya

The train, on its way south from the northern town of Alor Sitar near the Thailand border, had stopped at the town of Butterworth. There troops and their families were eager to board for their journey south to Singapore where a ship, was waiting to sail them on the last leg of their odyssey to Britain.

Dave Walters watched from his compartment window with envy as the troops boarded. Some were National Servicemen having completed their service in Malaya, while others were professional soldiers who had been here for three years or more. Most had spent the last few months fighting in the northern Malaysian jungles, pushing the communist threat further north, where it was now contained along the borders of Malaya and Thailand in the Provinces of Kedah and Perak.

With the hostilities in the north concentrated in small pockets and decreasing in resistance. In preparation for the day when Regular Malay troops would take over and defend their own country, some British units were being withdrawn from Malaya. Although that final day was still some way off.

As Dave scrutinized them, their kit by their side, patiently waiting their turn to board, his thought at that moment were, '*this must be a happy occasion for them, especially the National Servicemen, for now they needn't cross the days off their calendars, as their time here in Malaya was over, and they were now due for de-mob.*' Dave, like most of these young National Servicemen having been drafted grudgingly into the army. Over time, he knew, some had taken to army life and signed on as regular soldiers, however most will go back home better for their experiences, assured in what they wanted to do with their lives.

Observing the last of them to climb on board, Dave smiled at the thought of when they got home. As with all soldiers that have served in these tropics, some bad habits may still linger on, drinking, swearing, and walking about naked with only a small towel to cover their embarrassments. Their biggest problem he mused, when back home, asking local girls for some 'jig a jig' as if they were dance hall girls. His smile broadened at the thought of them spending the evening explaining what they meant.

On this journey the regular soldier's wives and children separated from their loved ones, travelled in the first-class compartments. Their husbands along with their regiments travelled economy. Over the last few years between skirmishes with the insurgents, these same troops had returned to their camps to regroup and have a well-earned rest.

Having lived a good life around Butterworth and on the beautiful paradise island of Pinang, that must now come to an end as their time here is over. Their husbands had done their stint for Queen and country, and another new chapter of their lives was about to begin. They were now all going home to dear old Blighty, in some cases with young children who having been born here in Malaysia, and only knew this country.

Casting his eye around the station, now emptied of troops, Dave, having been here many times over the past few weeks, was now quite familiar with Butterworth. A typical Malay town of size having a few thousand residents, a shopping centre, where most of the tradesmen were of Chinese descent, and lived above their shops. These businesses catered for the indigenous Malays and local foreign nationalities, like people from India, Indonesians, Burma, and the Commonwealth troops stationed around the area. There was also a small permanent market in the centre of the town, selling just about everything from watches to fresh fruit and vegetables.

A lot of the indigenous Malays though, preferred to live in homes built on stilts on the outskirts of town in small Kampongs or Villages, surrounded by the rice paddy fields nearby. The main asset of Butterworth was the ferry that plied its trade back and forth to George Town, on the Island of Pinang. Butterworth, he also learnt, was the main northern railway link and supply point for Commonwealth troops stationed in and around, and further north.

The station Master flagged the train out of the station at around twenty-two hundred hours that evening, and as the locomotive rolled along the track picking up speed, Dave picked up his western book and settled down to read, in hope for another peaceful night's duty.

Chapter 3

Where am I?

It began with a long loud screeching noise as the brakes were applied. Deep rumbling sounds followed as the wheels locked with a sudden thump. Carriages lurched throwing passengers violently around like rag dolls. The locomotive slowly slid off the track and stopped only after it rolled onto its side among the jungle vegetation, steam rising from its boiler. The carriages directly behind, creaked and groaned as they followed one by one, turning sideways, and jammed.

The remaining carriages broke their couplings, and luckily for most of the passengers, with a sudden jolt, stayed upright as the emergency brakes held.

The night air quiet, apart from the occasional peel of thunder, and a grating whirling noise as the locomotive wheels kept turning. Pissss, pissss, pissss, the hot boiler cried, as the raindrops vaporised on striking it. Then as though in its last throws of life, a sudden great whoosh as though death had come with the remaining steam being released.

Dave lay unconscious in his compartment, oblivious to all the mayhem that had taken place. Meanwhile, the humid damp night air hung heavy outside with smells of burning grease and wood, interspersed with the sweet spicy fragrant vegetation from the surrounding jungle.

Some soldiers, reacting quickly and with only the ghostly glow from the flashes of lightning, pulled away at the carriages with their bare hands helping others who were trapped. No one seeming to notice the heavy rain, with everything going on it did not seem to matter, as it only served to cool them down.

Other passengers, senses dulled, and initially stunned into silence, in the muted stillness of the night, they could hear nothing except the pounding of the rain on the carriages. After the initial shock passed, the muffled sound of voices from soldiers and civilian passengers along the trackside began to invade the distant surrounding air. Picking themselves up, they aided the injured who had been thrown from their carriages and were now lying at the side of the track. Others stumbled from their compartments, and as the shock of what had happened struck home, wandered around in a daze.

They were fortunate this time as the place picked for the derailment was on level ground. The terrorists had probably presumed an explosion on this stretch of line, with the train at full speed, would have caused more carnage.

The driver by his brave timely action had prevented a major disaster. Having managed to slow the train down when he had seen the warning flags further back the track, but at a cost to him, as seconds after his Fireman panicked and deserted his post, he was thrown from the engine footplate, and now lay badly injured by the side of the tracks.

When Dave opened his eyes, the compartment was in darkness except for the occasional eerie flash of lightning, and the stony silence in his head, broken only by the sound of distant gunfire. His senses, dulled with the shock of what had happened, but not enough to ease the pain he felt. Raising his right hand to his forehead, he felt warm blood running down the side of his face, then cradling his head in his hands he sat for what seemed a lifetime, but in truth, only a few seconds.

Confused at first, he did not understand what had happened, as all he could remember was a loud noise then nothing. Shakily he struggled to his feet and held onto the table until his senses began to clear. It was then he realised what had happened, and only then he heard the faint cries from passengers in the other first-class compartments.

Fumbling about in the dark he found his torch and slowly shone it around the compartment then onto the top bunk. His courier partner on this trip had been asleep there before the derailment, but in the beam, he could see only an empty bunk. Shinning the torch around the compartment again, he noticed it was lying at a slight angle and the bundles of mail previously made ready for the next drop, were now in disarray.

Tentatively he steadied himself before making his way to the compartment door. As he did, he stumbled over what he thought was the other mailbags until a grumpy voice called out.

'Oh! Fucking hell! what are you trying to do?' Sitting up the owner of the voice looked straight at Dave's lamp and quizzed, 'What's with the fucking lamp mate? And what is up with the bloody lights?' Pausing as he looked around, he then continued mumbling in surprise, 'What the hell has happened? The place is a bloody mess.'

That was his partner Doug, a Lancashire man, a regular soldier for the past eight years. So many questions, and at that moment Dave, stuck for words, tried to explain what had happened, but Doug did not seem interested. 'Some fucking mate you are, you might have wakened me,' he retorted.

Still dazed and trying to think straight, Dave, taken aback and surprised by his partners attitude, looked at him and angrily replied, 'Wake you! Wake you! You fell five bloody feet from the top bunk and that didn't wake you,' continuing,

Dave growled, 'You, asshole! You could sleep through a bloody atomic bomb.'

Doug, having fallen from his bunk, had been lying on the floor of the carriage sound asleep, oblivious to all that had happened. It was then the realisation dawned on him, he was still sitting on the floor. With a blank expression he looked at Dave then at the top bunk, then in a voice of amazement, he stuttered, 'B- bloody hell.'

Dave, through the pain in his head, thinking back about himself, surmised what had happened. With the first jolt of the train rocking the carriage, he must have been flung about and knocked unconscious. Some blood on the corner of the table seemed to point to where he struck his head. Then he deducted, as the train continued to lurch his momentum must have carried him backwards throwing him onto the lower bunk.

At that same moment, Doug must have rolled off the top bunk, unaware what had happened. Dave assumed, no doubt suffering a hangover, from a drinking session in the NAAFI the day before.

Sometime later, Dave found out that due to the heavy rain of the past few days, linemen had been checking the line, and had spotted saboteurs kneeling over the tracks. Their early warnings to the Malaysian army regiment near Ipoh enabled a unit to be on the scene quickly, but not quickly enough to prevent the line being blown up.

The heavy rain that morning was still dulling the sounds of the cries coming from the injured. Back up the track and away in the distance, could still be heard the pop, pop, pop sounds of gun fire from the pursuing Malay Regulars, intermittently mixed with rolls of thunder.

All this time the rescue of the passengers went on unabated. For some this journey will be delayed a while longer, for others, they may not complete it. Dave thought *'Is this just another reminder to the Brits why they're glad to be going home?'*

The time was just after O-one hundred hours, somewhere between Butterworth and Taiping one morning in September 1960.

Not a good time to die, but then, is there ever a good time?

With the realization and relief, he was ok and still alive; the two couriers looked at each other and burst out laughing. 'Welcome to bloody Malaya' Dave mused.

Chapter 4

Meeting the C. O.

When Dave first arrived at Paroi camp, in his interview with the Command Officer, Major Dunlop, a Dalkeith man, he was asked, 'What type of duty do you think would suit you?'

Dave answered confidently, 'I would like to do something that will keep me busy Sir. I heard that the Courier duty was a responsible duty, Sir.'

As the C.O. looked over his report records, he spoke quietly as though talking to himself, 'Hum! Walters, I see in your reports that you were recommended to stay at Ripon as an instructor,' Then looking at Dave. 'Any idea why that request was turned down?'

'Only, that they needed more D.Rs. for other duties at that time Sir.'

The C. O. then deliberated quietly with Lieutenant Lethbridge, who was sitting at his left-hand side. Looking at Dave again, and in an authoritative tone he declared, 'Very well Walters, I'm putting you into the Couriers section at the Signal Centre.' Then after another look at his records 'Son,' his tone changed as he spoke in a well-educated voice with a slight hint of a Scottish accent. 'This will be a nice job for you to fill

13

in your service time. All the trouble is over, and there is really no danger now. You will be able to see a lot of this beautiful country of Malaya, and on top of that, paid danger money, the sum of eight Malay dollars extra, (equivalent to one- pound sterling), each day on top of your standard service wage, just for carrying out your Courier Duty.'

Hesitating again, he looked at the files once more, then looking directly at Dave. 'I see you also played football back home. That is good, as we have a fine team here. I'll pass your information to Corporal Duff.'

As he passed the file over to Lieutenant Lethbridge, he instructed Dave, 'Keep your nose and your breeks clean, keep out of trouble and you will have a nice little holiday for the next nineteen months while you're out here. Now Walters, that cannot be bad, can it?'

After a sale's pitch like that there was nothing more Dave could say, except, 'Thank you Sir.'

Sitting on the edge of the bunk in the railway carriage that morning nursing his sore head, those words sounded like he was here on a holiday. Dave wondered at the time, *if it is a holiday, why the danger money?* His C.O, had omitted to tell him, that his duties would take him right into the area where the fighting was ongoing.

Dave having settled down to getting on with doing his NS, was serving with the Royal Signals, and stationed at 230 Signal Squadron, in Proi Camp, situated on the outskirts of a small town called Seremban. Seremban, the main town in the province of Negri Sembilan lay approximately thirty-four miles south of Kuala Lumpur, and inland, fourteen miles from Port Dickson.

Standing five nine tall, Dave was slim built, with army style short black hair, some would say good-looking with strong features. But a young man whose only ambition was to complete his service and return home to his girlfriend. To date he had completed nearly eight months of his N S, with over three months of these serving in Malaya, as a Military Courier.

His duties, carrying military mail, and this took him up and down the country of Malaya by train. The nature of the information carried, was mostly about troop movements, arms, stores replacements and personal letters. Some classified signals were clarification of orders from GHQ. The Top Priority mail was normally confirmation of orders previously sent by Cipher code over the wire to various Army Units. This mail was carried in a separate briefcase chained to his wrist.

Courier duties he found, contrary to what the C.O. had told him, were not without risk. This was emphasized to him by the training officer who warned, 'If the information you're carrying falls into the hands of the enemy, it will enable them to pinpoint troop movements. Therefore, it is imperative that you do your duty diligently.'

His last words on the subject though, proved prophetic, that in the past, derailment of the trains was a way insurgent could lay their hands-on weapons, as well as inflicting mass injuries to the troops.

Dave, recalled what one of his mates, a regular soldier on his second tour here had said, 'In the earlier years of the campaign here in Malaya, it was common for the insurgents to try to derail the trains, by blowing up the tracks.'

Dave rubbing his forehead, mused, *I am surprised that it has happened again tonight, as I thought the insurgents communists were nearly beaten, but by the look of things, this might go on happening until the threat is eliminated.*

This was his second time since arriving here in Malaya; he had been on a train that was derailed. The first time was through natural causes, when the bedding of the track had been washed away during torrential Monsoon rain. This time though, it had been by the hand of the commies, who seemed to be still trying to destabilize the Malay Government?

He shook his head as he remembered being confidently told, 'the Communist Insurgents are in the last throes of being pushed right out of Malaya for good.' At this moment, as he sat nursing his headache, they seemed able to still inflict damage to the railway line this far south from the border. He pondered as he shook his head; *it does not look like we are succeeding.*

He then recalled that not long after he had received his call up papers, he met a young man who had been wounded when doing his N.S, out in Malaya. What he said about the troubles made Dave, out of curiosity read about the Emergency, as it was called. What he learned was, it had been ongoing since 1948, and bloody battles had taken place all over Malaya.

It was said troops were there because of Britain's interest in the rubber trade, and in the beginning many rubber plantations were attacked. That was only the start of the troubles, as it escalated into a communist takeover attempt, which is why the Commonwealth troops were brought in.

In the early days, our troops did not have it easy, because the type of fighting they encountered was guerrilla warfare. The insurgents, well versed in this style and knowing the terrain better than our troops, were not easily trapped, as they had help from villagers and the vast jungles of Malaya to disappear into.

Over the years, the Commonwealth troops led by the British soldiers became more adept at fighting in the jungles. Eventually, along with the Ghurkha and Malay regular troops, they gained control over large parts of Malaya and to date, had pushed the insurgents into pockets nearer the Thailand border. The campaign has resulted in hundreds of brave young men having lost their lives or injured. All to give the Malaysian people a chance of living in a free democratic country.

In his short time here, Dave has seen troops from all over the Commonwealth being carried up north by train to eradicate the enemy in their last strongholds. In 1960, the mission is mostly complete, and most of Malaya now a pleasant place to stay.

This the world he and other N.S soldiers had been transported into, to do their service. Dave still felt a little resentment at being drafted, as he had been torn from a life he liked back home, his job, his girlfriend, his family, and friends, only to be thrown into this strange new world, all in the name of National Service for his country.

Looking around at the dishevelled carriage again, he thought, *Thank you, your bloody Majesty for remembering to pick me.*

Chapter 5

Day's before N.S.

There was a new optimistic mood around Scotland in the fifties, jobs were plentiful, and people were throwing off the last remnants of ration books. This was the age of Rock and Roll. Elvis Presley. Cliff Richard. Bill Haley and the Comets.

Leaving school at fifteen, Dave started work in MacDonald's Motorcycle garage in Falkirk, his hometown. Settling in with the help from his workmates he quickly learned his trade, and during these years, started to spread his wings.

In 1956 it was announced that the National Service might end soon, and being deferred from N.S. at that time because of his apprenticeship, Dave had been jubilant with great hopes that he might miss it all together. His life during that period, he felt was getting better.

He had just turned eighteen when a young girl called Jennifer Armstrong, entered his life. She was employed on the stores counter in the garage showroom. What he saw in her that first day, took his breath away. She was beautiful, with looks like film star Jean Simmons, stunning oval deep blue eyes he wished he could get lost in, shoulder length black velvety hair, flawless skin, slim well shaped figure, and shapely legs most women would die for; she was always very cheerful and had the cheekiest of smiles.

As time passed, they became good friends, and seeing her every day at work, they teased each other, and it was not long before people, even before he himself realised, noticed that he was besotted by her. She was sixteen when he first laid eyes on her, and at first desperately tried to avoid getting romantically involved, as he knew for sure he would get tormented by his work mates each morning. He also reasoned stupidly; she was too young for him.

At that time in his life, twice a week he was a member of a Badminton club, and on Saturday afternoons, played football for a local team in the Secondary Juvenile league. Weekend nights were out as well, as he and his mates went to the dances in the local halls. His life and time were taken up and was to full too start going steady with a girl so young.

Jennifer for her part, with designs of her own, started going to the same dancehalls with her girlfriends. On these occasions Dave asked her up to dance, but still tried not to get involved, that was until one special St Valentine's dance night. Ladies choice was called, and Jennifer crossed the floor and surprised him, 'Can I have this dance?'

Dumfounded, he at first was speechless, and without replying took her hand and accepted her invitation. That night as he walked onto the floor with her, he felt alive with emotions that changed his thoughts and his world. Knowing she felt as he did, they drew closer until he could not resist her any longer, and started dating her, but still he kept up with his mates.

On their first real date he felt so awkward, and so strange were his feelings he was unable to work up the courage to hold her hand, even though he desperately wanted too. Emotionally he was lost. On dates with other girls, he had never felt this way, but now with Jennifer, something was different.

Eventually they started going out more frequently, and becoming inseparable. They loved nothing better than to jump on his motorcycle and drive wherever the fancy took them. If not out on his bike, they loved long walks in the countryside, and when together, the sun seemed to shine on them every day, so wrapped up were they in each other. Their first real kiss, he wanted to last forever, and when parting that evening his emotions were all jumbled up. Until that kiss, he was not sure what love was, but if that was how it made you feel, he told himself, *I am in love.*

These feelings grew and from then on, he could not deny them in front of her any longer. The first time he nervously said, 'I love you.' He felt his world stand still. As he gazed into her eyes looking for a response, tears welled up within her and ran down her cheeks.

Thinking he had hurt her in some way, he asked, 'What's the matter? Have I said something wrong?'

Playfully punching him in the ribs, she whispered, 'I'm just so happy, I always hoped you felt the same as I do.'

Their relationship developed deeper, and their ambitions and dreams of having three kids, and plans to immigrate to New Zealand in the future were laid down during that time.

From day one though, he lay in his bed at nights thinking of the one obstacle he knew they would eventually have to overcome. Jennifer was a Protestant and a Sunday school teacher; he on the other hand, was a devout Catholic.

In the mid-fifties, he knew it was still a hurdle for couples of different religions like them to overcome. With both parent's strong churchgoers, the stigma of marrying in the opposite church was something he knew their parents were not prepared for. His oldest brother Brian had married out of the church, and he had seen how hurt his mother had been, but being the youngest of six and very close to his mother, to have her hurt again, was something he hoped to avoid.

His own impression of Jennifer's family though, was that they were a bit more prejudiced towards his religion, as at times he sensed their aversion towards him, very cold. He also felt her parents let Jennifer know their feelings when he was not there, as on some dates she would be incredibly quiet, and would meet him outside the house. With these thoughts, the pressure on him was mainly his own conscience, but even with that, he stubbornly believed Jennifer would accept his faith when they married.

As time passed, eventually when he did mention the question of what they would do when they got married, differences of religious opinions arose, and he found it difficult to converse with her. Love, he always thought would overcome everything, but this deep-felt religion was a different matter. When no solution could be found, he felt a wedge was being driven between them, and it was hurting them both deeply.

Dave was beginning to find their love, although strong, had been in ignorant bliss for nearly eighteen months, and now they were encountering the cruel face of the world for the first time. Cocooned, they felt their love for one another, and nothing else mattered. But now, the world they knew was breaking apart as the reality of the times encroached into their sheltered lives. From then on there were periods when he was not sure what to say to her, and that was when they started to drift further apart.

The saddest thing, he confided to a friend, 'neither of us knows what to do about it.'

This went on until one day when they were out walking, Jennifer was unusually quiet. 'What is the matter, you're so quiet?' he asked.

She shook her head, but gave no answer, and it wasn't until nearing her home, unexpected she said, 'David,' she was the only person apart from his mother who called him David. 'I think we should stop seeing one another for a while. I'm so mixed up, as our religions are making it impossible to think straight.'

Dave was devastated and struck dumb.

Stuck for words he did not know how to answer, in his mind he never thought it would come to this. He stood speechless, anger boiling up in him, as he tried to figure out what was going on. Finally, his anger spilled over. 'Has your mum and dad put you against me? I've had a feeling for a while they weren't happy about us going together.'

She didn't answer right away, and this made him more annoyed, turning as though to walk away from her, he heard her cry in anguish, 'David, I still love you, but I have to get things straight in my head what I really want for us.'

Still lost for the right words to say, he looked at her. She had tears in her eyes and the kind of look he hadn't been able to resist before, but this time his anger was deep and without thinking, dismissively said, 'Please yourself, I don't care what happens.'

He turned and walked away with the sound of her sobbing voice calling out, 'David please…. please, don't go away feeling like that, I still love you'

Chapter 6

Heart to Heart

On the way home that night, he felt his world had fallen apart and cursed their religions for destroying what they had. Entering his bedroom that had always been his refuge, he closed the door, sat down on the edge of his bed looked around, and hoped his troubled mind would settle. Then crossing over to the window he pulled the curtains back and stared at the starry heavens as he uttered a simple prayer, 'Please God; let her come back to me.'

In bed, he tossed and turned until exhausted, then drifted into an uneasy sleep. Next morning, with no appetite for anything, he skipped breakfast and drove to the Garage. Entering his workplace, he was not sure if he would be able to face her, or his work mates. Reluctantly, he scribbled a short note and putting on a brave face handed it into the storeroom for her. On it, it said, he would not see her until she had made up her mind about him.

Days past, but unlike his jovial self, he hardly spoke to anyone. Frank, his boss, who also happened to be Jennifer's uncle, noticed they had both seemed distant at work, pulling Dave aside he asked. 'What's wrong with you both? Jennifer's hardly spoken to anyone, and you are not that much better. Has anything happened between you?'

Dave at first, did not want to talk about their problem, but under Frank's persistence, explained their behaviour as best he could. After deliberation, Frank suggested, 'take a break away from here.' then offered 'Why not go and help set up my new shop in Linlithgow? Time apart might heal your problems.'

Dave, after some persuasion agreed and went along to the other garage that morning, but the following days and nights seemed to drag so much, he felt even to be in the same garage and just see her every day, was better than being apart.

The nights when out with his mates he was tormented by them, 'It's not the end of the world Dave, remember what they say, absence makes the heart grow fonder,' and 'There's plenty more fish in the sea.' but at that time Dave wasn't so sure about anything.

A week past, he was informed by one of his workmates that Jennifer had been on a date with another boy. Whether true or not, he decided to retaliate and went out dancing and dated an old girlfriend he knew. This did not prove successful, as there was a great hole in his life, and hard as he tried to enjoy his date, he could not. With Jennifer always in his thoughts, even going out with his mates and playing football had lost all appeal to him, and he started staying in more at nights. Their lives he felt were drifting further apart and he was lost.

One night while sitting at home, his Dad having noticed a change on him and asked, 'Not going out tonight?'

Not having spoken about his troubles to either of his parents, he felt it difficult speaking about it at first. Feeling as he did, he was a grown man and should be able to get over her, he replied curtly, 'No.'

His Dad sensing there was something wrong, and not

wanting to let him off lightly prompted, 'I thought you went out with Jennifer tonight?'

At the sound of Jennifer's name, he tried to choke back his feelings, trying to supress the tears and unable to face his Dad he looked at the floor. After a few moments he composed himself, then poured it all out about his dreams, his ambitions and his problems with Jennifer and their religions. When he had exhausted all this, he felt relieved at getting it off his chest. They then had a long heart to heart discussion.

Seeing how deeply hurt Dave still was, his Dad ended by saying, 'In affairs of the heart, nobody can say the right things to ease your pain.' Then hesitating, he went on to say, 'It will be of no comfort to you the now, but your grandfather always said to me when things weren't working out. Whatever is meant for you won't go by you.'

Days passed, and his dad's words of wisdom stuck fast in his mind, but still did not help ease his pain. The next week he was in town, he was met by Jennifer's favourite aunt, whom they had visited regularly when courting. In conversation she said, 'Jennifer has been around to see me and spoke about your problems. She is feeling very miserable since you stopped seeing her.'

The way she spoke made him feel guilty as though it was his fault, and she was the innocent party. Feeling as he did, he warily said, 'Well it's her own doing. She was the one who wanted to break off.'

Taken aback by his words, her auntie said, 'I'm convinced Jennifer didn't really mean for you both to break up permanently, as she doesn't know her self what she wants, but I'm sure the way she's moping about, she really wants to get back with you.'

'Well, she knows where to find me,' he said defiantly.

As her Aunt turned to walk away, her parting words to

Dave were, 'Go and grab hold of her and tell her, this nonsense has to stop.'

He mused, *if only it was as simple as that.* After listening to all she had to say about Jennifer, he thought long about their situation and that night realized he wanted to be with her no matter what, and knew in his heart what must be done, but not how he should go about it?

Around that time his boss Frank, seeing their separation was still affecting them, decided to play matchmaker, but Dave told him, 'I'm finding it difficult how I should approach her, because I'm not sure if she wants us to get back together.' In his heart what Dave really meant was, he feared rejection.

Frank suggested, 'Why not speak with Jennifer on the telephone?'

Dave thought about it a moment before replying, 'At least if she says no, I won't see the rejection on her face.' and eagerly agreed, although still feeling nervous.

'I'll arrange it for early tomorrow morning, and I promise you, you won't be disturbed.' Frank told him.

Feeling incredibly low and missing Dave, Jennifer wiped her tears away; she had been working away all morning and every now and then stopped to wonder what he would be thinking at that moment. Just then the phone rang. Not knowing about the arrangement between Dave and Frank, she picked up the receiver, and composing herself, tried to answer in her usual manner. 'Hello. McDonalds motorcycles.'

By the sound in her voice Dave sensed she had been crying, and this made him choke at first. He hesitated before speaking, as his thoughts in that moment were, *is she going to tell me it would not work and that she did not want to see me again*? His head in a spin, he tried to start conversing, but his mouth felt dry. Eventually plucking up courage, he nervously quietly said, 'I love you and I miss you. I want to marry you wherever you choose'

All was quiet for what seemed a long while, and only the sound of his heart pounding filled his ears as he wondered, *this silence, is this to be the last time she will want to speak to me.*

As though she had just suddenly recognized his voice she blurted out, 'I've missed you so much,' she sniffed, 'when I heard you were seeing another girl,' The tears rolled down her face, she sniffed once more, 'I thought you didn't want to see me again?'

'I've never stopped wanting to see you.' Dave replied. 'I want to spend the rest of my life with you.'

'I want that too.' She enthused, 'All I ever wanted was to be with you.'

Hearing these few words, his heart jumped for joy and the weight that had been pressing down on him lifted, and everything felt wonderful again. Jubilantly he replied, 'I've been so miserable without you, my life wasn't worth living.'

Through the tears of joy, she replied, 'David, I want to marry you too, as I love you.'

They talked some more of how they felt and calming down, the feelings he had before engulfing him, he felt, I can now hold my head up and smile again.

Having reconciled with one another, it was hard to put the phone down in case it had only been a dream. But knowing they had to break their conversation, 'I'll better go now, but I'll see you tonight.'

Excitedly she quickly answered, 'I love you lots and lots, and can't wait to see you.'

As he put the phone down. *'Now all I have to do is tell my mother'* he thought.

Chapter 7

Goodbye Again

That night, before she climbed on the pillion seat of his motorbike, he whispered, 'I love you.'

As they kissed, he felt her lips were so soft and sweet, and it was like falling in love all over again. Once settled on the pillion seat she wrapped her arms around and snuggled her head against him, no more words were needed.

That night in the cinema, although full of people, they felt alone, for they only had eyes for each other.

A week before her eighteenth birthday, they got engaged, and their parents were informed of their plans. Knowing how they felt for each other, they gave their blessings.

Once more, their dreams when married, were spoken of, and of how they would strike out on their own to New Zealand. These dreams seemed to fill their lives and brought them closer and nothing now they felt, could come between them. That was until May the 6th 1959, the day of his twenty-first birthday. This day brought them back into the real world.

Rather than opening only birthday cards, a buff-coloured envelope like hundreds more over the country with Her Royal Majesty Service printed along the top, had dropped through his letterbox. This was the long-awaited call up papers he was dreading.

His heart sank for he knew his world was about to change once more. Later that night as he stood with his arms around Jennifer, she sensed something was bothering him and asked, 'what's the matter?'

Trying to cover his disappointment, he shrugged his shoulders, 'Nothing really, just got my call up papers this morning, and I have to go to Edinburgh for my medical.'

'That's not so bad, they might not take you. Anyway, you might be too old,' jokingly she replied as she tried to cheer him.

'But if I am accepted, I could be sent anywhere and not see you for a long time.' he said, trying hard to keep his emotions in check, and not let her see that he was worried.

The rest of that night they discussed what it would mean for them both, and when she could see he still was unsettled, she whispered her promise, 'No matter what happens, I'll be here and will always wait for you.'

All was right, until it was time for him to go home. As they stood in the front porch, wrapped in each other's arms she sensed it was still bothering him. 'I told you no matter what happens I'm here for you, and always will be.' She whispered again, then tightening her embrace, 'I will wait for you for as long as you still want me.' Their parting kiss that night had a feeling of desperation and failed to settle him.

On the 20th August he passed his medical A1 and was declared fit for duty. What was left of that year seemed to pass quickly and before they knew it, his Draft papers arrived? In bold writing the letter stated he had been drafted into the Royal Signals and was to report to Catterick Camp in Yorkshire, by 12 noon on the 21st of January 1960. Travel tickets were enclosed.

Informing his mates of his imminent departure, they had

a boy's night out with a difference. After a few drinks most of his works football team decided to have one last kick about, this proved to be the daftest suggestion anyone could have made, for not only was it raining it was also played in the darkness. Nevertheless, they all enjoyed themselves and ended the night singing in the rain, and what a glorious feeling.

Next morning, he was still suffering from his night out when Frank called him into his office. In their chat he said to Dave, 'Your job will still be here when you return,' then smiling, 'if I'm still in business.'

He shook hands that morning with Frank his boss, and with everything in order he realised this was it, there was no way out for him now, so he decided, to make the best of it from there on in. The last few days and nights before leaving home he spent entirely with Jennifer. Just being there for one another, it seemed to keep the world at bay.

Around 8pm, on the 21st January, after saying goodbye to his own parents. Jennifer, her mother, and dad accompanied him to the Railway station to see him off. His goodbye with Jennifer was long and tender and when looking into her eyes, he could see all the fears she had about them. For this was the first time she would not be able to contact him easily.

This was the moment she knew he too had been dreading for weeks. The knowledge of not knowing what lay ahead and not being able to see her left him with a sense of despair.

Before boarding the train, they kissed a long lingering kiss and as they parted, he said, 'Take care and I'll see you as soon as I can get a pass to come home. And always remember. I love you.'

As he stepped onto the train, she replied 'I love you David, please don't forget me,' her voice weakening away, then gathering herself again, 'Please write to me whenever you get time.'

Standing on the steps of the train, Dave pointed to his heart and said, 'You know I won't forget you, for you are here always.' He moved inside and closed the door, for he did not want her to see his tears.

As the train picked up speed and pulled out of the station, standing at the carriage door he leaned out the open window to catch a last glimpse of her. What he saw pulled at his heart, she looked a lonely figure, tears were running down her face, waving and waving until the train was out of the station and out of sight.

The journey through the countryside passed him by that day. Looking out the window he never noticed the trees were bare of leaves, or that the land was covered with a white blanket of snow. Winter that day was just a word to him, for he was deep in thought of the love he was leaving behind.

In his thoughts he could still see her on the platform, looking sad and alone and a tear came into his eyes once more. The only consolation he told himself, *their love was strong enough to last*; and with that warm feeling he knew in his heart Jennifer would wait for him.

As the train took him further away from all that he loved, other questions were now running around in his head. He was on his way to an unknown adventure, and this would be his first time out of Scotland; he wondered; *will I be able to cope? Will I be able to fit into the army?* Deep in these thoughts he speculated what the future would hold for him, and at that moment felt homesick and all alone, and longed to have his Jennifer beside him.

Chapter 8

The Adventure Begins

Vimy Lines in Catterick Camp in Yorkshire on that cold winter's day, where Dave was to begin his ten weeks basic training with the 26th Signal Regiment. Around one-o-clock he arrived along with forty-five other conscripts at Richmond station to be welcomed by two Corporals. Bundled like cattle along with their belongings into the back of covered trucks, they were driven at breakneck speed the few miles to the camp. They were all in the same boat, so to speak, with hardly a word passing between these new friends.

At the camp reception office, formed in two lines with their personal belongings lying at their feet, a roll call was taken, Dave supposed, to make sure they were all there and that none had escaped. 'All present.' one of the Corporals called out. After standing in the falling snow for thirty minutes, they then were marched into a reception room where they were introduced to Captain Wilcox their training company officer (C.O.), an Oxford man. Tall and slim, very much a gentleman with a small moustache, his hair wispy but quite thin on top, he also spoke with an exceptionally soft voice. A silver spoon man Dave thought.

Their drill instructor Sergeant Horne, called them all to attention. His broad accent gave away his Scottish nationality. About five feet nine in height, stocky built and very fit looking, a force to be reckoned with by the look of his squashed nose.' Dave imagined he had been a bit of a boxer in the past. His assistants, the final part of their training team was Corporals Phillips, from Newcastle and Jenkins, from Coventry.

After induction, still wearing their civilian clothes they were marching round the drill square to a three-story U shape barrack building, all the while, the snow was appreciable getting heavier. Called to a halt outside what was to be their billets for the duration of their stay, Sergeant Horne said in a very civil manner, 'You are all in B troop and this is your new hame, look after them, laddies.'

Delighted to be directed in, they climbed up to the second floor, where stopping at the first room, 16 of them were allocated a bed, no questions about which bed. Corporal Jenkins called out 'That's yours, Walters, that's yours, Ellis,'. Once all beds were allocated, and next rooms were allocated, they placed their personal belongings beside them.

'Fall in.' Jenkins bawled, 'Not on your beds, but stand to attention at the end of your beds.'

Being late afternoon Jenkins told them, 'All you have to do today is collect your bedding from the Quartermaster's store.'

It was snowing more heavily as they assembled back outside and having just come out from a warm building Dave felt the cold pierce right threw him. Corporal Jenkins, still in charge, marched them for what seemed miles until they reached the store.

Inside, lined up along a lengthy counter, they were given bedding except a mattress, which were already on their beds. After signing forms for everything, it was the best part of two hours before they arrived back at their barrack room. Even though unfit and exhausted, the Corp did not let up on them until their beds had been made up army style, and only then were they informed that that was it for the day.

Right lads, the Corp informed, 'You can all now go down to the canteen hall on the ground floor, some grub has been prepared for you.'

Feeling cold with hardly any feeling in his hands, it was only then that Dave realized he only had had a sandwich to eat since his breakfast that morning. The supper that night tasted real welcome. Hunger satisfied, and back in their barrack room, tired, he was thinking he could now climb into bed, but no such luck. In marched Sergeant Horne, and all thoughts of sleep flew out the window.

'Stand by your beds' he called.

Most were up on their feet right away, but one or two had not fully understood what the Sergeant wanted. His expression changed, and the gloves were now off; he proceeded to explain to them in his own soft polite way. 'When I say, stand by your beds, I mean stand by your beds, not sit there scratching your fuckin balls.'

With a stare that would melt rocks, he looked at the lads who were slow to stand and growled in an aggressive voice. 'In future, I will only gee ye a command once and I want ye to jump.' That straightened out, the Sergeant in a gentler voice told what he had in store for next day.

That night, bushed, as he crawled into bed Dave moaned, 'It's been one hell of a long day!'

Early next morning it was a shock to his system to be greeted with loud banging noises and the lights switched on full. When he raised his head off the pillow, the sight that greeted him was the Sarge entering in full dress Uniform, red sash across his chest, baton tucked under his left armpit and toe caps of his boots, gleaming.

'Wakey! Wakey!' he bawled, and continued, 'Now is the day we start to make ye men. On your feet and be outside by O six hunner hours. But remember, make yer beds up.'

One lad called Bret, rolled over when he saw it was only five thirty a.m. and still dark outside. The Sarge walked calmly over to his bed, grabbed his bedding, and turned it over, spilling Bret and his bedding onto the floor. He then berated him in a manner Dave and most of the other lads had never heard before, words country lads were not used to. Bret got the message.

After that, a mad scramble ensued to get to the toilets, get washed, shaved, and then dress. Having only their civilian clothes to wear, it was a rush for everyone to see who would be first ready. It is amazing what forty-five men can do in thirty minutes. The beds were tidily put together as best as could be, then hurried outside to stand in the freezing cold with snow blowing all around them, wondering if it had been all worth it.

After roll call, their squad marched into the canteen for breakfast. The heat and the odours coming out of the cookhouse smelt fantastic, Dave thought, like music to his palate and made him feel even hungrier. That was until he joined the queue. What greeted him, porridge that looked like cement; eggs that looked like dead eyes and as for the rashers of ham and the toast the less said about them the better. Not what he had expected. Staring at the fare, he turned to the lad called Ron standing beside him and said, 'Please send me home.' They laughed but decided to suffer the food for the Queen's sake.

In no time at all they were being called to form up outside. In snow now heavier, they marched over to the Quartermasters stores. Wearing ordinary shoes this proved more difficult than they thought, as they slipped and slid all over the place. Ushered into the hall and formed in line, they were issued with standard equipment. First a kitbag to hold it all, then uniforms, two Tunics and trousers, two shirts, two pair of braces, and underpants that felt like were made from canvas, a greatcoat, and other items piled up in front of them until they had the prescribed kit.

With their loaded kitbags slung on their shoulders, they marched back to the barrack room, again this proved even more difficult with the weight of their kit. With underfoot slippery, some of the lads spent more time on their backsides than on their feet.

Struggles over and feeling glad to be back in their barracks, the sight that met them when they entered their room, was as though a bomb had exploded. The bedding covers were all over the place the beds were laying on their sides. While they were away one of the Corporals, part of the dirty squad, as they later called them, had in their absence decided that the display of bed making wasn't up to his taste, so he turned over every bed in the room.

As they stood looking aghast at the mess, with perfect timing in walked the Sarge. Standing in the middle of the room he looked around, shook his head, and tut tutting! 'Whit's this? I kin see I will have a lot of work to do, to make soldiers of you lot. This is the wurst display of bed making I've ever seen in all my army life.' Then raising his voice higher, he hollered, 'Pick up all those bloody covers, and stand by your beds.' He then roared 'Corporal Phill---ips.'

Corporal Phillips came running in and came to attention in front of the Sarge, as he bawled. 'What the fucking hell di ye call this. It is your job to make sure they awe make their beds properly. Right, starting from now you are in charge till they get it right. Understand.'

'Yes Sergeant' Phillips called out in an ominous voice. As the Sarge marched out, Dave watched him go and was sure the Sarge winked to Corp Phillips. Now in charge the Corp in turn, gave them a lashing with his tongue. 'You bastards, you have put me in the Sergeant's bad books, so now you will all need to work bloody hard to get me back in his good books or I'll make you all bloody wish you hadn't left fucking home.'

After the blue air cleared Corporal Phillips demonstrated how the bed should be made properly and then made them all practice repeatedly, until he said they were ok. Once that was done, he then proceeded to show them how to lay out their kit for inspection. That took most of what was left of the morning.

Because of the bad weather outside, what time was left that morning he demonstrated how to wear their uniforms properly, especially the beret, and how Jimmy their Signals badge should be worn. Later, how to polish their boots and shine the toecaps. 'Let me give you one word of warning.' He rapped, 'Make sure your boots are well polished, but don't fucking ever outshine the Sarge.'

Chapter 9

A Soldier Now

Now fully dressed in uniform, Dave started to feel like a soldier, and going for lunch with his new mates, he felt part of the army, as all the other squaddies were in uniform as well. Lunch over, Corporal Jenkins marched into the dining hall and called, 'B troop, outside in two ranks at the double.'

Outside, Dave, like all the others was stamping his feet to get the circulation going, as the air was cold enough to freeze brass monkeys, but thankfully the snow had now stopped falling. In his uniform he felt quite warm, but his feet were still cold. Sergeant Horne stood out in front immaculately dressed, his boots shining. Not even the snow would dare to dull his toecaps. Looking at the three lines of his new troop he called out 'Squad. AaaH--attention.'

The sound of their feet stamping down was more like a drum roll rather than one synchronized thump. Dave smiled inwardly.

'Dear oh dear oh dear,' the Sarge said, 'Ah thought ye hid to hiv good hearing afore they let ye into the army. Yi sees, attention means ye awe come to attention together.'

He then ordered Corporal Phillips to the front and told

him to come to attention, this he did very smartly. 'That's what I want you little boys to do.' said he sarcastically, then continued in a softer voice. 'Can you understand me now? Now that I have spoken in a, pish posh voice?'

Dave, along with the rest of B troop's feet, were very warm after spending the next hour stamping them as they practised coming to attention, until they were nearly synchronized in sound. By the end of that hour Dave was feeling they weren't too bad, only the odd thump of one or two out of timing, but with the Corp having it in for them he just kept swearing and telling them they were useless, and that they were all illegitimate.

Moved around in their lines according to height, they then started the serious part of soldiering, marching on the training parade ground. As the Sarge said, 'Only real soldiers are allowed on the parade square.'

It is amazing how difficult Dave thought, to march in time with a full squad especially when the lad in front does not know his left from his right, never mind his ass from his elbow. Their troop had unfortunately four lads in that category, and it made life difficult at first, as if one were out of step, they all suffer.

The days passed, and his first letter from home arrived. The way the letters were dished out, it was just one big rugby scramble to see who had one. Luckily, this time, Dave had two, both from Jennifer, one apparently written the same night he left home, the other written a few days later in answer to the one he sent her. In the first letter stained with tears, she said, were because she cried all the time, she was writing it. Her words were what he needed to hear. *I miss you darling, and I long to be by your side.*

He could sense she was desperately unhappy, and wished he were there to comfort her, to tell her he loved her, and that everything was going to be all right. Her second letter was more cheerful having now received his one; and knew he was still missing her even though he had settled down to the army routine. Letters from home he felt were what he desperately looked forward to, even though, they made it difficult to keep his concentration the rest of that week, as they unsettled him.

In the first two weeks, he seemed never to have much time to himself, even to think of home, but at the end of each day when lying in bed after lights out, he thought about life back home before the army came along. Like all the other lads, he did not look forward to most nights, as fatigues, like cleaning the barrack room, showers, and toilets, then bulling up their kit, had to be attended to. After all that, tiredness took over, and he was asleep as soon as his head hit the pillow.

The pressure seemed constant, orders to do this and to do that, but with encouragement from the Sarge and his henchmen, B troop began to get it together. As the training stepped up, he felt fitter and healthier, and the more he understood the army, he learned how to make more time for himself.

Heavy snow or rain in his early days of his N.S. meant they drilled under huge, covered sheds with no sides to stop the cold winds blowing in, and when the winds blew over the Yorkshire moors, which was often, he was sure they headed straight to Catterick Camp.

Before long B troop were trusted with rifles. This was a step up in training. Marching, Dave thought, once mastered it was easy. But carrying a rifle, that is another story, as the first week with rifles he nearly lost teeth when the lad in front turned quickly and too close during a marching exercise. Bruised with a swollen lip, the Sarge said after examining him, 'Laddie yer just a casualty of stupidity,' he then had to carry on.

The drill with rifles intensified until B troop started to work as a team in unison.

After the first three weeks of marching, running and physical education to build up muscle, B troop lost seven conscripts for some reason or another. One big black lad from Birmingham was a bit of a pain in the backside to the Sarge and tried very hard to get thrown out of the NS. He even attempted in front of the troop to their astonishment, to pick a fight with the Sarge in the dining hall. His feet hardly got time to touch the ground. He was shipped out very quickly, and rumour had it, he was sent to join the Military Police.

Another with weight problems was sent to another camp to lose some weight. No one heard if he managed or not, Dave mussed, probably he is an officer now. One other lad dropped his Gun as he politely referred to it and for his trouble the Sarge made him run around the parade ground with his Gun above his head.

As the Sarge said 'This, bonny laddie, is what you will do until you can remember it's, a rifle.' He was then moved on. The other four lads were luckier, Dave thought, as they were discharged from N.S for one reason or another for health reasons.

Derek Ellis, two beds from Dave, must have wished he had been one of the lads kicked out of the N.S. after a kit inspection. Everyone laid out their kit in their beds neatly before going down to breakfast, as inspection was first on their orders for the day. Returning to their Barrack room, they all changed into battle uniform, and as they all stood patiently by their beds waiting for kit inspection, a noise could be heard of things scattering on the floor from next room. Dave looking in wonderment at the lad across from him, shrugged his shoulders, but thought, *I am not worried, I am confident my kit's all right.*

Sarge was still shouting at the top of his voice as he left the other room and tension mounted as they could hear the click-click of his footsteps coming along the corridor, and, even before reaching their room he was calling out 'Stand by yer beds.'

Entering the room, he ordered them to attention, and then starting on the bed opposite Dave, in turn, he proceeded to take apart the layout of the kits on each bed. When he arrived at Derek's bed he stopped, looked closely, then said, 'Gid kit lad pity you hivnae got a fork.' He then faced Derek nose-to-nose and called him all the pansy names under the sun, some Dave had not heard before. He then scattered everything on the floor and proceeded to do the same with the rest of their kits. When he left, Corporal Phillips asked Derek 'Where is your bloody fork?'

Derek quietly replied 'Don't know Corporal. It was on my bed before I went for breakfast.

Corporal Phillips looking at Derek shook his head and told him 'In this bloody army when you lose a part of your kit make sure when it comes to kit inspection you have all yours intact, Savvy.'

The lesson Dave learned that day, no matter how much he thought he knew his new friends, there might be the bad apple in the barrel. Next payday Derek learned he had been docked the price of a fork from what paltry army wages he got.

Looking like real soldiers and marching as a unit, Dave felt, had bonded the lads together and as they progressed, instead of marching on the training ground, they marched straight onto the parade ground. Which was some two hundred yards square and was much better he thought, as they could all now hear the noise of their boots click in step. The only drawback to being on the parade ground was, they were now under the watchful eye of Regimental Sergeant Major Bigley, who when not amused with their performance, let the training group know it, then our squad came in for more tough exercises.

Tea break around ten hundred hours Dave never looked forward to, as it was a bit like a scramble. All the other units were given their break at the same time, and that led to about three hundred conscripts charging to the NAAFI at the same time. With only thirty minutes for everyone to get served and drink your tea before being called out to parade again, it was always chaotic, and friendship went out the window.

Dave was sure all the NCOs had a streak of masochism in their blood and took great delight watching all the troops scrambling and fighting to get first. So, it was important to make sure your squad stopped close to the NAAFI. Depending on how the Sarge felt that morning determined where B troop finished, but by the number of times they were last, Dave thought the Sarge, the cruellest of them all.

Days past, and B troop were moving as a slick unit, which was when Captain Wilcox joined them to oversee the marching and rifle drill. Rifle inspection become important and greater emphasis was put on cleaning the barrel. As Wilcox says, 'A dirty rifle means a sloppy soldier and not one to have at your side when trouble starts.'

Dave did not know if he was meaning the rifle or the soldier, and believed Wilcox spent more time telling them how important it was to keep the rifle clean than it was to be able to shoot it. Later Dave jokingly said to one of his mates, 'Remember when attacked, tell the enemy to wait while you clean your rifle before you can shoot him, you don't want him to die because of a dirty bullet, do you?'

The trips to the rifle range were something B troop looked forward to, as Dave found he was quite a natural at shooting and recorded quite high scores, so much so the range Sergeant asked if he would like to join the shooting team. For some reason never confined to him, Captain Wilcox refused this request. Wilcox though, became more involved as their training progressed, and took over the education in Map reading and cross-country travel, and officer rank recognition.

'Finding your way by reading maps,' he told them 'means you should never get lost.'

Dave smiled at his remark and thought, *he should have given us a map of the* Camp, as *sometimes we cannot find the bloody NAAFI without getting directions.*

Wilcox also said, 'Recognizing the different ranks may keep you all out of trouble while in the service.' This left them wondering; was he meaning for them to hide?

With training being stepped up in the gymnasiums, Dave thought with all the sport he played back home, he had been fit before joining the army, but this training had taken him to a higher level of fitness. So fit he felt, that by the end of his fifth week, he sensed bullets would bounce off him. This can also be a curse for healthy young men full of testosterone. He mussed, with the lack of sex, some nights the barracks were alive with the sound of flesh slapping.

Training with the other companies on the parade ground each day was stepped up for the big day. That day, their passing out parade in front of all the top brass.

Chapter 10

Dreaming of Home

Since leaving home, Dave always looked forward to Jennifer's letters, twice a week she wrote to him of her love and to let him know she was there for him, and waiting patiently for the day he would be home. After the first unsettling weeks her letters in the beginning helped him get through that period. Now though, it would not be long before he would see and hold her in his arms again, as a forty-eight-hour pass, was their prise once their pass-out-parade was over.

That was a day to look forward too, he thought; *not because of the passing out parade, but because he will be going home.*

As the big day drew closer, bulling their kits for the final inspection took up all their spare time. Over the weeks they had learned everything from hygiene to laying their kit out, and to be able to bounce a coin on the top of the bed, whatever for, he never fathomed, but that was the army way.

Inspections became more frequent, and on one occasion, Sergeant Horne, while inspecting their kit noticed that Peter Cantrell, one of the lads in Dave's barrack room, had bulled his toecaps so bright that they outshone his own. Without saying a word, the Sarge just grabbed all the bedding covers, kit and all and threw the whole lot out the window. Bad enough they all thought, but this was a more sinister ploy committed by the Sarge, as there was about three feet of snowdrift under the window.

For that small insult to his pride, all of B troop had to do their kit all over again. Peter with some help from the lads, had to dig his bedding and kit out of the snow, and start all over again. It was a harsh lesson to learn Dave thought, but in the army, it taught him one thing, follow orders, and stay within the bounds of what is expected and that should get him through. After all, this was only, he kept telling himself, for two short years.

During the last few weeks, they had grown more into a team that worked together, the spirit of one for all and all for one was true at this time and leading up to Pass out day they were warming to the Sarge and began to appreciate what his training methods had been all about.

After all the hard work that had gone into bulling their brass buttons and buckles over the weeks, into the barrack room marched the Sarge, 'right lads I want all your brass buttons removed from your tunics and great coats and I want these new ones sewn on.'

They all looked at each other; as if it were a joke. Having just finished polishing the brass buttons that last evening, now they had to start all over again, polishing these new buttons.

Like him he was sure; they all said a few words of thanks, or words to that effect very quietly in their heads. The Sarge called out and in marched the corporals with boxes, handing one to each rookie, they were ordered to open them up the boxes, low and behold the buttons just about blinded them, for they were all sparkling and bright.

Sarge, with a twinkle in his eyes said, 'Ye didn't think I wis going to be bad tae ye, did ye. Ye lucky lads, the army his decided to issue these new stay bright buttons as they call them, so you won't hurt your wee fingers polishing those old brass ones.'

That day, the Sarge and his henchmen were genuinely nice to B troop; little did they know, it was all a swindle, for they wanted the old brass buttons, so they could make some money on the side.

The following Monday they had a good piece of news, a forty-eight-hour pass for that next weekend. Now they were starting to look like soldiers, the top brass must have thought they deserved a little holiday.

The rest of that week seemed to fly past, and on Friday with no duties, around eleven a.m., you could not see anyone for dust.

Dave managed to catch the eleven-forty-five train to Scotland. As the countryside flew past and being too late to let Jennifer know he would be home, all his thoughts were concentrated on surprising her. Lady luck smiled on him that day as he managed to catch his connections and arrived home just before she finished her work.

When he walked into the showroom, she was standing behind the counter with her back to him and did not hear him approach. Still dressed in uniform, and trying to disguise his voice, he said, 'Is anybody going to serve me.'

At the sound of his voice, she turned and screamed with delight, her face beamed with a smile as bright as the sun. Running around the counter she almost knocked him over as she flung her arms around him and smothered him with kisses. As their lips met, the past weeks seemed to just melt away and embracing her in his arms was like he had died and gone to heaven.

Pulling away she asked in surprise, 'Why didn't you let me know you were coming home?'

'I couldn't, this was sprung on us at the last moment.' He explained.

All was forgiven, as all she wanted was to hold on to him. Just then his old boss Frank, who had been watching them through his office window, walked in and coming over, shook his hand, and said, 'Welcome home Dave. My, you look smart in your uniform.' Then turning to Jennifer and jokingly inquired, 'I suppose you will want to finish early tonight and even have tomorrow off, now that he's home.'

Jennifer coyly replied, 'Yes, please, please. Boss,' and with a cheeky smile, wasted no time in getting her Jacket.

The weather that weekend was not particularly good, it had been snowing just as heavily as it had been at Catterick. With it being so cold, that night and most of Saturday night Dave and Jennifer, spent most of their time wrapped in each other's arms, sitting in front of a coal fire in her room upstairs. With the scent of the woman he loved, surrounding him, he felt wonderful. It was the best feeling he had had since the night before leaving home.

He was also surprised by the welcome from Jennifer's mum and dad, who made him feel at home. Over dinner for the first time in all the time they had been dating, her dad started to treat him like one of the family. Getting his feet under the table, he told himself. Dave thinking back to before that night he had often felt her dad just accepted him because he was a mechanic, and he, himself being a keen motorcyclist. Now it felt different.

All too soon though, their time together was over, and it was time to go back to Catterick. Before leaving, he told her, 'Next time I see you, will be when basic training is over, and that won't be for another four or five weeks.'

As Jennifer kissed him goodbye, she softly said, 'That will have to keep you till your back in my arms once more.'

Chapter 11

Back to Camp

Arriving back at camp and meeting all his mates took away the sting of having to leave Jennifer again, but over that next couple of days the conversation between his mates always seemed to return to talking about their girlfriends. It was then back to reality and the completion of their training in preparation for their pass out parades, which was scheduled for around mid-April.

One day, he and the rest of B troop were wakened incredibly early. There was a big flap on, so they were told, and ordered to do all sorts of cleaning jobs around the camp. The daftest of the jobs, Dave found himself on, was covering dirty parts of the snow-covered ground with fresh snow. The reason, later they were told was because a top brass Brigadier was making a visit next day. Whatever the reasons for his visit, B troop were never informed, but there he was along with his mates in the freezing cold with brushes, shovels and barrows trying to do nature's job, all for one man.

To finish off his day, he and two others were selected for guard duty, as the Sarge said to them, 'Just to get some experience.'

That night was the coldest Dave had ever felt in his life and to top it all off, as it neared the end of their guard duty, the snow turned to sleet and, on the ground it turned to slush. So much, he cursed, for all that good work covering up the dirty snow. He stood shivering on guard as day light approached, and mused, pity the Royal Signals had not phoned up for a weather forecaster station before they panicked.

The weeks rolled in, and he could not write as often to Jennifer, but still looked forward to her letters, as she kept sending them twice a week. In Catterick Camp he and his group now gaining in confidence, so much so, they knew they were ready for what faced them in the future. In the last week of their Basic Training, they were put under even greater pressure with kit inspections sprung on them at odd times and marching drill to perfect their march past, which would be taken by a Brigadier of the Royal Signals.

Because such a high-ranking officer was taking the salute, Captain Wilcox became very fussy and scrutinized every move B troop made, even inspecting their kit himself. By this time, the training group had done a good job on Dave and his mates, as no complaints were received from Captain Wilcox.

On Thursday, the twenty-first of April 1960, the big day, as it became known arrived. B troop, along with the four other groups made up the company for their passing out that day. The weather was dry with a hint of blue sky and just the touch of frost on the ground. *'All in all, not a bad morning for our pass out parade,'* he thought.

As they marched onto the parade ground around ten hundred hours that morning with their boots all bulled up and shining as bright as the morning sun, he thought B troop looked smart and they were trying to impress the other companies that they were the best. To be fair he assumed, they were all probably thinking the same.

As they stood to attention, under the watchful eyes of the R.S.M. Sergeant Horne passed between the company lines, stopping at each soldier he checked their uniforms and calming nerves, 'I'm proud to have been your sergeant and I'm proud to say you have been the best batch of conscripts that I have had the pleasure to train.' Dave knew he was buttering them up, but it did not matter, for like the rest of his mates he felt what he was saying, was true.

Waiting for the next command gave Dave time to reflect over the weeks, to when he walked through the gates of the camp a young man who did not have much to say for himself and hadn't been out of Scotland before. But here he was with his mates from different parts of these British Isle, moulded together to form this company of soldiers. At that moment, every other thing was forgotten, and feeling proud to have experienced this time, he stuck his chest out a little bit further.

'Paar-rade at Ee-ease' was shouted in a loud voice, more like a scream, by the R.S.M. They all stood at ease, and then Sergeant Horne and the NCOs walked along the lines double checking all their uniforms again.

Dave felt they had been standing for an eternity, when on the far side of the parade ground a Land Rover carrying the Brigadier came around the corner, slowly it drove up to the back of a stand that had been erected for this occasion. The moment the Brigadier mounted the stand the brass band struck up playing the Royal Signals anthem. The R.S.M. called out in a long-drawn-out way 'Parade.... attention.'

At that moment, the officers left their companies and marched forward and came to attention in front of the stand. After pleasantries, they all returned to their places in front of their companies. The orders were then given for the troops to shoulder arms and then to march.

The march and the presenting of arms were carried out

without a hitch. The band played marching tunes and as they passed the Brigadier, as one, they turned their heads in salute. He was sure a little swagger was in their steps at that moment. When it was all over, it was straight into the dining hall for their special pass out lunch.

The next day he felt was a kind of an anti-climax, but he cheered up with the news, they had all been given one-week mid training furlough. A mad scramble then ensued, as they dashed to check the order board, to find out where they were being transferred to for the rest of their training.

The posted orders read, Sig. David Walters, transferred to 25th Signal Regiment, Harper Barracks, Ripon, Yorkshire. The army in their wisdom had decided that he was to report to Harper Barracks to be trained as a Dispatch Rider (D.R.). He mussed, *considering I am a Motorcycle mechanic, with army logic, I thought they might train me as a cook.*

Three of his mates, Scouse Tom Chivers, Londoner Derek Willis, and Brian Edwards from Durham, were also posted to the same DR section in Ripon. Over basic training, they had formed a close friendship, so it was good Dave felt, that they were still going to be together for a while longer. But now it was time to think of a well-earned rest.

Before departing Catterick on leave, they still had one last mission to accomplish. The Sarge and his henchmen had put them through hell these past few weeks and now it was payback time. It snowed heavily earlier that last night, and he and a group of B troop, concocted a plan to let the Sarge know how much they appreciated all the help he had given them.

Gathering loads of snowballs, they laid them on the windowsills around the entrance to the Barrack Block. Waiting patiently until they saw the Sarge come to call lights out, once he was within range of the outer court door, they let off a salvo of snowballs, so many, he must have thought world war three had started. Luckily only one or two hit the mark, for their aim was not as good as their intentions. As the last snowball was fired, they scampered back to their rooms, and by the time he had climbed the stairs up to their rooms, they were all sitting or lying on our beds.

Entered, snorting fire from his nostrils he blasted out. 'You bloody lot, ah know it wis you. Fur that! There will be no lights oot the night.'

Dave along with his mates muffled a silent cheer but then the Sarge went on, 'No you bugger's, you hiv some snow clearing tae dae afore ye turn in, so get ready, and be ootside in fifteen minutes.'

Their prank had backfired against them. Reluctantly they readied themselves and assembled outside in the now heavy snow and waited for the Sarge to arrive. After another half hour past, still standing freezing and now covered in snow and looking like snowmen, they were just about to desert their position when the Sarge appeared.

With a big grin on his face he said in mock, 'Sorry lads, Ah completely forgot about Ye, Ah was just having a wee dram in the mess when someone said to me, there's a lot of bonny soldiers standing out there looking a wee bit lost.' With that, he turned about and said in a way that meant, got you! 'Ye better awe get to bed afore ye catch a cold. Gid night lads, sleep tight.' With the wave of a hand, he marched off.

Dave looked at his mates next to him with a blank expression as they all realized how stupid they must have appeared, and said, 'we've just been had, well and truly been had.' Dave learned a lesson about rank that night and vowed it would be the last time he would ever try to get his own back on any rank above him.

Chapter 12

Soldiers Together

Feeling fitter and having enjoyed his first twelve weeks training at Catterick, it was here in Falkirk, back in the arms of his girlfriend Jennifer, that he wished he could stay. One full week, they spent every moment they could together, and the world just passed them bye. Having been apart for all those weeks their lovemaking became more intense, so much so, that he went against his conscience and his Catholic belief. He at that time would have loved to consummate their relationship, but the last thing he needed in his life at that moment was, Jennifer to be expecting a child. They had talked often of having children, but he was sure, in her heart, as it was in his, it would have only made more problems than they could handle at that time.

The days passed by quickly and on the Friday of that week, as his birthday would fall on a day he was away, Jennifer's parents organized a birthday party for him at her house. Both his mum and Dad attended, and it seemed to seal the approval of all our parents, that when he came home from the army, they would be married.

The day before Dave left to return south, they went for a

long run on his motorcycle, with Jennifer snuggling up behind, and wrapping her arms around him, she whispered loving words in his ear. They lost themselves in the countryside that day, and even though it was still cold, they could have driven forever.

Their final evening, they spent with some friends having a good time, having a drink and a laugh. Then all too soon it was time for him to say goodbye again.

While standing on the platform in Waverly station in Edinburgh waiting for his south bound connection; he met another young soldier called George Harris, who also was returning to Catterick., Little did he know then, they would become best mates for most of their NS time together. George, Dave found out, had been in one of the other companies at Catterick, but this was the first time they had bumped into each other.

On the way down to Ripon They got to know one other, and surprisingly, had a lot in common. George also was a keen motorcyclist and had his call up time deferred because he had been an apprentice electrician. He too, had just left his fiancée to whom he was hoping to marry once his NS was over. In George's company, the journey seemed to pass much more quickly than before.

Arriving at Ripon station on the second of May they met up with some mates from the same Barrack room in Catterick, and some from the next room, who also had been posted here for DR training. Some other lads there, were coming to train as Signal operators. It was nice meeting them all, as it was their friendship that took the sting out of leaving home again.

Approaching the guardhouse gates of Harper Barracks, Military policemen were on guard. One of Dave's mates whispered 'God, it's not a training camp, it's a prison camp we've have been sent to.'

The guards, after checking I. D's, pointed them on their way to the Admin building for indoctrination. Inside they joined up with more of the lads from their previous companies. After standing around for ten minutes, they were introduced to Lieutenant Chadwell, unlike most of the officers they had had to deal with, this one was a little bit on the heavy side, but at six feet tall his height helped him to carry his weight well. This was the first time Dave had met an officer that spoke like one of the lads, no airs, or graces, and seemed a very down to earth man. Later Dave found out his first impressions were right.

Given the appropriate books and paperwork for our individual training courses, they were then allocated different barrack rooms according to their respective trades. Out of all the companies that had passed out that day in Catterick, only twenty had been detailed to train as DR's. Lieutenant Chadwell informed them their training group would meet them at their allocated barracks. Room C was to be his home for the next five weeks training.

Assembled outside the Admin office, a corporal Thomson took charge and marched them over to the barrack rooms. Stopping outside Hut A, he called out some names then the remainder proceeded to Hut B and so on, then it was Hut C. His new home turned out to be a long wooden building divided in the middle into two rooms that could hold ten, Dave was put into room C-1 along with nine other lads. Entering the building even though the heating was on, the smell of damp cold musty air just about took his breath away. It appeared the rooms had not been used for a while. At one end, a smaller room nearest the entrance door was the duty corporal's quarters,

Once allocated beds, it was off to the Quartermaster store for bedding, but this time they had transport, so it didn't take as long. When they returned and had settled in, they met their Instructor, Sergeant Coningsby. Among them, they nicknamed him, Sarge Con, as he was always trying to con them out of everything they owned. Once he found out that Dave was a Motorcycle Mechanic, he singled him out, not for punishment, but so he could repair his 500cc Royal Enfield motorbike. Dave thought, *this might turn out to be a good move for me*, because he missed some very dirty fatigues.

Having his first weekend at Ripon off, On Friday morning, Dave got the opportunity of a lift to Scotland in a Motor van owned by one of the Sergeants from the L.E.D. garage. Knowing he had no guard duty or fatigues that weekend, and that he would be able to leave at three that afternoon, he took the chance to get home, thinking; *I can surprise Jennifer, and spend tonight and all Saturday with her.* His thoughts were also, he wanted to drive his motorcycle down to camp for future weekends.

But before that could be accomplished, he had a kit inspection, taken by Lieutenant Chadwell, that Friday morning. This inspection though, was much more relaxed than at Catterick. Even though their kit was up to the same standard as it had been at Catterick, the Lieutenant just walked along between the beds hardly looking at our kit but stopped at each bed to ask their names and where they came from. All very cosy, and that was how he continued with them during their training. The dirty work it appeared was left up to the Sarge and the two corporals.

After kit inspection Dave made a bee line over to the L.E.D. and spoke to the Sarge about a seat in his Motor van. Chores finished by late Friday afternoon, along with George and two other lads they sped up the A1 road and then through some back roads onto the A68 road. The way the Sarge drove Dave wondered if he would survive the journey because the Sarge knew only one speed, pedal to the floor. With all the bumping and swaying Dave was convinced the van had no suspension or maybe they really had crossed right over Hadrian's Wall. On they sped, onto Carter Bar where Dave was beginning to feel seasick; such was the rocking and rolling of the van.

It was quite late that night when Dave arrived just outside Falkirk and was never so glad to get his feet on steady land. By the time he had walked home it was too late to contact Jennifer, and decided to wait till next day before surprising her.

When he walked into the shop, on seeing him her eyes lit up in delight, and in her surprise was stuck for words. 'What are you doing home?' she stuttered.

'I've went AWOL,' he said jokingly, 'Just so I can be with you.'

She smiled as she embraced him. He then told her his plans about taking his bike back down with him. That pleased her, but then she asked, 'The roads down there aren't dangerous, are they?'

Dave gave her a comforting squeeze. 'No, the roads are pretty straight and quiet most of the time. Anyway, it will mean I will be able to get home every weekend to see you, unless I am on guard duty.'

Over lunch with his parents Dave explained his plans, his mum wasn't too pleased. But he supposed, like all parents, they find it difficult to loosen the apron ties. His mum asked Jennifer 'How do you feel about it? Don't you think he should take the train?'

Jennifer looked at Dave as she replied, 'He said the roads are good and quiet. Even so, I will worry until he is home, and that he has returned to camp safely.

Dave looked at the two most important women in his life with love as he said. 'You both know I know what I'm doing when on my bike. I will be ok. So, you do not need to worry. Anyway, you will see me nearly every weekend.'

With the knowledge he could be home every weekend, Jennifer was feeling very amorous the rest of the afternoon. At night they spent in the company of her sister and her fiancée. They, Dave learned, had just set the date for their marriage, but unfortunately for him, he could be away at that time and not sure if he would be able to attend.

Not being familiar with the road down to Ripon that Sunday, Dave decided to leave a little earlier that afternoon. The weather was calm and sunny, good for driving. The motorcycle engine purred beautifully as it sped along. With the wind in his face, he had the wonderful feeling of being free, and was ecstatic. With the roads quieter than they might have been, the countryside zipped past him as he weaved round the corners and speed down the straight roads. It was as though he was at one with his bike. The journey south that day, was a blur, and the good thing about it, the weather stayed dry, and the journey was uneventful.

The first person he met as he pulled alongside the guardhouse was Sergeant Coningsby. Coming over he had a good long look at Dave's bike, it was an AJS 350cc, but with a few modifications. These modifications intrigued the Sarge so much he questions Dave at great length about them and seeing Dave's AJS was no ordinary bike he whispered, 'You'd better park your bike beside mine in the bike shed. In the open carpark it might get stolen.'

That is what happens with, I scratch your back if you scratch mine. Taking Dave over to the L.E.D workshop he opened a door into a round roof corrugated shed, what greeted Dave was like something out of an old museum. There in three rows were motorbikes most of them old side valve BSA M21's. Some had the old pre-45 Girder forks and ridged back ends on them.

As Dave looked them over, the Sarge told him, 'The

engines are still exceptionally reliable.' And went on to say, 'these are the bikes you'll be doing your training on.'

Dave laughed as he said, 'That should be a bit of an experience for the rest of the lads.'

Coningsby smiled, they both left the garage and locked the door. Back at his Hut, Dave found George and some other lads had already arrived, but some lads who lived near bye would not be in till just before reveille next morning.

Chapter 13

The Army Motorbike

Monday morning the sun was splitting the heavens but was spent inside a classroom being put through a motorcycle mechanic course. Before the start Sergeant Coningsby took Dave aside and said, 'Just sit there and listen, and go through the motions.' Dave thought, *probably because I knew more than Sarge about mechanics.* Most of the lads had not at this time known that he was a motorcycle mechanic and were made none the wiser.

After lunch they were all issued riding trousers, just like the ones that were worn pre-war. Then they were introduced to what was to be their motorbikes. This could not have come at a worse time, as the heavens opened and it poured, the wind blew strong making the rain blow horizontally across the yard. With only six of the group having ever driven bikes before, Dave thought, *A nice start to riding these old heavy bikes, especially for the ones that had not been on a motorbike before.*

Undaunted by the weather the Sarge and the other instructors proceeded to demonstrate to the novices how to ride the Bikes the army way. Then the fun began, skin and blood were lying all over the yard after an hour of teaching the lads how to stay upright on the bikes.

One lad called Brian Hays, really had them all scampering for cover when he lost control of his bike, he apparently opened the throttle instead of closing it and ploughed into some parked bikes. Thankfully only his dignity suffered with a sore backside, and a skinned elbow. When the Sarge asked in a demanding way 'What the fuck happened? What the fuck were you trying to do?'

Shaking, Brian apprehensively replied hysterical 'I don't know Sergeant.'

Dave, thinking back to their early days of marching as a unit, Brian was one of the lads that had had trouble marching in step with them. The Sarge shook his head, looked at Brian, and bawled, 'You wouldn't know your ass from your elbow. Would you?'

One lad could not resist called out from the back of the group, 'He does now Sarge.'

That brought a laugh from the group and got Brian off the hook. The Sarge joined in and could not stop himself from having a laugh as well. At the end of their first day of learning to drive bikes, it was more like some had been in a war and not just training. The MO was busy that afternoon.

At the end of each training day the most tedious of jobs were washing clean their motorcycles that were covered in mud, and only when the Sarge was happy, were they allow to fall out for the night. The following days were spent learning how to drive other various vehicles, particularly how to reverse a Land Rover with a trailer full of radio equipment. Dave found, it was not an easy job with the trailers being very heavy, and a mind of their own. Having learned to drive cars at home before conscription, but not passed his drive test at that time, for Dave this was one thing the army would put right.

When they had free time during the week, he along with his mates went into Ripon town Centre to a Café just off the Market Square. The big attraction was a Jukebox, and the local girls. The number 1 song at that time was 'Running Bear.' and every time they were in the café that tune seemed to be playing. It was a nice change to have some freedom just to walk about the town, especially as they could wear civilian clothes.

Training stepped up on the Tank training ground near Catterick, as cross-country work on these old bikes was difficult especially when on different difficult terrain. One section, an old quarry with a path of about four feet wide cut round the sidewall of the quarry. The test was to drive down this path to the base of the quarry and out an entrance at the other end. Sounds easy, but with a drop of about twenty-five feet, even Dave being an experienced driver found it was a daunting task, but for lads learning to drive, it must have been frightening. Other times when crossing rocky shallow rivers, a few involuntary baths were taken.

Each day out training was long and tiring, but one day turned out longer than the rest. They had started back to Camp when Brian Emery from Leeds got stuck up to the axles in a muddy hole. The Sarge took one look and shouted at him 'What the hell were you trying to do by straying off the road.'

Brian moaned, 'Thought it was firm ground Sergeant!'

'Well, you fucking know now.' Bawled the Sarge. At that he took a spade from his own bike and threw it towards Brian. 'You got it in on your own, so you can bloody well get it out on your own.'

Dave looked at his watch, saw it was nearly four-o-clock and with still a half-hour drive back to camp. Looking at Brian, who was just staring at his bike,

Dave approached the Sarge and volunteer, 'I'll stay behind and help him get his bike out Sarge.'

The Sarge reluctantly agreed, and they all drove off. It took twenty-five minutes to dig around the wheels but could not pull it out. Just about to give up when a R.E.M.E. Land Rover stopped, and the driver called over, 'want a tow out?'

Dave accepted gladly. Once out and most of the mud cleaned off, he managed to get the motorbike started and they then trundled back to camp, arriving around six-thirty. With the bikes still to be cleaned, and dinner missed, they settled in the end, for NAAFI food.

Next day, the Sarge pulled Dave aside, 'Listen Walters, volunteering shows initiative, but I'm happy that on this occasion, you're prepared to put yourself out to help others.'

Dave thought before replying, 'It's my upbringing and my training. That was the reason, I volunteered.'

Chapter 14

Four-wheel Training

Most training days from then on, were instructions in the controls of four-wheel vehicles of all sizes, but mainly driving Land Rovers, normally three trainees to one instructor at first on an old airfield nearby, which was laid out with proper roads, signs, and roundabouts.

On one infamous excursion to the airfield, Dave driving along about one hundred yards behind the Land Rover in front, as they approached a roundabout they all gasped as the Land Rover in front, like in a scene from a Keystone cops movie went straight over the Roundabout, and as it did, the two lads sitting in the back were bounced out onto the ground. Dave's instructor shouted stop, and jumping out, ran towards the lads on the ground.

As they watched him stop to speak to the lads on the ground, they just had time to see the Land Rover in front disappearing into a wilderness of bushes and trees. After a few moments, the driver who just happened to be Brian Hays, staggered out and was confronted by an irate Corporal, screaming, 'What the fuck were you thinking about?

Brian replied matter of flatly, 'Just carrying out your orders Corporal.'

The other Corporal, pulling off his berry, threw it to the ground, took a deep breath and then let rip. 'Have you got cloth ears? You stupid bastard! I said to go straight when you come to the Roundabout, not straight over it. You fuckin well could have severely injured the lads in the back.'

To say Brian learned his lesson, maybe not. Probably it was the instructors who learned more that day, which was; do not let Brian behind a wheel again. Within the next week Brian was transferred to another section to learn to become a cipher operator, where he did not need to march or drive.

Once competent with driving in the eyes of the Sarge, the training took them all over Yorkshire Dales, from Skipton to Harrogate to Bolton Abbey and down the coast to Scarborough. Dave looked forward to their trips to Scarborough, what young man in uniform would not? Chatted up the local lasses was to no avail, as their time there was too short, and it was time to return to camp.

Time passed quickly during this period, with getting home at weekends to see Jennifer, which both looked forward to. During the week at camp, time was spent in class learning about convoying, and then practicing on the road, In-between they had map reading exercises. Dave preferred this time, as it got him mobile on his army bike on his own.

Reading map references and finding the markers, felt good fun. But behind it all, he knew was a serious part of his training, nevertheless enjoyable. These exercises took him all around the Yorkshire Dales and through some exceptionally beautiful villages and countryside. An area of the country he might never have considered visiting before.

The weather up on the moorland he found could be very rough and had been changeable most of the time crossing over them, but with the onset of summer and much warmer conditions, it was becoming more pleasurable driving around the Dales.

Next big day on his calendar was his driving tests, which took place in Harrogate with civilian testers conducted the tests. The days leading up to their tests they had had a few runs around Harrogate, so he felt ready for what lay before him. When it was his turn, in typical fashion the civilian testers changed the route, but still he managed to drive around the streets and answered all the Highway Code questions. He felt confident at the end of the day but was not told if he had passed or failed.

All the tester would say was, 'You'll be informed once back to camp.'

It was next morning before the results were posted. At the top of the notice board, it said Seventeen had passed and three had failed, Dave excitedly looked down the list, but before he came to his name, George Harris leaning over his shoulder and shouted in his ear, 'You lucky bugger, you've got an A1 pass,.' continuing he chipped in with, 'Humm! That stupid tester needs his eyes tested for failing me, the best driver in the army.'

George, Dave found out, was like that, always seeing the brighter side of life. Turning to eye him he said, 'George maybe he just enjoyed your driving so much he wants a repeat show.'

'Aye yae may be right; if that's the case I'll gee the bugger the thrill of his life next time.' Next day he took his test again and passed.

Their last week of training in Ripon was a series of kit inspections, which Lieutenant. Chadwell passed by without even a glance. He spent much more time asking how each one was getting on with life in the army, and had we been writing home. In-between these inspections, some marching to polish up in preparation for their final pass out parade, on Thursday the 2nd of June 1960.

Dave looked forward to that day with trepidations as that day was also when they were to be told where they would be posted. Two weeks previously the Sarge pulled Dave aside and told him, 'I've applied to keep you here as an instructor, which will mean a home posting for you.'

Dave was happy with that and said, 'That would be great as it will mean I'll be able to get home often.'

The morning of the parade the sun shone, and it was ridiculously hot when all the trainees marched together onto to the parade ground. This time their inspection and salute were taken by the OC of the camp, who then gave them a talk, 'You all should be proud that you are now soldiers and I'm pleased with all your marks in the tests, the highest for years,' Dave knew flattery when he heard it. The OC finished off by saying 'You are all an example of why the British Army is so respected all over the world and I'm sure you will make your parents proud of you, I wish you all well in your new postings.'

At that Major Harrower of the training division called for three cheers, hip-hip hooray he called out and they all responded. Dave inwardly gave an extra cheer in the thought he might be kept there for the remainder of his service. It was quite an emotional time as they all knew that they might be split up and sent to different places.

After two hours of parade, they marched back to their barrack room in a sober mood, Dave was still elated. The order board was the first place they all made too, to see if their posting were up. Dave looked down the list, his heart fell when he saw that instead of a home posting he was being sent out to Malaya.

Later the sergeant told him, 'Sorry about your posting Walters. My request to have you stay had been turned down as they needed thirty DR's and there were only twenty in that intake. Eighteen DRs, have been posted out to the Far East, to Malaya and Hong Kong, while the other two were posted to Germany. Sorry for building your hopes up.'

Dave felt a little jealous of the two lads that had been posted to Germany, as he was thinking it would have been easier to get home more often. He swallowed his misfortune and wished the two lads well. When they broke up camp, the only conciliation he felt at the time was that all his mates were being posted to Malaya as well. But for now, they had fourteen days embarkation leave to look forward to. Before saying goodbye to his mates, they all agreed to meet up in Chester before going on to the Transit Camp.

On the road home that day he couldn't make up his mind how he was going to tell Jennifer about his posting, he knew it was going to be the hardest thing he ever would have to tell her, and the feelings he had at that time were as bad as the time they split up. On the journey north that day, he was on autopilot, the fields, and the villages he passed were just a blur. Arriving home too late to see Jennifer that night, he settled into his bed and as he wasn't expecting to see Jennifer until the Friday, his last thoughts before drifting off to sleep was, *how do I break the news to her.*

Chapter 15

Home to Relax

Fourteen glorious days, it seemed a long time, but trying to cram every minute he could with Jennifer, it was only but a moment in time. The first day together he tried to break the news to her but found it difficult. It wasn't till later that night, she asked, "Well, when are you going to tell me where you're being posted to?'

Dave knew if he told her outright, it would be a shock to her and tried to let on it was not so bad. 'I'm being sent someplace hot.'

She punched his shoulder playfully as she said, 'Tell me or I'll just have to torture you till you tell?'

'Ok, ok. I'm going abroad.'

'England's abroad to us Scotch.' She persisted as she once more playfully punched him. 'Are you being kept on as an instructor like you said might happen?'

'No not that either.' looked at her, as the smile left his face and became more serious. 'I've been posted out to Malaya.'

Her head dropped, and she went quiet. He pulled her close and could feel her body shuddering as she tried to gather her thoughts together. Once she finally realized I was being sent further than they both wanted, a tear ran down her cheek.

'I don't won't you to go too far away, what am I do without you not getting home at weekends.' She sobbed.

Dave for once was feeling the stronger, kissed her tenderly, then teasingly said, 'You know what they say Absence makes the heart grow fonder.'

She looked at him with tear filled eyes, and with a strangest of feelings, he melted into her arms. Clinging tightly to one another, they showered each other with all their love as though they had no tomorrow.

It was a couple of days before they settled down with what it would mean to them, and when looked into each other's eyes there was something foreboding in the background and a sadness that they were unable to chase away. This sadness though, drew them closer together.

The days past and as hard as they could they were unable to really enjoy their selves, even when away for a run on the motorcycle, the countryside did not look the same. A change had taken place, and their love became more desperate. Jennifer got very emotional when he asked, 'Do you want to talk about me being away for such a long time,'

'I don't know. I just want these moments to last for ever.' She whispered.

'I know, I know. I wish they could as well. I also wished it had not made our time together so awkward. I had hoped being home with you would have filled us both enough to see us through till I come home, but this is not how I had felt our time together would have been.'

At night leaving her was harder than before as the passion between them was much stronger. Jennifer hung onto him desperately and refused to let him go, it was as if she believed he would not come back, and as for Dave's part, he found it extremely hard to resist not staying with her.

Time passed and as the day drew nearer, Jennifer told Dave, 'Uncle Frank has given me the keys to his holiday home.' It was not really a home, more a big shed done up as a summer hideaway. Trying to convince Dave she went on, 'We spent many wonderful days during our time together walking among the hills. It's only an idea, but we could spend some time alone there, with no telephones or anyone to bother us, it would be perfect for us.'

Convinced, he replied, 'Sounds a great idea, somewhere we both like, but what about your parents, what do they think?'

Looking seriously at him she whispered, 'They think it will do us good to be alone for a while.'

Setting off with only the clothes they wore and a few sandwiches, the intention was only to stay just for the day. That day the sun shone and was the warmest day they had had, and just being together released them from all the pressures they had been under. Wondering hand in hand through the woodland she asked of their aspirations 'Once we're married will we still emigrate? After all you will be away for at least nineteen months and might not want to go away again.'

'I wouldn't mind as long as you're there with me, but let us not talk about that the now, let us just enjoy what we have here and now.' With arms wrapped around each other, they continued until reaching the little stream that flowed down the valley.

The sun now high in the sky and the meadows looking colourful, he thought, I wish I could stay as happy as this with Jennifer forever. Nearing the widest part of the burn Dave said, 'Let us go for a paddle?'

They clown around for a while, then sat by the stream holding hands as they watched the water ripple over the stony bed. After a fleeting moment he looked at her, 'You know, you mean more to me than life itself. I love you so much; to have to go away from you will be the hardest thing I will ever have to do. I hope you will still want me when I come home, if you do, I promise we will never be apart again.'

Her eye glazed over with tears, 'I love you too, and I'll wait forever for you, so you hurry back home and marry me, as I'll never love anyone as I love you.'

He pulled her to him and kissed her, the feelings that engulfed them at that moment as they clung to one another, it was as though life depended on it. They stayed that way for a long, long time, captivating the moment.

Time passed and as the sun sank behind the hills, a dark ominous shadow began to engulf them. 'I think we should think about starting home?'

The moment had gripped Jennifer so much she whispered, 'I don't want to go. I want to stay here, just the two of us together.'

'What will your parents say? Won't they be annoyed? After all we are not married.

'I don't care what anyone says, I only want this to be special and that you will always remember that I love you. She said as she snuggled into him.

That night, the gentle breeze that funnelled down the valley cooled the air in the cabin, and as they lay naked under the blankets in one another's arms, they gazed deeply into each other eyes, their bodies heating one another as they made love. For the first time together, their love was blind to the consequences, as they knew it may be the last time for a long time, that they will be like this again. It was this special moment in time spent together that their love seemed to lift them to a new level.

The next morning Jennifer woke first and lying beside the one she loved she just watched his face as he slept. Her thoughts were of how much she will miss him when he is gone, and of how she will cope. He turned to face her at that moment and opened his eyes, his first thoughts were, *she is beautiful, and she is all mine.*

'Good morning sweat heart,' she said with a kiss. Dave embraced her and feeling her soft body against him aroused a need again. She playfully tickled him, he returned the gesture and before long they were making love again, this time slowly and with much more tenderness. They stayed in bed long into the morning whispering of their love for one another.

After sharing their last sandwich, left from the day before, they spent the rest of the day just strolled around the hills locked in this perfect love that surrounded them.

Before long, sadly and with great difficulty they had to with great reluctance return home.

As she sat on the pillion seat, her arms rapped around him, she whispered in his ear, 'I hope I'm going to have your baby after last night,' she then snuggled into him as kissed him on his ear.

Dave at that moment was feeling good just having her so close to him, as he knew it would not happen again for a long time after tomorrow. With the wind blowing in their faces, at that moment they were free from all their problems.

When they arrived back at Jennifer's home neither of her parents commented about why they had stayed the night. In those days, which was not the proper thing to do before marriage. Dave was sure though, they both had their thoughts, but the time for them to vent them was not now.

Leaving Jennifer that night, Dave expressed, 'I hope you don't get into trouble because of us staying over,'

Before completing what he was trying to say, she put her hand over his mouth and with a tear in her eyes, said softly, 'I wouldn't have change anything we did over the last two days for anything in the world,' she hesitated then said, 'Except have us stay there forever.'

Chapter 16

Time to Say Farewell

Tuesday the 14th of June 1959, Dave was up very early and sitting on the edge of his bed looked around the room at all the possessions he had gathered since childhood, it began to dawn on him that this was possible the last time he might do this here in the privacy of his own personal world. A lump came into his throat as thoughts of all his childhood memories came to him and of the times spent there, and he knew he would miss this space he called his own.

After breakfast, which was a quite affair, his mum and dad probable, would have had their own thoughts of this day, but now that he was off for a long time he knew in his heart, he would miss them as much as they, him. He put on his uniform and packed the rest of his kit along with family photos, and his special photos of Jennifer, into his kit bag. Standing at the door he gave one last glance around his room, and in his heart, he said farewell.

Earlier in the week through some tears and handshakes, he had said goodbye to his sister, his brothers, and friends. He also sold his beloved 350cc AJS motorcycle to a friend with the promise of buying it back when he returned. He was now as ready as he would ever be.

Before leaving that morning, he sat with his mother and dad in the privacy of their home, it was a difficult farewell as he was sure they still looked on him as their bairn. He kissed his mum on her brow and as he turned away tears formed in her eyes. He did not dare look back at her, for he did not want her to see, that he too was trying to hold his emotions back in that moment. It was with a sad feeling that the cord had finally been cut, he walked out the door.

His dad, a quiet reserved person, accompanied him down the stairs and onto the Street carrying his kit bag. Laying the kit bag down on the pavement, then placed his hands-on Dave's shoulders, looked at him for a long moment as though he knew something Dave did not. Dave could see the love he had for him in his eyes, as he was his bairn, his youngest of six children, and although he knew his dad was proud of him, seeing his youngest all grown up into a young man and off to serve his country, and although sad, he showed he was also proud to see him go.

His parents had raised him up to be a person, who respected people, always to tell the truth and never to get into trouble. Embracing his dad in a hug, they stood like that for a long moment, and he could feel his dad's sadness, then for the first time in Dave's life his dad shook his hand as a man.

His dads last and only words to him that day were 'Take care and come home safely.'

As Dave walked along the street, he had a strange feeling in his gut, but, he put it down to the sadness of leaving home, or maybe just the excitement of the day he thought, and the new adventure he was about to embark on. At the corner of their street, he turned and saw that his dad was still watching him. The tears he was trying to hold back welled up in his eyes, as they waved to one another. In his thoughts Dave said, *'Thanks dad for everything. I hope I make you proud of me.'* He turned the corner, and into a new era of his life.

Standing on the station platform embracing Jennifer as they waited for the ten-a.m. train to arrive, He asked 'Why so quiet?'

Jennifer replied in a very quiet hesitant voice, 'I'm missing you already, and I can't help thinking that you're really going to be gone for a long time and I won't be able to see you.' Sighing deeply as she continued, 'I'm trying to be brave for both of us as I know you don't want to go.' Dave wiped away the tears from her face and lingered in that tender embrace. Lifting her head up, her lips felt so soft and warm as they kissed long and passionately.

The spell surrounding them at that moment, they did not want to break, but break they had to. Pulling away reluctantly from her lips, it felt like he was losing a part of himself. Her eyes filled with tears as he whispered, 'Remember always, I love you more than words can say, you'll always be with me here,' as he spoke, taking hold of her hand he placed it on his heart.

Dave had said goodbye to her parents and uncle who had drove them to the station. They had stayed back a distance allowing them space to be alone, for they knew this moment was for the two of them alone. The world was outside the cloud of love that engulfed them, and in those precious minutes, they felt as one. These precious moments he knew, were to last them for a long time, as who knows what distractions the future holds for them. But for now, they were together.

As the train, smoke billowing from the engine slowly came along the track towards their platform; she tightened her grip around him. He tried to pull away from her, her head dropped as she sobbed uncontrollably, and tears ran down her face again, he pulled her to him once more to comfort her and felt her tears on his face as he himself tried to control his own emotions.

At that moment, her mother came forward and putting her arm around her shoulder, gave her a comforting hug. Looking at him, she said. 'Don't worry David, we'll look after her till your home by her side again.'

David slowly stepped back from her and felt a sudden jolt in his heart. Jennifer slowly lifted her head, and looked at him with a look he would never forget as she whispered, 'I love you darling, please return home to me.' She blew a kiss to him; he raised his hand and caught it then pressed it to his lips.

At that moment, the air of his world went quiet, and only the sound of his boots carrying him away was left. After boarding the train, he stood leaning out the door window. Jennifer broke free from her mother's attention and ran forward and grabbed hold of Dave's hand. The train by this time slowly at first started moving, still she held on saying repeatedly, 'I love you!'

The train picked up speed and she could no longer keep up, and as their hands parted, he felt a jolt in his heart. The train was carrying him on his way out the station, and he sighed as though the breath of life was being pulled from him. All he could do was watch, his eyes not wanting to let the sight of her go, with his heart breaking, he stared at her lonely figure, at the platform end, still waving until she disappeared into the distance, and then he was alone.

Chapter 17

Transit Camp

Dave's destination that afternoon was the 3 SQN, 11th Signal Regiment embarkation Depot Camp, near Chester, Cheshire. He had to report in by the following morning, Wednesday 15th before 8am, so this journey had to start the day before. It turned out to be the longest and loneliest journey he had ever taken. The first half of the journey he spent fighting back the tears as in his mind, he could see Jennifer still standing at the platform end.

Arriving in Chester station he met up with some of his mates and a few other lads from their group. They were told to notify the camp on arrival and transport would be sent to pick them up, the journey to the camp outside Chester only took a few minutes. It is amazing how with your training you fall into routine once back in the confines of army barracks. About three quarters of our Company were present by evening, the rest who live near bye, arriving before reveille next morning.

Over the next few days, the troop changed their old uniforms for tropical ones and were told what the itinerary would be. They were also briefed on where they would be going and on the type of transport use. It seemed to be all go, Dave thought, taking them away from their loved ones it was the best thing to happen to them, as it concentrated their minds on what lay ahead.

A thorough medical check from the M.O. was next, and then came the inoculations to protect them from everything except the army. Some of the lads did not take kindly to these injections and were laid up for the day. Dave was fortunate he did not come down with any side effects except a sore arm for a short time. Others though, could be seen swinging their arms and walking about, just as the orderly had said, 'Swing those arms about lads, that's the best way to get the inoculations through your system quickly.'

One lad piped in with the comment, 'Pity there weren't more officers about, as while we're swinging our arms, we could practice saluting.'

The next two days after inoculations they were given time off and allowed to go site seeing in Chester. The weather that June was ridiculously hot, one of the hottest for years. The town centre was quaint and beautiful in the sun, and showed its best side to them, as it did that day as they strolled along the Dee river side.

This was a good time to be healthy young men, for this was the start of the Rock and Roll era, the time when the young ladies wore their short summer dresses and looked their best. It was a morale booster to their egos at that time, they chatted up and charmed the young women knowing that they would be gone for some time and might not see a beautiful young English rose for a long time.

Sitting by the riverside Dave mused, because the weather was so hot, *this might be good preparation for what they might expect when they reached Malaya*, twenty-one thousand miles away by sea.

Dave was sure it was a journey into the unknown, he and

most of his mates really hadn't a clue what Malaya would be like. So ignorant of that country, no one talked about their future destination. Dave's knowledge of Malaya was that it was a small country, a peninsula at the bottom of Burma and Thailand. Even his own idea of the citizens, was of people who lived in houses made of bamboo and used blowguns. So much was his ignorance of Malaya, he had decided to borrow a book from the army library. What he read, changed his mind about Malaya, the country that was to be his home for more than eighteen months.

The day, Monday the 20th of June 1960 was to stay in Dave's memory for a long time. He stood silently on the deck with his six mates watching the shoreline recede into the distance, in his mind he could still hear the band playing the tune 'Will yae no come back again.' he couldn't look at his mates or say anything as he had a tear in his eye, as he was sure they all had.

The thoughts going through his head he felt sure, were echoed in the thoughts of his mates. The only comfort they had at that moment was, that they all literally speaking, were in the same boat and their thoughts were of their girlfriends, families, and the lives they had left behind. All that was about to change now, they were on their way and there was no turning back.

Earlier they had travelled down from Chester by truck to the docks at Southampton to board their troop ship HMT Oxfordshire. This ship carried, they were told, over five hundred passengers and had done so many times since it was commissioned in 1957. The journey down the road was uneventful, stopping only to stretch their legs and have their pack lunches in comfort. The sun had beat down on the truck canvas cover, making it extremely hot for sitting inside, so it was a pleasure just to get out onto the roadside for fresher air.

Arrived at the docks, lots of people were waiting to board. Soldiers, who had families travelling with them, had already boarded. Other soldiers who were travelling without families, said their goodbyes on the quayside, there was much crying and hugging. Dave having already left his relatives watched the proceedings from the top deck, feeling very nostalgic.

He scanned the throng of family groups on the quay and thought of his own back home. His eye was attracted by one family group, a soldier holding a baby up as he kissed it, then cuddling a little girl before giving the woman standing beside them a formal sort of farewell. At that moment, among the crowds on the quay, this one family whom he had not met before, was destined to change his life.

Chapter 18

Bon Voyage

When all were aboard, the brass band struck up with tunes to wish them bon voyage, the mooring ropes were taken off the capstans. At that moment, Dave felt for the first time the power of the engines pushing the ship slowly away from the quay, it was then that the band struck up playing 'Will yae no come back again.' People were waving both on the deck and on the quayside. There were very few dry eyes at that moment, as it was a happy and sad occasion in that same moment.

It was a strange experience for Dave, his first time on such a large ship, however one he was looking forward to as the ship sailed out of the docks,

Dave and his mates were still standing on deck watching the land recede further and further into the distance. It was his Scouse mate Ron, who spoke first, 'Well lads, no more crying you're all big boys now.'

They all looked at each other, then without a word they started pushing Ron about, then one another like a bunch of kids having a laugh; tears dried from their eyes as they tried to come to terms with their situation and to enjoy the rest of the moment. Side by side with his mates, Dave felt they had formed a bond that would stand them in good stead while together.

Settling into life on the ship was not easy for them, first they had to negotiate a hammock and that was not as easy as it appeared, especially while the ship was swaying and rocking about. Another problem was trying to find where places are on the ship, and what parts of the upper decks were out of bounds. With all the squaddies restricted to the bow of the ship, and the officers and family quartered at the stern, and off limits to them. In many ways Dave thought, the stern would be like sitting on a bus facing backwards and not able to see where you are going.

The English Channel, calm to start with, had Dave thinking, this is going to be easy, but the further out into open sea they sailed, the rougher it became. Without using the ship stabilizers, it was rock and roll time, and by the time they reached the Bay of Biscay, there was not much room around the ship railings. Not so much all hand's on deck, more like all heads hanging over, being sick. Dave along with the rest.

The Medical Officer had a steady stream of sick people trying to get relief, but the ranks were told to toughen it out, as the MO was busy with the families and their children. So, for the next few hours they had to watch where they put their feet, so messy was it, the safest place for Dave to be in his hammock below deck, where he could get the cool air blower on his face. After a while he thought he was over his seasickness until he decided to go back up on deck for some fresh sea air. It was nice to feel the breeze on his face and he started to relax.

Dave was just sitting on top of one of the hatches having a quiet think, when two lads rushed past him running like seasoned sprinters over to the deck fence. One lad did not make it and spewed his stomach contents up in front of Dave.

That was Dave's time to join them by the deck fence polluting the sea once more.

Next morning, enjoying the gentle breeze, things were a little better. In conversation with his mates Dave mentioned, 'You wouldn't think there were any Officers or NCO's (*Non-commissioned Officer's*) on board.'

George, his Edinburgh mate countered, 'I don't blame them, how could you control that mob! I was nearly tossed overboard when I tried to shove my way to the fence last night.' Smiling he continued, 'All I wanted was to have a wee pee overboard and they kept shouting at me. This is for sickies only.' His sense of humour kept us all in a chirpy mood the rest of that day.

The top brass, Dave surmised, must have known it would take the few days for the troops to find their sea legs, for some a little longer. In his case, he was one of the latter and it was not till they had cleared the Bay of Biscay that he started to find his sea legs and was able to join the other lads.

Once most of the troops had recovered the NCOs took over and installed discipline among them and explained to them what the program would be each day. One thing was, after some exercise each day they would have plenty of time to acclimatize as the ship sailed along. One order repeatedly given, 'Don't lie in the sun too long, as sun stroke will be treated as a self-inflicted injury, and you will be put on a charged.'

Sailing onward with the coast of Portugal to the left of them was just a dark line on the horizon, Gibraltar was to be their first port of call. Dave by this time began to enjoy being on the ship. More relaxed, he started thinking about what lay ahead. On the third day at sea, while lying on deck he heard the speaker announcement telling them that they would be docking in Gibraltar within the next two hours, and that they would be allowed some shore leave, for a few hours. What a welcome announcement that was and was greeted with a big cheer.

Seeing Gibraltar for the first time Dave thought, *places like this I might never have been able to see if I had not been drafted into the NS*. He had only ever read about Gibraltar in books at school, but here he was, and it was an impressive site to see up close. This was a first for him, to set foot on foreign soil, so along with his six mates they hurried down the gangway onto the quayside. Their first thoughts, post letters to loved ones back home, then see if they could get a taste of the local cuisine and maybe a cool refreshing pint of beer, for that was the one thing in short supply on the ship.

The local Senoritas were out in force by the time they got right up into the town and tried hard to entice the innocent young lads into compromising situations. Some, Dave thought, didn't succumb to their wayward ways. With all the distractions around them, by the time they reached the town centre the bars and restaurants were so crowded, there was not enough room to swing a cat. In the end they settled for a sandwich from a street kiosk. That was his memorable day in Gib, not as exciting as he had imagined it would be, but nevertheless it was a pleasant change from being on board.

Arriving back on board he was informed by the duty officer that he was on fatigues duty in the Galley next day, something they all had to take their turns at, so he was not surprised when he was selected. That night as they sailed away from Gibraltar, he made the most of the pleasant calm weather as they sailed into the Mediterranean Sea. The weather now much warmer even with the sea breeze, had most of the troops on deck. The talk among his mates was all about what they will do once they returned home.

Dave smiled and looked at the rest of the lads for here

they were on the deck of a big ship sailing on a calm sea with a gentle breeze, a cloudless sky and on the start of their biggest adventure of their lives, and all they talked about was when they would be back home. He slept well that night.

Next morning before breakfast, the duty sergeant wakened him at dawn to start in the Galley. A quick shave and wash, into his fatigue uniform and then off to report in. On arrival at the Galley, waiting there as he entered were five other lads whom he had never met before, being from other units on board. He was paired off with a twenty-seven years old lad called Michael Higham; a regular soldier in the Royal Signals for about eight years, and on his way out to Malaya for a second tour. Their job in the Galley was mostly cleaning up around the floor and generally helping the cooks.

During their time together, Dave like Mike, as he wanted to be called, got to know about each other. Dave felt very much at ease with him, and in their conversations, Mike told him, he was married, and his wife's name was Lynne, they have two kids one aged three and the other fourteen months old.

'Hopefully,' he said, 'they will be joining me out in Malaya later this year.'

Their conversation took in their possible postings and individual duties. Mike mentioned a duty called a Courier. He said, 'It's a good duty to be on as you have plenty time to yourself.' He also said, 'The duty was delivering mail to the different units.' Dave had not a clue what else was entailed, but one other thing he said, 'You also get extra pay for food, while away from camp. That certainly was an incentive to try for that duty.

Their duties finished in the galley; they exchanged deck numbers. Mike was on the deck directly above him. Before parting they arranged to meet on deck later. That was Dave's fatigues over for the journey he hoped, and maybe he could now sit back and relax, then again, he was sure the duty officer will prove him wrong and have other ideas for the rest of their trip.

Dave's other mates were doing fatigues cleaning the deck; two of them even boasted that they saw bathing beauties when up at the family end of the ship. One also bragged, 'I sat by a small swimming pool and chatted up some of the ladies while dipping my feet in the pool.'

'In your dreams.' Dave told him.

Chapter 19

The Suez Canal

With the Mediterranean calm, it was plain sailing all the way. One night on deck it got so busy with over three hundred other lads trying to find space, but Dave and his mates managed to get a spot where they could all sit together. Feeling the cool breeze on his face Dave started telling them about the soldier he met while on fatigues, and as he was speaking, Mike walked over to join them. 'Ah, here he is now.'

Dave introduced Mike to the lads and was not surprised they all got on so well, as Mike had a very disarming way about him. It was also nice to hear someone who had had experience, telling what it was like out in Malaya. The rest of the evening Mike filled them in on the do's and the don'ts of what to expect once they got to Malaya. He also said, 'The country may be different, but a lot more modern that you might imagine.'

Early the next morning, Egypt loomed up on the horizon, because of the mirage effect. What land could be seen in the distance Dave was informed, was much further away than he imagined. Staring at the mirage he could feel the heat strengthening each hour as the ship ploughed its way towards their next stop.

It took nearly the rest of that day before the anchor was dropped outside Port Said at the entrance to the Suez Canal. That evening, more provisions were brought on board for the next leg of our journey. Once loaded up, the ship moved into position to await a pilot to guide the ship through the entrance and then down the Canal.

After breakfast next morning, while their ship was still waiting to enter, Dave went up on deck and met up with some of his mates, who were all leaning over the side. Joining them he was surprised to find the sea full of small craft called bumboats, long slender and very flimsy, all full of tourist gifts. The merchants standing precariously on their boats, threw ropes with gifts attached up to the passengers, obviously hoping for a sale and their sales talk very persuasive, so much so, Dave feeling sorry for one scruffy young boy, was conned. Thinking of the handcrafted photo album he bought, supposedly genuine Egyptian leather, only to have it fall apart later when he tried to open it. His mates laughed and never let him forget the day he was stung by an Egyptian Bumboat boy.

Once more the anchor lifted, and they sailed through the entrance into the Canal. At the end of the pier one lad pointed out what looked like a statue lying on its side and quizzes Mike, 'What is that all about, someone they didn't like?'

'It's a legacy from a few years back when the Egyptians tried to block ships travelling through the Canal. 'I think it was when Anthony Eden was Prime Minister.' He replied.

'Now that you mention it, I think I read something about it, but it was too far away for me to bother about it then.' Dave then thought, '*but here I am now, looking at that event of history.*'

Sailing down the Suez Canal they found a bit weird, for when standing in the Centre of the ship they couldn't see the sides of the Canal, it was as though the ship was sailing over the desert, but disappointedly no pyramids were in sight. What little they saw of Egypt, Dave thought, was a backward country, very dry, with sand that seemed to go on forever on either side. Because of the restricted speed, due to obstacles still blocking parts of the Canal, it took the best part of the rest of the day to travel down to the Red Sea. Then, the shoreline on both sides started to recede away on both sides. The ship had now passed their only barrier to sailing all the way to Malaya.

Next day those without duties, were invited to a party, all because they were now crossing over the Tropic of cancer. Tradition has it, they were all informed, that when boats pass over this imaginary line people are usually ducked under the water. Dave said to his mates, as they pushed him forward, 'Not this boy they're not.'

On this occasion it was a Major General, the highest-ranking officer on board; it was his fate to suffer this dipping on all their behalf. The biggest cheer of the day went up when he went under the water, poor soul. After the party it was back to their own section where they had a special meal, and, at night a film show; starring John Wayne in the western 'She wore a Yellow Ribbon.' Since leaving home, that was the first night they felt in a party mood as the top brass had opened the Bar, so they could have a beer.

The following morning Dave woke up feeling a bit squeamish and skipped breakfast. With no duties, he went up on deck and with the air incredibly still he decided to lie in the shade. A short time later he was wakened by the movement of the ship rising and falling. Opening his eyes, for a moment he thought the ship was going under the sea and then it was up in the air. This movement went on, up and down, up, and down like on a roller coaster ride.

George came up on deck a few minutes later and smirking, strolled over to his side. 'Missed you at breakfast! Feeling all right?' then teased. 'Do you want me to fetch something for you to eat?'

'No,' Dave answered 'Just felt a bit squeamish so I decided to pass breakfast and come up on deck to lie down in the fresh air.' Then pointing, he drew his attention to what was ahead, 'Only to open my eyes to this.'

George gave him a slap on the back and shouted, 'Brilliant, isn't it! Just like being on the big dipper at Portobello Beach.' Then going as near as he could to the bow of the ship, he turned and shouted again 'Brilliant.'

Just then two other mates came over and asked, 'What's the matter with you? Missed you at breakfast.'

Dave didn't answer them, he just said, 'That stupid Scotsman has gone off his heed.'

Brian Emery looked at Dave, then over at George and back at Dave, 'I meant you, not that idiot.'

They all had a laugh at George's antics and shouted 'Dive! Dive! Dive!'

George turned to look at them; a big smile filled his face. Leaning on the railing, he called out, 'Throw me a spear me hearties. Thurs a whale a beckoning.'

Brian shook his head, 'There's nothing that would put him down. I'm told on good authority, when we sailed through the Bay of Biscay, it was George that was steering the ship, because the captain was down sick.'

They then all sat quietly watching the ship rise and fall until the Red Sea started to flatten out a little. It was just after that a deck hand was passing bye. 'Mate' George call to him, 'What makes the sea like this.'

The deck hand was of an African nationality, but could speak reasonable English; said 'Land narrows. Before going into big sea, its normal, Sab.'

They learned that day, it was due to the water of the Red

Sea tapering as it got near the Bab el Mandeb straits which leads into the Gulf of Aden. This eased to a gentle sway as we neared the straits and then they were through into the Gulf, sailing on a smooth sea with porpoise skimming on the bow waves as onward the ship went to their next Port of call, Aden.

The Ship anchored off Aden to take on some fuel and drop off some army personnel. While this was taking place, the Captain announced that those who wanted, were allowed four hours shore leave. Taking advantage, Dave, George, Mike, and Brian ventured into the town. Aden, but found out as they walked along the sandy road, it was a very dry, hot place, and even though they were becoming accustomed to the heat, this was the hottest they had experienced. It was hot enough to have fried eggs on the sidewalk. Luckily, they found a place to get something cool to drink.

Wearing only tropical gear, shorts, shirt, and their floppy Jungle hats as they were called, Dave thought at that moment, *the ones who stayed on board, had made the right decision.* To stay too long, they all agreed, would have been folly, so back on board they headed and down to their deck where the air conditioner was blowing cool air. At least Dave mused, *I stood on the soil of Aden.*

It was during that stop, all his letters he had written to Jennifer and his family, along with the other mail, were taken off ship and sent on. With more provisions and mail redirected on board, the ship set sail again.

The next leg would take them all the way down the Arabian Sea and into the Indian Ocean to their next destination, Port Colombo on the island of Ceylon (Sri Lanka), off the south tip of India.

Dave sat many times on deck just marvelling at this vast expanse of sea, thinking, he was in one of the loneliest parts of the world, but often proved, that this is not so. While crossing the Indian Ocean, day after day, he was fascinated that they were often accompanied by shoals of porpoise diving through the waves made by the ship, and occasionally whales could be seen. Sometimes it would be shoals of flying fish that would skip over the surface and fly for distances before diving under again. Other times it was shark fins that could be spotted.

Dave was mystified more than anything with the number of cargo ships that plied their trade across these lonely waters, for even at night in the dark, lights could be seen from other ships going about their business. To Dave, the crossing was now becoming more interesting, as at last, he had finally found his sea legs and was topping up a good tan. From there on, he felt at ease on the ship.

It took around four and half days to cross the Indian Ocean and each night he managed to find some time and space to write his letters, which was not easy with so many soldiers on-board.

All the while the rhythmic heartbeat of the ship engines kept chugging steadily hour after hour, until as the pirates of old would call out, 'Land Ho! Thur be land, captain.'

Chapter 20

Terra Firma

Having travelled south until land was again sighted on the distant horizon, where five hundred miles north of the Equator, lay the jewel of the east, Ceylon (Sri Lanka).

On deck with his mates, they impatiently stared at the horizon as the fuzzy black line of land rose higher and higher until the shimmering coast could be seen. Beaches lined with coconut palm trees, and white sand stretching into the distance. The translucent water of the blue ocean sparkled in the sunlight as the waves lapped onto the beaches and with a beautiful blue-sky overhead, all together, it was a magical scene.

His eyes took it all in, having never seen anything so beautiful as this tropical scene before him. Dave said excitedly, 'This is paradise! I'm going to enjoy this kind of life if Malaya is anything like this.'

It was a magical moment, only to be shattered by George roaring 'Where's all the burds in gress skirts.'

Typical George. However, after the long sail and feeling travel weary, Dave was more interested in just going ashore, inquired, 'Wonder if we will be allowed ashore?'

Brian seemed to speak for the whole crew when he said, 'I hope so, as my feet are desperate to stand on land.'

Before this trip, none of them had been out of Briton, so it was left up to George again, who in his wisdom said, 'Well lads, look at all this wonderful stuff.' Then in a sarcastic voice, 'You'd never have got this far to feast your eyes on this, if it hadn't been for me pulling the strings to have us sent out here.'

As Dave grabbed hold of George, the rest joined in, lifting him up as though going to throw him overboard. George squealed. 'I can't swim!'

'Just as well,' Dave responded, 'or you might be still floating in the sea when the ship sails on.'

The ship's anchor dropped with a splash around three in the afternoon, just off the coast near the capital city Colombo. Meantime, with nearly eight hours needed for refuelling and replenishing food stocks, they had time to kill. Four hours to be precise. Motor launches were ferrying civilian passengers over to the harbour, and Dave, George, and Brian managed to get on board one to get some shore leave. The OC said it was not so much shore leave, but mainly to help the civilian passengers, so they jumped at the chance to put their feet on the soil of Colombo.

Walking part way up into the city from the harbour, Dave was not particularly impressed with what he saw. The streets were dirty, dusty, and very run down looking, probably typical dockland area. The local inhabitants where pretty much the same, and not what he had pictured, like something from the Arabian Nights. It left him with the distinct feeling. This was an extremely poor place, as every second person seemed to be a beggar. This was the first experience he had had of real poverty in the Far East and of the style of shops with no windows.

Trying to barter for goods was something else; Dave

turned to his two mates, 'We'll have to sharpen up on our bartering ability.'

They laughed, and Brian smirked, 'Just like you were at Port Said.'

Just then a street vendor came up to them and asked, 'Johnny you want buy?'

He was trying to sell some beads like gemstones; Dave took one look at this scruffily dress character and said to his mates, 'This Choggie is trying to sell us some gems, but look at him. If they are real gems, he'd be better using them himself to have a good feed.'

The Choggie smiled. Whether he understood or not, he just carried on with his sales pitch 'They good Johnny, you get plenty rich!'

'Not interested,' Dave reacted, but by just speaking, the scruffy man stuck to him like a leech and followed them as they walked up the street. Further on, a corporal, with R.M.E flashes on his tunic came over towards them, seeing the local character was bothering them, shouted at the pedlar, 'Fuck off you scrawny Bastard.'

You could not see the Ceylonese for dust as he scampered away back up the street. The corporal then asked Dave. 'Did that shite sell you anything?'

'No, I wasn't interested.'

'Just as well, as those gems are just colour glass and aren't worth a penny.' Then as an afterthought, 'By the way, where are you from with that ascent?'

'Falkirk,' Dave replied.

'I'm Jim McFadden, from just across the river in Alloa.'

They shook hands, and Dave said, 'These are my mates, George, and Brian.'

They spent the rest of what time they had left, finding out more about each other and went sightseeing before meeting up with other lads. Then together they all ended up on the beach clowning about, until the sun slowly sunk over the horizon. It was then time to catch the last launch back to the ship.

On board later, waiting their turn to go for a late dinner, Ron Chivers came over and shouted 'Guess what lads. We're getting another film show later tonight after grub.'

'Goodie, goodie'! George exclaimed, 'I hope it's a sexy porno film.'

'Who would you like to see in it?' Dave asked Ron.

'Jane Russell or Marilyn Munroe,' He replied. 'I'd even settle for seeing my girlfriend in it.' He looked up to the stars with a glint in his eyes.

They all said at once. 'You wish.'

Mike at this point came over dressed in fatigues. 'Been busy?' Dave asked.

'You could say that, and more,' he said, 'I've been scrubbing and washing dishes in the galley sinks for hours.'

'You must have been a bad boy to cop fatigues again?' Dave queried, But before Mike could answer, 'Ron tells us we are being shown a movie later, will we see you there?'

'No fucking chance mate. Anyway, I've seen it before,' he replied.

'What's it like?' George asked him,

He replied curtly, 'Porno.'

George stood up, grabbed hold of Mike, and jumped around with him in circles shouting, 'Great; that will do me.'

After tea, it was one big rush to get a good spot to watch the film. The dining mess hall doubling up as a cinema was packed, with the ones who had the job of rearranging the seats and tables grabbing the best seats before anyone got in.

After a noisy half hour, in marched the officer who was OC of the day, and everyone stood up. 'As you where,' he said, and continued, 'Settle down now lads, I want to introduce you to Captain Fuller, the Chief MO on board. He wants to have a little talk with you all about personal hygiene and your health, and then he will show you a little film.'

The OC and no sooner finished the introduction, when in walks the MO or should it be said, wobbles in. A small stocky built man with a chubby red face, his glossy jet-black hair looked as though he had used his shoe polish on his head instead of his shoes. Certainly not in the army for his physique, it must have been his medical skills.

Standing at the front of the makeshift stage, he placed his hands on what was assumed his hips; looked around, and then in a very effeminate jovial voice said, 'What a lovely bunch of healthy well-tanned lads I have before me. I hope you are all as healthy looking when you return back home.' He smiled, then continued, 'As many of you have never been away from your mummy's side before, it has been left up to me to give you some information to help you all return home safe and well.'

He then gave them a lecture for about an hour on the do's and don'ts of what to look out for, when in Malaya. 'Keeping clean,' he said. 'Have a shower as often as you can, and make sure you clean into all the little cracks, crannies and orifices.' He then explained to them, 'The kind of heat you can expect in Malaya will make you sweat a lot, and it's important that you remember to take your salt pills.' At that, he turned to the projectionist and said, 'Roll the projector.'

He then turned back to face the assembly and with a big grin, continued. 'I tried to get you a nice comedy film, but they have sent me the wrong one. Never mind lads. This one will help you to understand about life and hopefully keep you all safe, so that when you all return home to your girlfriends, you won't give her anything other than a baby.'

A big cheer went up.

As the film rolled the MO explained, 'Having sex without

a Johnny, as there're nicknamed, for those who don't know what a Johnny is, it's a condom.' He then went into greater detail about how to avoid, as he said, the evil side of sex. Stopping the film, he then said, 'My advice to you all is, if you are really stuck, use your best friend Palm.'

One lad in the front shouted out 'I don't have a best friend called Pam, its Tommy.' A laugh rippled round the room,

'I mean.' Said the MO, hesitating, then after he stopped laughing. 'What I was about to say," he laughed again, then continued jokingly, 'there's always one, well in your case, use Tommie's palm and for the rest of you, your own palm of your hand,' He lifted his hand up and pointed to his palm, and continuing his advice, 'If you feel the need, just masturbate yourself until your sexual feeling subsides. That's the safest way to do it, so you don't catch any nasty diseases.'

Another voice from the room chipped in with 'Corr! That means I'll be up all night again.'

That brought more laughter from the rest and brought a smile again to the MO's face. After about half an hour explaining about the medical side, he stopped a moment to let what he had said, sink in, then spoke again, 'This next part of the film will graphically let you see what can happen if you are not careful when you have sex with a prostitute.'

George, sitting to Dave's right, nudged him, and said, 'I told you; we would get a porno film.'

The film rolled again, and before long there were gasps coming from around the room. As for Dave, coming from a quiet up-bringing, it was a very sharp shock. Never had he heard or seen some of the things that appeared on the screen and never imagined diseases that were depicted ever existed.

The film as the MO said, 'This graphically shows the consequences that are associated with venereal, gonorrhoea, and other sexual diseases, and can be passed or picked up by having sex with prostitutes.'

Before the end of the film, some the lads with low constitutions were leaving the room to be sick, not because of the sea this time but because of all the ugly, withered and diseased genitals that were displayed on screen.

When back on deck for fresh air, there was quietness around the friends. With not much conversation-taking place, only the deep sound of the engines throbbing away as the ship ploughed through the waves and only the fluttering of the flags in the sea breeze could be heard. The sea at this point was a little rougher than it had been crossing the other leg of the Indian Ocean, but it was the film that was on their minds, not the weather. You could say the film left an impression on them.

After a while on deck, with hardly a word spoken Mike joined them, 'Well, did you enjoy the film?'

'Rotten sod' George growled 'you might have told us what we were in for,' then carrying on as though in disgust, 'That's it! I am off sex for life. I don't want a blobby knob.'

Ron Chivers, who was a bit of a lady's man, said softly, 'Don't know what I'm going to do without a shag for twenty months?'

'Well mate,' George piped in, 'don't ask me to toss you off.'

With the tension eased, the rest of the evening their conversation was about sex, or the lack of it.

The night wore on, and the weather took a turn for the worse, the gently warm breeze during the daytime gradually became stronger and colder. At first the sea churned up slowly in a rhythm like a flamingo dance, then as the tempo increased the waves stirred up like the dancers, petticoats. The sea was becoming more violent now, and the waves larger with white crests of violence erupting all over the ocean, trying to engulf everything, forcing the ship to sway to the beat. It got darker and darker until it became hard to distinguish where the sky ended, and the sea started. The ocean now became a cruel sea, and it was time to batten down the hatches, as it looked like they were in for a very rough night.

Later, Dave lay in his swaying hammock thinking, '*now will be the time to test my sea legs, if I have any.*'

Chapter 21

The Last Leg

Throughout the night, the stormy sea tossed the ship around, Dave for once, during the roughest time through that night slept well and was thankful for the inventor of the hammock. Wakening next morning to the sound of the Claxton horn at reveille, the wind had blown itself out and the ship, having passed through the storm, was now sailing in calmer seas. Some lads though, especially those who were lying on fixed bunks had not slept well, when the morning rise call came, with most of the NCOs having suffered through the night themselves, this allowed a lot of the lads to catch up on sleep.

Dave on the other hand felt good. Unlike crossing the Bay of Biscay he got up right away and went to the toilets, which he found where cunningly situated on his deck, as those feeling unwell had to pass by the kitchen door. As he trooped along to wash up Dave thought, this must be poor hell for some, as the smells from the kitchen that morning were wonderful to him, but for others was too much, and the railings up on deck where full of nodding heads again. He felt quietly chuffed sitting eating breakfast that morning, because it was noticeable by the empty seats that quite a few of the lads had had a very rough night.

On the forward deck after breakfast, with all the absentees, it was incredibly quiet. With no duties that morning he had plenty of space to himself and decided to answer the letters from home he received while anchored off Ceylon.

My darling Jennifer, he started, *I miss you very much. As I lie here on the deck in this warm sunshine, I am thinking about you and the warm caresses we shared together. I hope you are looking after yourself?*

We had some terrible weather last night and now we are nearing our destination, my thoughts are not on what lies ahead, but on what I am missing back home with you.

As his pen travelled over the paper writing and nearing his destination, this letter made him feel home sick, and he longed to be home in the arms of his sweetheart. He sat imagining home, and enjoyed the cool breeze that was taking the edge off the heat. He stopped writing, looked out over the sea, and fantasized about the future. He looked at Jennifer's photo and convinced himself, it will not be that long and started writing again.

He was just finishing off his letter with '*I love you and always will. David,*' when Mike, joining him on deck, brought him out of his melancholy mood.

'All alone, where are the rest of the lads?' He asked.

'I think they're all recovering from last night's buffeting.' Dave replied.

'Writing home to the girlfriend?' he queried

'Yes, just replying to her letters.'

'Is that her photo?' Mike enquired.

Dave always looked at her photo when writing his letters

to her, it gave him the feeling, she was near. He handed the photo to Mike,

Mike took a long look at it, and returned it to Dave, saying, 'Beautiful looking girl.' At that he took out his own wallet and removed a photo and passed it to Dave, 'That's my wife Lynne with our kids.'

Dave took the photo and studied it for a few moments. He liked what he saw, Lynn looked incredibly beautiful, and the kids were bonny. He handed the photo back and said 'You must be proud to have such a wonderful family like that. Lynn looks fabulous.'

Mike smiled, put the photo away and suggested, 'If we are posted to the same camp, you must meet her and the kids when they come out.'

Just then, George, looking terrible, and feeling sorry for himself, came forward and sat down, put his head in his hands and groaned.

'Rough night' Dave asked, and was surprised. Of all the soldiers on board George was the only one whom he had not seen being seasick,

Mike, with less concerned of his wellbeing, jokingly asked him 'Something you ate last night not agree with you?'

George looked at each in turn, and was going to say something but only nodded, and then put his head back between his hands again.

Mike, not wanting to let George off the hook, said teasingly, 'I take it you won't be thinking about sex for a while then.' George groaned again. Mike continued mischievously teasing him 'Have you had anything to eat this morning?' At that George groaned again, jumping up and ran across to the side of the ship where he delivered what contents he had in his stomach into the sea.

'Great conversation, George,' Dave called over to him.

The rest of the day on deck was noticeably quiet with not much activity, but then over the next few days they saw more activity on board concerning the troops fitness, and briefed on where they would be posted. They were then informed what would happen on their arrival at our destination in Singapore.

Luck was with him, along with Dave, George, Derek, Brian, and Mike, they were all posted to a camp called Paroi, near the town of Seremban. Ron and Bret along with Peter Cantrell were posted to the main Signal Centre Camp on the other side of Seremban.

Mike, having spent some time in Malaya before, put them in the picture where Seremban was in Malaya, and what it was like last time he was there.

Over the last eighteen days they had had the occasional exercises to keep them from getting too lazy, but now there were kit checks as well as more frequent exercises. They also had some classes about the people and the land of Malaya.

Nearing the northern tip of Sumatra but still too far out to see land properly, the ship steered a different course and slipped through the Great Channel and was now going in a southerly direction. Later Dave learned; they had entered the Straits of Malacca. This stretch of water was a particularly important highway for trade between the islands and separates the Malaysian mainland from the Island of Sumatra. It was from here that they started to feel the difference in the heat as it turned more humid at night.

Next morning Dave and his mates were up early and after breakfast were all out on deck. Now beginning to feel a little bored with ship life after such a long trip, the ship engines chugged away as they sailed on, still in a southerly direction until in the distance they could see faint lines of land on both sides on the horizon.

By lunch time under steady knots, the ship swept aside

the waves as they travelled deeper into the Straits of Malacca. It was now noticeable to them that this was a busy shipping lane, as there was a constant passing of cargo ships at regular intervals.

On the distant horizon to their left, the land was rising higher, and they could make out that the beaches and coastline of Malaya were not to dissimilar from the coastline of Ceylon's. Here also, white sandy beaches and palm trees stretched right down to the water's edge.

The Oxfordshire, with every beat of its engines, was nearing Singapore, which is situated just north of the Equator and the night sky darkened by the minute.

That last night on board, Dave and his mates sat quietly watching small islands, silhouetted by the setting sun, pass by. Quietly he felt, they, like him, were all looking forward to getting their feet on dry land, any land, for this trip had lasted twenty-one days and was now becoming tedious.

All eyes were fixed on the distant horizon until the rays of sun disappeared, then the darkness was transformed by billions of stars twinkling brightly all over the heavens. At that moment, his breath was taken away with the stillness of the night and the display overhead. Meanwhile the ship slipped through the water and all that could be heard was the quiet chug-chugging of the engines.

The date was Monday the 11th of July 1960. They were informed earlier that because of their late arrival they would spend one last night on board and in the morning, they would be transferred to a transit camp in Singapore.

Early next morning before sunrise, they were all up and packed, had breakfast and were ready to disembark. When the order came to parade on deck, the sun was just starting to rise. Standing beside George and Mike, Dave said, 'Looks like it's going to be a nice day for our first day here.'

Looking out over Singapore from the deck, the sun now climbing higher in the east, shrinking the shadows fast and exposing Singapore, which stretched far into the distance? The deck of the ship, being quite high, they had a good view out over the city. Surprised at the size and height of the buildings, turning to George,

Dave whispered 'Looks a fair size place.'

'That's an understatement. It's a big place,' George ventured, 'Bet there's plenty of nukie here.'

The mates all laughed, 'Good old George, back to your old self again, and still thinking about your dick and not your stomach.' Dave continued to tease him, 'Have you forgotten the film we saw? And what about your resolution about not having any more sex.'

With a mischievous look on his face he said, 'Nah, that was all just movie stuff and fairy tales anyway. That film was to put us all off nukie, so the officers can get it all to themselves.'

'Well,' Dave laughed 'Don't you dare shake my hand after you've been playing with your dick, as I would never know where your hand or your dick had been.'

That was our only few well-chosen words spoken, and there might have been more if it had not been for the order to disembark. They had been on deck for more than half an hour and were getting impatient to get off the ship. The trucks arrived, and with kit bags on their shoulders they marched down the gangway and climbed onto the back of the awaiting transport.

Chapter 22

Singapore

Driven along busy roads in convoy, they arrived at their transit camp around ten hundred hours. This camp, so they were informed, was for the next three days until their dispersal to the various camps of assignment. Once billeted, they had a quick medical by the camp MO. Unfortunately, they were all past fit for duty. The only place in camp for a cool drink was the NAAFI. That is where a group of them were sitting when Dave recognised a lad at another table. With a wave they both instantly acknowledged each other. He was an old school friend called Peter Hunter from his hometown. Dave was taken aback, as he had not seen Peter since leaving school. As he crossed over to speak to him, Peter came to meet him.

Shaking hands like long lost friends, Dave said, 'Small world! Imagine meeting you here? I haven't seen you since we left school!'

Looking bewildered he replied, 'I saw you coming in with your mates and thought, I know that face.'

They had a beer and past pleasantries of old times. Dave then asked, 'Have you just arrived?'

Peter replied, 'Yes from up north. I'm going home on a ship called the Oxfordshire tomorrow.'

Dave surprised him when he said, 'That's the ship I arrived here on this morning.'

They spent awhile talking about their school days, making Dave start to feel home sick. Peter must have recognized it in his voice when Dave said, 'I wished I were returning on the ship.'

Peter replied, 'I felt the same at first, but it passed.' He then said, 'Where I was stationed was alright and my days here have been good most of the time.'

Dave could see by the RASC badge on Peter's shoulder that he was in the Royal Army Service Corps. Peter went on to tell him, his duty was transporting ammunition and supplies to the frontline troops, and that he had also seen some action up north. His mates after a while, started calling to him as they had been playing cards. They shook hands and parted with an invitation, 'I'll see you once you get back home, we can talk about old times again.' Then like ships in the night, they went their separate ways.

'How did you get on?' George asked Dave as he returned to his own table, 'Did you manage to score? They say the only sex you can get in this camp is with a fairy.'

'Don't tell me you've been trying already,' Dave joked.

Mike, sitting next to George added 'George couldn't get a jump here, even if it were over a vaulting horse in the gym'

From then on, George took some ribbing from the rest of the mates. Dave then told them about his old mate Peter, and what he had told him about his time out here in Malaya. He had enjoyed his time here, but was glad to be going home.

George tried to get back at Dave, 'You should have told him to look up your girlfriend once he gets back home,' then with a sly grin he continued, 'On second thoughts if he hasn't had sex all the time he has been out here? and your girl hasn't had any since you left? Ah! Well, you better not tell him.'

Before he said more, Dave gave him a shove and George fell off his chair.

The next days were spent time being indoctrinated on life in Malay, and familiarized themselves with what they were to do about their health. Then they had to top up their kit with other items needed while here in Malaya. Some of the lads, who were posted to camps in Singapore and in the southern parts of Malaya, left early that day. Dave and his group, having been posted further up north, were scheduled to leave early next day from Singapore station at seven hundred hours.

With each passing hour their group was being whittled down.

Next morning in convoy with six others, they drove through the city centre to the Railway station. Dave's first sight of Malaysian railways, surprised him at how modern it was. The carriages, not much different from home except for the windows, no glass only metal bars and all open with only a blind for shade, only the first-class carriages had glass windows. With the humid heat now reaching thirty-four degrees, he found out why later.

The engines were remarkably like the ones back home, and on closer inspection a plate attached to the steam cylinder told him why. Made in Sheffield. The only difference being the front of the engines had some sort of shield fitted to them as though built to remove debris from the tracks.

They all patiently stood waiting in line on the platform awaiting the order to embark. Once the officer in command of the troops had walked to the front, he gave the order. It was then an almighty scramble onto the carriages that were reserved for them, and after fighting for the best seats, they eventually settled down for their journey up north. For some of them, that would be Seremban, approximately one hundred and seventy miles up the line.

Others in their group would leave the train for transport to their respected camps earlier, while others would travel further up the line past Seremban. On this journey Dave's eyes were being opened to this strange new world.

Sitting quietly taking in everything, he smiled at all the hustle and bustle in the station. Little did he know at that moment, this was for him to be the first of many trips he would make on the trains that travel the length of Malaya.

Chapter 23

New Destination

The Singapore station that Thursday morning the 14th July, heaved with locals trying to get onto the other carriages. People were selling drinks and other kinds of food. The whiff of all the fresh fruit and curries, mingled with the smells of the railways, gave a unique taste of their new home. It was with excitement he heard the Station Master blow his whistle and the train pulled out, heading towards the manmade causeway that joins Singapore to Malaya.

Picking up speed, they were soon over the causeway and onto Malaysian soil in the State of Johor, then the first stop, Jahor Bahru. After that the country marshland gave way to thick jungle on both sides with the occasional clearing. Progressing up the track, more clearings appeared, then rice paddy fields with people busy planting rice shoots, taking over the scene. Most buildings around this area were built of Wood and corrugated sheeting roofs. Dave quietly taking in this scenery, noticed the houses did not look very safe.

Their next stop was a small town called Kulai just a few miles into Malaya. Later, he learned, this area had been where the Commonwealth troops trained in jungle warfare before going on to engage the enemy. The terrain of his new home he would learn, consisted of two-thirds Jungle down the Centre of the Malaysian peninsula, with towns and population mostly on the western side.

Like most of the Far Eastern countries, Malaysians staple diet was rice from their paddy fields. In this strange countryside that passed by Dave's window, paddy fields and vegetable fields stretching for miles, only intermittingly broken by remnants of the ancient jungle that once covered the whole peninsula. A great variety of fruit and vegetables was also grown locally for sale in the various town markets, on railway station platforms, or by the roadside venders.

As the train sped on, even though he was enjoying the breeze, the humidity that day was sauna like, and his perspiration-soaked shirt stuck to his back. His thoughts at that moment were of the soldiers who had been here before him, fighting insurgents in this humidity, even in these jungles. Before starting on this journey, they had been told that the area they were going too had been clear for two years, but then again, as with any terrorism there are some sporadic bombings at anytime, anywhere.

His mate George was happy with what he had seen so far and let them know it. 'Fantastic all this heat,' he said, 'It looks like I won't need to wash myself while I'm here with all this sweat running out of me.'

Brian Emery was the strange one, very into classical music and reading a lot. He reminded Dave of Stan Laurel from the old flicks and looking at him, he thought he was going to have a hard time out here, as Brian was always looking for shade. Even on the ship he stayed as much as he could out of the sun. Still, he managed to get a reasonable tan on his face. George kidded him on about this, calling him a lollipop, because of his thin white body and his red face and occasionally teased him with, 'Stanley, this is another fine mess you have got me into.'

Derek on the other hand was more concerned with getting a good tan before going back home. From the docklands of London, Derek a slim lad, standing five-ten tall, had a strong cockney accent, but quiet for a Londoner. Out here, it was as if he had just found out all about the countryside. He kept going on about the trees and the bullocks in the paddy fields. Even though he had travelled up to Yorkshire to do his training, the countryside still seemed to overwhelm him. I am sure he would have preferred a post in Singapore.

Coming from a smaller town himself, Dave felt comfortable as the countryside was in his blood, open spaces to him infinitely much better than cities and was looking forward to learning over the next year and a half, about his new home.

The rice paddy fields eventually gave way to rubber tree plantations, fields of pineapples and other fruits. As he gazed at the plantations of rubber trees, he remembered reading that the Gutta Percha resin to make rubber was part of the troubles in 1948, and treaties with the Sultans of the various states was the main reason the British Government became involved in the war against the communists, who were trying to disrupt this industry. Rubber in those days accounted for nearly fifty per cent of all exports from Malaya and with British interests very prominent in the commerce of the country, hence the presence of the British troops.

Because the track was only single line, their train had to stop at a small station called Kluang, to allow another train to pass travelling south to Singapore, stations were the only places where this can happen. It was a twenty-minute stay, giving time to buy some ice cool pineapple or coconut and sugar cane juice from the stalls on the platform. Being so hot, the drink although cold and sweet, was a very welcome thirst quencher.

The talk between the mates as they travelled on, turned to what duties they would like, when George asked Dave what he would apply for, Dave replied, 'Mike told me about the Couriers job but with only a few needed there might not be much chance of getting it, so I'll just need to settle for babysitting you.' Then he put his arm around George's shoulder for fun.

George shrugged his shoulders and pulling away said jokingly, 'Hey, not now while everyone is looking.'

Meanwhile, Mike, unable to get a seat beside them, sat a few seats further back, engrossed in a game of cards with some of the lads from his own unit. Dave thinking about the duties, recalled what Mike had said, that he had been a courier for a short time last tour here, but then had said, they changed the Couriers around back then, and thought it might have been because of trains derailments at that time.

Derek on the other hand, said 'I'm not fussy what I do, as long as I get plenty free time off.' A man of many words was our Derek, but that would change the more he got to know them all.

Their attention was drawn to some kids trying to pinch fruit from one of the stalls when at that same moment the south bound Singapore train arrived in the station. No sooner had it come to a stop; theirs was on its way. With the sun now rising higher, the heat was increasing and making the atmosphere almost unbearable. Pulling down shades did not work, as that stopped the breeze, so they were in a difficult situation. George who was a bit of a ginger top, burned very easily, so he moved into the centre isles away from the sun rays.

On the next part of the journey, the plantations and fields were left behind and now on both sides thick impenetrable jungle shaded the train, effectively cooling down the compartment. The strong odour of burning wood and vegetation drifted out of the jungle sending off a strong sweet pungent smell, unlike anything he had experienced back home. Later he found out it was coming from the other big Malay export industry, tree logging.

The train steamed on with the rhythm of the clickity click of the wheels over the tracks. Thick jungle was still on both sides with only the occasional small opening, and here the machinery that was used in the timber industry could be seen, but try hard as he could, he couldn't see any of the many wild creatures they had been told existed here.

Their next stop on this long journey was a place called Labis. Only a short stop, but time to eat the pack launches, a sandwich with bullied beef, one with cheese slices, a chocolate biscuit and an apple given before leaving Singapore. Off again, the country became open and flooded paddy fields was the scene before them all the way up to our next stop, a town called Segemat. Then on to Gemas the next town, where the railway lines split. Here some carriages were disconnected and shunted back, while other carriages were added to our train. This operation seemed to take ages. Dave learnt that day, there is no hurry to do anything that can be done later, or the next day.

From Gemas the train chugged westwards towards the town of Tampin, on the border of the States of Malacca and Negri Sembilan, their last stop before reaching Seremban. It was noticeable the country had been developed in recent times and the jungle land gave way to palm trees, with small Malay villages dotted here and there. Their houses in Kampongs, were built on wooden stilts for ventilation. I supposed to keep wild animals out too. The railway tracks now closely followed the main road, right up to Seremban. Dave's first impression was that the road was not a busy highway.

On arrival at their destination, they never had time to

see much of the town itself. Disembarked from the train and assembled outside the station, names were called out and it was onto one of the three trucks they climbed. Mike, George, Derek, Brian, and Dave along with five other lads in one, as they were informed were all going to the same camp called Paroi. The rest of the troops who disembark at the station travelled onto the main Seremban camp. Without wasting time, they were on our way out of Seremban and heading up the Kuala Pilah road. Fifteen minutes later they turned into Paroi camp, home for the duration of their stay in Malaya or until transferred to another post.

His first sight of the camp was of a light airplane, taking off from the camp airstrip. The truck past the guardhouse and swung left up a slight incline road until it came to a stop outside the C.O.s office. Sergeant Major (S.M.) Wilmot was standing waiting for them as they climbed down, all ten of them lined up and he called them to attention.

After a few moments Major Dunlop, an Edinburgh man, came out and was accompanied by another officer called Captain Hansen. After introducing himself, he then briefed them on what he expects of them at Paroi Camp. After a brief inspection Major Dunlop told them that he would interview them the following Monday. This, he said, was to give them time to settle in.

Dismissed, they were then shown to their quarters by a Lance corporal whom Dave learned later was nick named James Bond after the character in the spy books. His real name was Lance Cpl James Barry.

Chapter 24

Paroi Camp

Not much to look at, at first glance, but over time it grew on Dave. Built on a slight incline that rose about thirty feet to the top, situated about three and a half miles from Seremban town centre and further four miles from the main Royal Signal Centre Camp, where all the real business took place.

The Camp he learnt, was only a place to put his head down, and store his belongings, The main reason for the camp was an Airstrip to house the air reconnaissance unit, also the workshops for the Royal Electrical Mechanical and Engineering unit. With around thirty in total number of Royal Signal lads in Paroi Camp, they were outnumbered by the R.E.M.E. lads. Although they were all housed in different part of the camp, they used the same Mess Hall facilities.

Lance Cpl Barry marched them up the hill to their new sleeping quarters, in building F, or Basher as they called them. A long wooden structure with a thatch roof, open windows with night shutters, bare interior except for eight single beds, wardrobes, and a small cabinet at the side of each, all standing on a smooth green painted concrete floor, their home from home.

Cpl Barry said as they went in., 'Any bed except the two beds to the right-hand corner.'

Dave, first in, grabbed the bed in the left-hand corner, which had a window to one side and looked onto the parade ground at the top of the compound. Not the best view, but at least he could see over the parade ground and the land behind the camp, which had been deforested about fifty yards, no-man's land before the jungle. Better he thought, than the other side which looked onto the back of another Basher. Brian grabbed the bed next to Dave, and the other lads just fell on beds that were nearest to them.

Over that weekend the mates found out where everything was, especially the NAAFI, a place they spent most of our time relaxing and sampling Tiger Ban beer, the local brew. With time on his hands, he wrote letters home. Lance Cpl Barry during this time was a good help and filled them in on what to expect from the Major Dunlop.

Barry, when not talking about the army, did a very funny impression of a German, speaking in broken English. He strutted about the Basher like a German officer slapping his glove on his trouser leg as he said 'Ah, so you are British soldier are you not? Ve have nice camp here have Ve not? Remember one thing, if not you are a good Ve kinder, Ve vill send Helga to you, and her sexual methods of interrogations you vill not like.'

He had many more little sayings, which they all heard in the days to come. Over the coming weeks as fate would have it, Dave got to know him a little more.

The heavens opened that Saturday night giving them, their first experience of the kind of rain to expect more like buckets of rain than just raindrops. The four feet deep monsoon ditches around the Basher filled to overflowing within minutes. With it raining, the air turned colder and for the first time since arriving, Dave put on a jacket. Half an hour later the rain stopped as suddenly as it had begun, and as the ground dried a blanket of fog stirred up by a gently breeze wove patterns over the ground.

Cpl Barry talking as an old hand said, 'That gent's, was a small shower, just wait till the monsoon comes,'

'Can't wait for that,' Dave chipped in, and then muttered 'we'll be able to swim down the hill if it rains heavier and longer than that.'

Sunday morning at breakfast, it was announced there was Mass over in Seremban Camp and any Catholics wanting to go, should report to the guard house at nine hundred hours, transport is laid on. Derek, whom Dave knew was a Catholic but had not attended mass for years, asked him if he was going to go, at first Dave said no. After promising Jennifer about marrying her in her church he did not think it proper, but Derek explained that he had been thinking about going back to church but felt the need of company on his first time. Dave reluctantly changed his mind and agreed to accompany him.

Sitting in church that day all sorts of questions came into Dave's head, his faith he felt was still as strong as it had always been but his love for Jennifer was just as strong. He felt awkward sitting there, but in a way he also felt calm. He put all other mundane thoughts out of his head that day and just sat thinking about all the things that had made life so difficult for them and of his decision to marrying her in her church. Was it the right decision or the wrong one? He prayed that the lord would bless him and help him to overcome his doubts.

Back at Camp, still feeling a bit home sick and missing Jennifer, he hoped in time it would ease, but at that moment felt he could not mix with the other lads. He went down to the Airstrip, where he sat a while with his own thoughts of home to keep him company.

About an hour later he heard, 'There you are! I've been looking for you.' It was Mike. 'Thinking of home, are you?'

'Ye, a wee bit.' Dave replied.

Mike sat down and asked, 'What's bothering you?' He was a good listener, and that day Dave spoke of his doubts about his decision to give up his faith. As their conversation continued, he found out that Mike had had some problems in his own marriage, but said, things have a way of working out in the end,

'I hope so' Dave said.

He echoed that by saying, 'I hope so too, for once Lynne comes out here, I hope we will be able to overcome our own problems.' Then standing up he said, 'We need some cheering up,' and pulling Dave up onto his feet they went into the NAFFI and had a few beers. Dave slept well that night.

'Wakey, wakey, Up and shine' S.M. Wilmot, called out 'Let us be having you! You are still in the army and your work starts today to pay Her Majesty back for all the hard cash she has spent training you.' He continued 'After breakfast, I want you all on parade in full dress, at eight hundred hours.' At that he left and one of the lads asked what time it was, as it was still dark outside.

'It's only fucking half past five,' George shouted after looking at his watch, 'Shite! What the hell is this army coming to when a chap can't get a long lie in.'

From Cpl Barry's corner a voice could be heard. 'During zee vor, ven ve vere in zee trenches, because of all the noises our neighbours made with zer big guns, ve did not even get to sleep.'

'Good morning, Malaya,' Dave said as he put his feet on the floor. It was then that he just realized that he had had too much to drink the night before.

Flip-flops on his feet and a towel wrapped around his

waist, he was off to have a cold shower and shave. Mike, having already beaten him into the shower block jokily said, 'God you look terrible. Are you feeling as bad as you look?'

'Flaming awful.' Dave replied.

'I bet you can't remember what you were worrying about last night, can you?' He asked.

Dave looked at him and said, 'I can't even remember where I left my head last night, because I must have picked up somebody else's one, and stuck it on my shoulders.'

The water felt magnificent, he stood, enjoyed the soothing feeling as the cool water ran all over his body. About twenty minutes past, and as they left the shower block, they were hit by this blinding light they called, the sun. He was amazed at how quickly it turned from dark to light, as last night, he could not honestly say when it turned light into dark. *Strange land this*, he thought.

Now very warm outside, dress was shorts and flip-flops to go down for breakfast. He had heard it said before he had joined the army, that the grub was not particularly good, but the grub that morning even in his condition smelt wonderful.

On parade it was very clammy; even the dry shirt he put on was now damp with sweat. He now realized why the S. M. wanted them at this time, as later; the sun would be too hot. Their parade was basically just a roll call and from there they marched down to the (C.O) Commanding officers office. In turn they were called in before Major Dunlop, asked a few questions then allocated their duties. He finished by saying to Dave, 'Well Walters I hope you don't let me down now that you have the duty you wanted,'

Dave replied, 'Thank you sir.' Saluted, about faced, and marched out of the office.

Once all the lads had been in to see the C.O. Outside again, they fell into line and marched round to a classroom where the S.M. explained about their jobs. It turned out Mike was given a Courier's job as well. George, Brian, and Derek were to work in the Signal Centre office over in Seremban Camp. Their jobs, unlike the Couriers, was more of a local delivering of orders to the camps within the near bye vicinity, or working in the offices.

Once back at their Basher, Cpl Barry filled Mike and Dave in on what their duties entailed. These included, along with six other Couriers, in turn, after collecting mail from the main Signal Centre camp, from there, driven up to Kuala Lumpur railway station. The mail was then collected at each station the length of the line north of Malaya by soldiers from camps in their area, and the couriers pick up mail for delivery north to other camps up the line.

Chapter 25

Training Again

Over the next two days, they were ground on all aspects of their duties by the S.M. even down to the importance no one got near the mail at any time until it was passed onto the proper people. 'One other thing,' the S.M. said, 'Some mail will be classified 'Top Priority.' This must not be allowed to leave your side at any time, until it's handed over to an officer who would be designated to collect it.' It was at this point he said, 'This mail will be stored in a case which will be chained to your wrist.'

All very secretive, Dave thought, but the importance of the duty got through to him when they were told that they would be issued with firearms for protection.

The S.M. finished by saying 'Couriers travel in pairs and must always look out for one another at all times during the tour of duty.' With that they dispersed, and for the rest of the day, spent time in the NAFFI relaxing until it was time for dinner.

On the third day breakfast past: it was something different, after more briefing they were outside again being driven by Land Rover to a rifle range near the main Camp for revolver practice. Never having held a real handgun before, George, Derek and Dave found this a new experience.

Mike said as they were being driven over, 'there's nothing to it, just watch the kickback.'

On the range unlike firing the rifle where they had lain down, with the pistol they stood when firing. For Dave, it turned out to be a very enjoyable experience, and after strapping on their handgun holster, they clowned and strutted about like cowboys until the range Sarge in charge, pulled them up.

That day they learned to respect their weapons and then it was onto the twenty-five-yard range for practice. The targets although close, were not that easy to hit because of the recoil from their Webley pistols and on top of that, the Sarge let them know about the waste, as the missed targets proved. A few more rounds later they were hitting their targets, and once mastered the stance and how to aim, Dave was becoming confident at hitting the target. Derek on the other hand found it difficult, but eventually was given pass marks. Dave was now ready to get started on his first assignment.

Next day, on the way down to the mess hall, Dave looking at the Duty notice board found he was to go on his first trip that night with Cpl Barry. He sat beside the Cpl, who filled him in on the procedure for later that day, he was collect his Courier armband first from the Quartermasters store, then after tea collect his handguns from the armoury. Dave was excited and looked forward at last to be doing something positive.

After collecting their armband, which had Courier written boldly in black on a pale blue fabric band, he was informed with it goes great responsibility while on duty, as no officer of any rank can give him an order that contravenes the courier's orders.

The day passed quickly and after dinner weapons collected

from the armoury, one handgun, one holster and six rounds of ammunition, and all dully signed for. Arriving to take them up to K.L in a Land Rover was their driver Cpl Morgan, nicknamed the Terrible, from the Royal Army Service Corps. He, Dave was informed, being their usual driver would also collect them on their return.

At the Signal Centre at Seremban Camp, after picking up the mail for camps up country, they drove the 34miles north to Kuala Lumper Railway Station. On the way Dave quizzed the driver, 'why are you nicknamed the Terrible?'

His reply 'Because of all the fucking idiot Malay drivers.'

Not having seen many Malayan drivers on the open road, Dave pursued the matter, 'What's wrong with them?'

Cpl Morgan smirked and replied 'Well at night they are like moths and drive into your headlamps, I don't know why the Bastards do it, but I keep a few half bricks at my side and if they venture to close I throw one at their headlights, and that makes them move over.'

Dangerous Dave thought, but he had to laugh.

The Cpl was an amazingly fast driver over the winding road, however Dave hung on as he was sure, passengers had been lost before. Maybe it was just as well it was dark, and they could not see much. Arrived in one peace in K.L. at a building Dave thought at first was a palace. He sat looking at it when Cpl Barry, who said, 'Right let us be having you. This is our stop.'

Astonished, Dave asked, 'I thought we were going to the railway station?'

'This is it,' He said.

Dave looked at him in disbelief and thought he was kidding, 'This building looks more like a palace than a railway station.'

Cpl Barry retorted, 'Magnificent isn't it?'

Dave agreed it was and with all the other rundown buildings they had passed in the city on their way there, this was an oasis of perfection.

Whilst waiting on platform four, lads from units stationed around K.L. arrived, dropped mail off and collect some to take back to their units, it seemed a haphazard way to do business on the platform Dave thought, but with no office to use they just had to get on with it.

The train pulled into the station and once on board he was surprised to find they were in a first class, the compartment consisted of two bunk beds and a table. The lower bunk was used to hold the bags of mail, while the Courier not on duty used the top bunk. Once settled in, more soldiers from other units arrived and the mail starting to gather. Looking at the pile, Dave knew then that they had their work cut out.

Cpl Barry gave Dave the list of stops and left him to it saying. "Dave you take first duty."

Around twenty-two hundred hours the train pulled out of K.L. station. Their first scheduled stop, seventy miles up the line at a place called Tapa and would take the best part of two hours. Cpl Barry who had been away for a cup of tea arrived back and decided that he would instead do the up duty. With nothing to see outside and only the strong smell of burning wood filtering through the top window, Dave helped him sort the mail.

With the mail now all in bundles, not feeling tired Dave decided to have a walk himself, just to sample life on the train. The carriage next forward was the dining Carriage, Then after that the second class. On this journey and his many trips later he learnt, Commonwealth soldiers and Malay regulars were traveling to new postings or going on leave. Further forward the carriages nearer to the engine mostly, carried local Malays, Chinese, Indians, and other nationalities, with the windows open he could smell the dank sooty smell of the smoke from the engine.

Back in his own compartment he tried to sleep on the top bunk, but not being used to night trains he found it difficult. That night he thought, will be just the matter of resting rather than sleeping with all the rocking of the carriage and the clickety clack noise of the train and people walking about.

James, as he told Dave to call him while on duty, had been in the army six years and out here in Malaya for eighteen months, and on Courier duty for the last seven of these, and was an old hand at dropping off to sleep for an hour at a time.

Reached Tapah station, still awake, Dave watched a flurry of activity with soldiers collecting mail and leaving some for other camps further north. Then the train quieted down as they waited for the down line train to pass, Dave finally drifted off to sleep and the next thing he knew was the train lurching forward and moving again.

James was sitting reading when he opened his eyes. 'Jing's! I've only shut his eyes for a minute and that's us off again' Dave sleepily said.

'What do you mean, a minute?' James replied, 'You've been asleep for an hour or more while the train has been sitting in the station.'

This Dave learned; the trains stop for an hour at most of the stations every trip. With just a single track all the way, it was not prudent to have passing places anywhere other than at town station. To have a train sitting in a passing place out in the countryside during the hostilities, would have made them easy targets for the insurgent communists.

The rest of the journey with stops at Kampar, Ipoh and Taiping passed without a hitch. For his part he managed to catch a few winks of sleep here and there. The last section of their journey from Taiping would take them all the way up to

Butterworth, it was here they had to split up. Being Dave's first time on courier duty, on reaching Butterworth James stated, 'Dave, seeing it's your first trip, you go over to Pinang Island, and I'll go on to Sungie Pitani.

It was six thirty-five when they arrived in Butterworth and after instructions, Dave proceeded to the ferry which was not too hard to find, being only a short distance from the Railway station. The sun was rising over the horizon brightening up the Island of Paula Pinang as he stepped onto the ferry. The time was just after seven hundred hours when the ferry left the pier. The crossing over to George Town the capital of the island, was very smooth. For the fifteen minutes it took the ferry to cross the straits, he just relaxed and enjoyed the nice cool morning breeze coming off the sea.

Chapter 26

Paradise Island

Standing on the Pinang Island pier waiting for Dave, were two tall soldiers dressed in the uniforms of the Royal Australian Signal Division, stationed here on the island.

'Gid Morning Mate,' they greeted Dave 'Had a gid trip, had you'

'Yes, thanks' Dave replied.

The Ausies looked at one another, and then one said in a slow manner, 'Not another Jock?'

Dave smiled as he replied, 'You noticed?'

'Mate, I can just about tell you what house you stayed in with an accent like that,' and continuing 'Nice to meet you, What's your name Mate. I'm Gerry and this here's my Mate Chip.'

'Dave, Dave Walters.' They shook hands.

Once on board the jeep, he was whisked through the streets of George Town and out to the camp near Sungie Dua. Head Quarters, Home of the Royal Australian Air force and First Royal Australian Regiment. (1st RAR)

A beautiful place for tired eyes in the morning, Dave thought. Well-groomed lush green lawns, palm trees and bright white buildings. Across his left shoulder he could see the blue seas, and the waves lapping up onto the beaches. 'This surely is paradise, and to be posted here must be fantastic?' Dave enquired.

Turning into the camp, Chip said regretfully 'Beaut isn't it, pity I'll be splitting here to git home in a couple of months, but Gerry here will be around a lot longer to keep you right.'

After a pause Gerry asked, 'Who's on with you this trip, Mate.'

'Lance Cpl Barry,'

'Not that twit that thinks he's a German. Is it?'

'Yes.' Dave said, and smiled at the thought.

'You poor bloke' retorted Chip.

Dropping Dave at the Signal Centre, Gerry told him, 'Make your way over to Basher H,' He pointed to a basher up the hill, 'There's a spare bed there for the Couriers to have a bit of shuteye.'

That sounded a good welcome to Dave for he was bushed, and the heat was not helping. Signing into the Signal office he handed over the mail, and his weapon. The duty Sergeant looking at Dave asked, 'New on the job, are you?' Not waiting for an answer, he continued, 'Well, you're done here, but, remember to report back to the Signal Centre at twenty hundred hours, till then, you're on your own.'

Picking up his personal belongings he made his way up to Basher H. When he entered, Chip was there and showed him to a small room at the end, which measured about fifteen-foot square.

'There you are Mate, get your head down there and I'll give you a shout at chow time.'

The room air was cool due to a big fan in the middle. Dave took of his uniform, and with only his underpants on, lay down. The bed smelt fresh and clean, and it felt like heaven when his hot body touched the cool sheets. No rocking or rolling about like it was on the train, just a steady bed. He fell asleep listening to the methodical squeak coming from the fan. The time was around eight thirty a.m.

It was just after noon when Gerry woke him. 'Chow time' he blurted out 'When your decent, I'll take you over to the mess and get you a billy for your coffee.'

Coffee! Dave mused, *I haven't had that since Chester and that was only once.*

While waiting in line in the dining hall there was a bit of banter between Gerry and some other Ausie mates, Dave sensed he was the brunt of some of the comments about his height, all in fun he hoped. Most of these young lads were conscripts, but they seemed to have a different attitude to their being in the army, Dave's first impression, they were treating it like a holiday, as, when an officer entered and ask them about the food, jokes were thrown at him, but he just laughed along with them.

Dave mused; *they would not get away with that at Paroi camp.*

Their meal that day consisted for starters, Cooks' special Soup then a choice of thick Tuna steaks, tatties and vegetables, or various sliced meats. Another table to one side was covered with all sorts of fresh fruit, some Dave had never ever seen or even tasted before. For drinks, Coffee, or lemonade till it was coming out their ears. It was a revelation, Dave thought, *these Ausies know how to live.*

Sitting listening to the banter going around the table, he realized that they were not that much different to the Brits, brassier like the Yanks, but just young men trying to get through and along the way having a good time.

Back at the Basher, Gerry told him he had to go on duty but would see him later to take him over for evening dinner at six. Dave asked him, 'What did the other couriers do with their spare time here?'

'Sometimes they hitch a lift into town,' he said, 'if you do go downtown, try the Broadway Café!' He then gave a slappy salute, 'Must skip now or I'll be late for duty.' With that he left.

Dave found himself alone with only the noise of crickets clicking away in the undergrowth, and it being his first time here, he decided to sit outside under the veranda that had a view out over the sea, and write a letter to Jennifer. As he wrote he tried to capture the moment and the mood of the place.

My dear sweetheart, I'm sitting here in one of the most beautiful places anyone could imagine, but I feel so sad, as you're not here to share it with me. Although I am settling into life out here in Malaya, each minute I am away from you gets harder and harder.

You are in my thoughts always, and everywhere I go; I take you with me in my heart. I hope you are looking after yourself and like me, are longing for the day when we can get married.

As I look out over this wonderful scene, the sun is shining brightly, the sea is a deep blue, and palm trees are swaying in the gentle breeze. In the distance I can see the ferry that brought me over to this Island of Pinang, its waves brushing aside little fishing boats

Dave let the pen drop as the heat and tiredness caught up and he dozed off.

It was Chip coming back off his duty that wakened him. 'Sorry Mate, if I woke you. Thought you might have gone into town,'

Dave rubbing his eyes replied, 'No, I decided to catch up on a letter to home.'

135

'You're Sheila, back home is it?' Chip ventured.

'Yes' said Dave, and showed him a photo of Jennifer.

Taking it in his hand he whistled, and said, 'A real beaut isn't she. Are you going to get hitch when you get back home?'

'All going well we are hoping to,' he replied.

They sat, and talked about their girls. Chip then handed Dave a photo of his girl. 'We're getting married later this year once I'm home.'

'Where's home about?'

'It's only a short distance from Melbourne. About ninety miles north, in a small town called Mooralbark,' he replied'

Dave listening to him talk, realized there was a big difference in mentality between them, as Chip took for granted that ninety miles was only a short distance.

Time passed, and Gerry joined them. After chatting for a while, both went to change for Dinner. Before leaving, seeing Dave sitting there in his shorts, and a pair of flip-flops, Chip told him they normally went for dinner at night a bit dressier.

As Dave had only his uniform to wear, walking into the dining hall he stuck out like a sore thumb, but to his surprised no one seemed to notice. Waiting in line for his turn, and seeing what was on offer, Dave thought the meal at launch time had been good, but this was a banquet with beefsteaks and a good variety of veggies, washed down with a pint of beer. All very civilized he thought.

After dinner, Chip took Dave over to the NAAFI where he met some of the other lads, too many to remember except one lad whom he got to know well, his name Gilbert Homes, from Sidney. A laidback sort of guy, in conversation he told Dave, he felt at home in Malaya, because the weather was not that much different from his home area.

The minutes passed quickly, and it was time for Dave to

get organized for his return trip. Saying cheerio to the lads, he thanked them for their hospitality.

It was just before twenty hundred hours, when he walked into the armoury, took charge of his handgun, and checked it over before inserting the rounds in the chamber, he then made his way down to the Signal Centre.

Two bags of mail were stacked up ready for him to check, one letter was marked 'Priority, Confidential' destined for K.L. This had to be treated differently, and was put into a small case which was then chained to his wrist. First trip he thought, to have this thrown on me, but this was part of the job.

It was with a new driver and escort that took him down to the pier and waited with him till the ferry arrived. On this occasion they never exchanged names just the usual friendly banter.

The ferry arrived and people disembarked. One escort he found out later was called Brad. He went on board with him over to the mainland and escorted him to the waiting train, to make sure he met up with Cpl Barry. The escort then promptly returned to catch the ferry back to Pinang Island.

On board the train James asked, 'Well! How did you get on with the Ausies?' Then changing the subject, 'Some place for a posting isn't it. Did you manage to go into town?'

'No'! Dave replied, 'I was a bit bushed, so I slept all morning then had a lazy afternoon writing letters. Oh! by the way, Gerry sends his regards.'

'Good lad Gerry is,' he replied, 'We've had some good times downtown. Did he tell you about the Broadway?'

'Yes.' Dave replied, 'We had a good blether about a lot of things about the town and what to do' pausing, he then asked, 'but what is it about the Broadway?'

'Next time your over there you can find out for yourself.' He replied with a grin.

'I got on very well with a lad called Gilbert Homes. He told me he'd show me around the next time I'm back.' Dave said casually.

'Never heard that name before. What unit is he in?' He asked.

'One RAR' Dave replied, 'Gil they call him, had been stationed on the mainland at Butterworth and only transferred over there a couple of weeks ago to work as a wireless Op.'

As Dave spread the mail on the table he asked, 'What do I do with this case?

'We don't have a key, so it's attached to you until the train arrives in KL.' He replied.

They settled into sorting the remainder of the mail, some of which they had carried, was distributed to the lads from the camps around that area of Butterworth, the rest they put into bundles.

'Right! Tea break.' James said, and asked 'Want a cup of tea and a sandwich?'

Both settled for a pineapple and ham sandwich and a mug of tea. They had just sat down to eat, when on time around twenty-two hundred hours the Station Master blew his whistle and the train pulled out of station bound south. With it being a fair time before their next stop Dave put his feet up and enjoyed the break.

James had been on the top bunk for over an hour when they pulled into their first stop, Taiping. Four different units handed over mail and collected mail for their own units. Having the use of only one hand it was awkward to say the least. The remainder of the trip was a mirror reverse of the journey north. In between stations, to keep him from dropping off to sleep, Dave caught up with reading his Zane Grey Western novel. Without it, the journey would have been boring.

Apart from the snoring from James, who by this time was

fast asleep, only the sounds of the wheels clickety clacking, and the occasional banging of carriage doors were all that could be heard.

At Ipoh, while waiting for the up train to pass, Dave stretching his legs, stood in the passageway at the carriage door listening to the night noises of the crickets and other animals that came out of the jungle. The only consolation he thought in that moment was, he was paid an extra pound a day and given expenses, which was supposed to cover his food ration. So, all in all he was better off than most N.S. soldiers at that time.

Chapter 27

A New Dawn

The skies overhead, were starting to brighten around twenty-five minutes past six as the train pulled into K.L. station. Without a hitch through the night, all the mail had been handed out, and some taken in. Waiting for them on arrival in K.L to pick up their mail, were lads from six different units around the city, and an officer from GHQ, who removed and took charge the case.

Meanwhile, Their own driver sat patiently waited outside, with transport to take them back to Seremban. Feeling weary, Dave settled down in the backseat thinking, *first trip over.*

Having not had any sleep on the journey down from Butterworth, he began to feel the long journey taking its toll. With the sun shining in his face, even with the cool breeze on the road back to Seremban, his eyes were smarting, and he had difficulty keeping them open. James earlier, had expressed to him; the first few trips were the worst and after a while he would learn to pace himself.

The way Dave felt, he hoped so.

After handing over the mail into Seremban Signal Centre main camp and signed off, they were whisked back to Paroi

Camp, and a welcome bed. Before turning in Dave showered and washed away the aches and last night's perspiration, then went down to the canteen for breakfast. On entering the canteen, he found his mates were still there. The conversation was all about, what his trip was like.

When telling them about his trip over to Pinang, George grumbled, 'You lucky sod! I got stuck in the Signal Centre all day and they lucky sods,' pointing to Brian and Derek, 'Got to run about the countryside swanning, while I was slogging in a hot office.'

Putting his arm around George's shoulder, Derek said sarcastically in his cockney accent, 'There, there wee man. I put a good word in the ears of some girls on Malacca beach for you, so next time you get the chance. Get yourself down there, and dip your wick.'

'Oh'! George replied with gusto, 'He's found a bit of humour at last.' There enthused a bit of playful wrestling.

They all departed to go on parade leaving Dave sitting on his own. Having just come off duty, he was excused parade. In the basher with everyone away. Cpl Barry having slept through the night, left to go into Seremban. Peace at last, Dave thought, and lay down on his bed, just at that moment in walked their Dobby Walla to clean, and change the bed sheets. With the heat and the noise, Dave knew he was not going to get sleep at that moment. He turned on the overhead fan to cool the room and to ward off the flies. The Dobby Walla continued to work away, trying to be quiet.

All the while, lying on his bed he was thinking of home, when his eyes were attracted by a Chit Chat lizard running over the walls. He supposed, just like counting sheep, it might help? Next thing he knew, he was wakened by a loud buzz and a thump. It was a large flying beetle nicknamed a Buzz bomb, which had lost its way, and thumped into his locker.

Looking at his watch, it had just gone One-o-clock, time for him to get ready and stroll down to the canteen for dinner. With Mike away north and his mates on duty it was a quiet lunch, and then back up to the basher and time to think of what had gone before.

After a few more trips up North, and settled into the routine. On the first Saturday in August 1960, along with most of the lads who had no duties, he volunteered to go to K.L. The occasion, a Independence Parade to mark the end of the Emergency, even though fighting was still on going up north.

The parade that day, wound its way around the city streets and the Merdeka Square, past the Sultan Abdul Samman Buildings, where the salute was taken by the King, Yang di-Pertuan Agong.

There were approximately three thousand troops from the Malaysian Army along with other Units from the Commonwealth armies, plus armoured vehicles, heavy artillery, and marching at the rear of the parade were school children and religious groups who were also taking part in the march past.

It was a very noisy and colourful, and with this being a very special day that year, the streets were thronging with people. With the parade having taken around two hours, at the end with time to kill, and as it was also the first time most of his group of mates had had a chance to visit K.L, they decided to explore the City centre,

Dave being the only one who had been there before, and knowing where to go, led the way to look around the area known as China Town. After exhausting all the stalls looking for souvenirs and places for eating and refreshments, they then collectively, decided before making their way back to the assembly point, to try the bars near the City Centre.

After a few drinks, Dave, and his mates, thinking they

would be last back, arrived somewhat merry from drink, and for their penance, they had to sweat out time in the searing heat waiting for late comers, who, all were worse for drink. Without any ceremony, they were all bundled into the trucks like baggage.

On the return trip to Seremban, with all the drink that had been consumed, the truck was full of merriment with boisterous singing all the way back to Paroi Camp.

Chapter 28

The Day of the Gun

Every trip over night for the next five weeks, Dave became more comfortable in his Courier job and had travelled back and forward up north to Pinang and consecutively to Sungie Patani. But the world of the Couriers was suddenly brought into prospective. His next duty had started like all the others. Tea with his mates, collect his Handgun, put a few civvies in a bag for the trip, then off they would go. But this time it was different for on returning to the Basher he was confronted with Corp, James in a panic.

'What's wrong?'

James had all his clothes out of his locker and scattered over his bed. A look of dismay on his face and near to tears he said, 'I've lost my Handgun, it's been stolen.'

'How did that happen when you've only just collected it,' Dave continuing, 'Where did you lose it? Could it have been on your way here from the Armoury?'

'No!' He said, panic in his voice, 'I was stupid. I left it in my locker. When I got back here the locker had been forced open and the gun was fucking gone.'

Sitting down beside him, Dave quietly asked, 'Didn't you get your Handgun after tea?'

'No! I got it before. I've done that before, and locked it in my locker, and nothing has ever happened before.' He replied.

Dumbstruck, Dave could not say anything to console him knowing. Having been foolish, he had disobeyed standing orders regarding the collection of arms, he was in deep trouble.

As they had to leave on duty soon, and time was running out, together they went to see the duty Sarge. When told about the gun, the Sarge was livid and tore into James with a barrage of words that made him visibly shrink in height. After calming down a little the Sarge turned, look at Dave and quizzed, 'Are you OK to go?'

'Yes sergeant, but who will partner me?'

He turned to Cpl Duff sitting at the other desk, 'Go tell Signalman Warrington to report here for duty.'

Cpl Duff left the office, leaving Dave a bit bewildered as he had muttered, 'I hope he is sober, for he has been off all day and will probably have spent his time in the NAAFI?'

Half an hour later Dave met Warrington, or Doug, as they called him, had been in the services for years, and an old hand doing the Couriers job. His condition to say the least was nearly sober but with a long way to go.

Cpl Duff pulled Dave to one side before they left and said, 'watch him, he's known to disappear from time to time.'

This Dave thought, this I can do without. After having collected the mail from the Signal Centre, and were being driven up the road, to be fair Doug moaned, 'It's your duty. You say how you want to work it.

Looking at the state he was in Dave quickly replied, 'I'll take the first shift, you can get your head down for some sleep.'

On the road the talk was about Cpl James, Doug shouted,

'The stupid baster! He'll be for the high jump; the army takes a dim view about losing a weapon.'

All that night, the lads from various camps collected their mail with questions on all their lips, where's Jamesy? Dave not wanting to speak ill of James, explaining that he didn't have all the facts, but before he could finish Doug dived straight in, 'Oh! He will be spending his holidays in Changie Prison.'

That brought a laugh from the other lads. Doug thankfully spent the rest of the journey asleep. Thinking over who should go where, Dave decided that once they arrived at Butterworth, he would go to Pinang, and send Doug up to Sungie Patani. With what Dave knew about him. Letting him go to Pinang, there was no telling what state he would be when in arriving back at night.

Dave smiling smugly thought, *'there aren't many bars in the village of Sungie Patani, and the NAAFI in the camp wasn't geared up for British personal.'*

Next morning, before Doug was fully awake Dave caught him of guard and stated, 'It's my turn to go over to Pinang.'

Doug tried to make him change his mind, but he lied and told him, 'Having been to Sungie Patani on my last trip I've made arrangements to do something on Pinang this trip'

In Basher H, in Sungie Dua camp on Pinang, although a little tired, Dave refreshed himself up with a cold shower. Learning Gil was on duty, and that breakfast was over, Dave a little more familiar with the area, made his way down to catch a lift into George Town, for a look around. George Town, was different from the mainland in many ways, as it still had lots of old colonial style buildings with an assortment of shop signs in Chinese and various other nationalities, a very cosmopolitan place.

In town he took a trishaw out to an old Fortress called Fort Cornwallis, he learned was built by the Governor General of the East Indian Company around 1808. Relaxing on the Old fortification wall in the sunshine, he sat, watching the sea craft sail bye.

Around twelve noon, after having had his fill of history, he went back into town and the Broadway Café. On an earlier trip, Gil had introduced him to a young prostitute Chinese Girl, called Nee Nee Than. She had a slim well shaped figure, which filled her red Chung-San dress to overflow, extremely attractive light tan face with flawless skin. Her best feature being her oval deep dark brown eyes and full well-shaped soft lips, which he sampled when they parted last time. She had the most beautiful long blue tinted black hair, which fell, all the way down to her waist. Nee Nee worked out from the Broadway Cafe?

The second time he had been in the café, he was sitting on his own and she had walked over, her strong oriental perfume surrounded him, 'You like nice girl Johnny, I give you good time. I clean girl. I show you certificate.'

Dave shook his head and explained, 'I have a nice girl back home and not interested.'

But she sat beside him anyway. He bought her a drink. As they talked, he learned about her life. Speaking broken English with a nice oriental accent. 'I sold when twelve years old and trained as dance girl, Now I nineteen years old, my master send me be goodtime girl.'

Dave at first did not understand what she meant, but after she explained he could not but admire her candidness; considering her lifestyle, she was still very nice looking. Continuing her story, 'I kept in touch still with family who are poor and send money home to help with food.'

He was taken aback, as he had never given much thought about these girls who were prostitutes, but his eyes were opened when he began to get to know her better. Nee Nee realizing quickly how he felt about his girlfriend Jennifer, and how he was saving himself for her. She thought it very romantic and warmed to him as though a sister. From then on, each trip he was in Pinang, in the mornings, she showed him around the Island sites that he would never have seen on his own, like Ayer-Itam temple. She also liked telling people in her oriental accent he was her Scotty boyfriend Daveny.

Their meetings were always relaxing and friendly without the pressure to take their friendship further. When leaving her, he always gave her some money, she tried at first to refuse until he told her it was a gift to send home. Since then, they had become very friendly

One trip, when he walked into the cafe she came over and letting the other girls know he was special to her, she greeted him in her usual bubbly broken English voice 'Hello Daveny, you want company.'

'Yes, Nee Nee. How are you today?' he enquired.

'I velly happy, I see you.' Typical prostitute he thought, always praising in case you might be a client. But he felt, since getting to know her, she did really mean it. Starting her work, as she called it, was never until late afternoon, so his time in her company was spent in conversation or sightseeing.

This first trip with Doug, arriving back at the Butterworth station from Pinang, on the train, he was surprised to find Doug on board, sober and ready to do his shift, which pleased him. As they sat arranging the mail, they spoke of how their day went.

The train due to leave at twenty-two hundred hours, never seemed to, although, always arrived on time in K.L. This night though they were three quarters of an hour late, which normally means there are rail works somewhere down the line, and the lads would have a longer wait at their respective stations.

After something to eat, Dave climbed up onto the top bunk and fell asleep. The next thing he knew was, with a shunt of the train he wakened. Looking out of the top window he noticed they were pulling out of Tapah station. He lay back thinking another three hours to go. Next time he woke, it was starting to brighten up outside and they were nearing K.L. Climbing down he was greeted by Doug, 'Morning Jock. You must have been tired, to have slept practically all night.'

Stretching and having a yawn Dave replied, 'I walked far too much yesterday, and was bushed, that sleep was desperately needed.'

'Walk! where did you walk to?' He asked.

I told him, about meeting Nee Nee and going to see some temples on the other side of Pinang

'Crafty man, got a bit on the side already have you? I didn't take you for someone like that.'

Dave not making him any the wiser, just thought, *that will keep the rumour mill going.*

Arriving back at Paroi Camp Cpl Duff told him to report to the CO, at ten hundred hours. He showered, shaved, and grabbed some breakfast. At five to ten he was standing outside the CO's office all spick and spam in his best uniform, waiting to report to Major Dunlop as ordered.

Cpl Duff came over, and Dave inquired, 'What's it about Corp?'

He growled, 'That clown Lance Cpl Barry.'

'Where is he the now?' Dave asked

'In the Guard House' was the reply.

At that moment Dave thought to himself *'Am I in trouble because of all this.'*

Cpl Duff got a signal and told Dave to come to attention then, 'Quick march. Left right left right left right.' Into the office, until he stood before the CO.

'At ease,' the CO barked. 'Now Walters, the theft of a handgun, this is a profoundly serious situation, can you enlighten me on any other thing that took place before you left on duty?'

'Only what Lance Cpl Barry told me Sir. When I went in to meet him to go on duty,' he said, and then proceeded to tell the CO. the events as they happened yesterday.

'Very well Walters,' he said, without looking up at him and fingering through the papers on his desk, 'there's no blame on your part, but you may need to appear as a witness when his trial comes about.' Looking at Dave, 'Have you any questions?

'No Sir.'

'Very well you are dismissed.' Left right left right left right, and he was outside again

As Cpl Duff dismissed him. 'Before you go Walters remember there is a training session for the football team this afternoon.'

That was his afternoon taken care off, no forty winks this day, but his time was not wasted, as he learned all that had transpired with the saga of the handgun, from the Cpl

'The thief who stole the handgun' he said, 'turned out to be the fucking Dobby Walla who cleaned your basher. The bastard has had clearance from the army for years, and a pass to come and go about the camp.'

'Did he leave the camp with it?' Dave asked.

'Yes! once he stole the Handgun, he went into Seremban town Centre and robbed a shop. In the process he shot the shopkeeper in the arm and stole some money, outside the shop he panicked and threw the handgun away.' He went on, 'Some kids found it and were seen playing with it before accidently firing off another round. It was then that the local police apprehended them. The CO informed the police about the handgun as soon as he knew it was reported stolen, and fortunately, the police were actually out searching even as the thief was robbing the shop.'

'What about the Dobby Walla, where is he?' Dave asked.

'Last night he was apprehended in a dance hall in town.' Corp Duff replied.

Later the other lads said MPs stormed into the camp, closed it down, and went through every Basher, rounding up all nonarmy personal and questioned them about who did what and where. The upshot of it all was that new stringent orders concerning the collection of weapons were issued.

What happened to the thief? Dave could only guess but was sure he would be out of circulation for some time. He heard the shopkeeper was treated for a grazed wound on his left arm. Just as well he thought, it is not as easy as people think to shoot off a handgun and hit the target without taking proper aim.

In the outcome of the court case against Lance Cpl Barry, one week later, he was found guilty of negligence and disobeying a direct order on the procedure in uplifting his Handgun. He was sentenced to a six-month term in the Military Changi Prison in Singapore, and was also stripped of his stripe. Dave wasn't called to give evidence.

A harsh punishment Dave thought when he heard about it at first, but he supposed it could have been worse and a soldier or a child might have been killed, so all in all the punishment may well have fitted the crime.

Two days after the case, the couriers were ordered to collect their handguns from the armoury just before leaving the camp, and were not to be loaded until they were placed in imminent danger.

Dave jokingly said to some of the lads while trying to impersonate the CO. 'Now listen here lads, if you are challenged at any time, do as all British men do, have a stiff upper lip, and fearlessly tell the enemy, please wait a moment till I load my little thingy gun?'

Dave thought it was a silly order because of one silly corporal's mistake at the time, but orders are orders.

Chapter 29

Getting to Know You

Football training was an order, and there was no way out even if you felt tired after a night on duty. Twice a week in the afternoon the team trained. The next game the following Saturday, was against one of the local teams that is made up of different Indian religious sects, and the following week another team made up of Chinese. These games were usually played in the sports arena gardens in the Centre of Seremban.

When off duty on these days, Cpl Duff selected him, 'Walters, you'll need to play in both games as most of the lads are away or on duty.'

Dave replied in a sarcastic tone, 'Thanks for nothing, I take it the other twenty couldn't make it?'

He looked at Dave and smiled, 'Listen, I couldn't get a team out of the other twenty. At least I know yea can kick a Baw.'

'Right Cpl, I hear you. I suppose you'll buy the usual pint afterwards?'

He walked away and laughed out loud saying in his gruffly Scots accent, 'That wull be the day.'

Cpl Duff wasn't a bad spud; he could give and take a bit

of banter like the rest. As for the games, they generally were a walk over for the boys. In the team were three lads who were signed for professional teams back home in England and the rest of them had played in teams at various levels before coming into the army. The teams they were playing against though, hadn't played at the same level. As Cpl Duff always said, it was more an exercise and training games for playing against other army units in the coming weeks.

To say, only mad dogs and English men play in the noonday sun, well here he was running about the football field chasing after a ball in temperatures reaching thirty degrees Centigrade, all in the name of sport. He now knew who the mad dog was. One thing though it did for him, he could lose all the weight he put on with drinking in the NAAFI at night.

After the game it was generally straight into the canteen to replenish the fluids lost, with a warning not to drink alcohol until they had drunk a few pints of orange juice or plain water. Cpl Duff said it was to prevent dehydration or something to that effect. Dave personally thought, it was to give Duffy time to get into the NAAFI so he could get his pint in first.

That first September in Malaya the weather was getting wetter, this was the start of the Monsoon season and the trips up to K.L. by road became very hazardous, especially when caught out in the open road. When the rains came down and with Cpl Morgan driving, Dave was sure it was going to be exciting, as Morgan only knew one position to have the pedal, and that was to the floor.

At this time Mike was taken off the Courier duty in order to prepare his married pad for his wife Lynne and kids arriving, they were due around the sixth of this month. Dave thought, that will put the locks on Mike and his attraction for the Prostitutes down in Seremban. On the few nights they were off, and together in town. After a few drinks in the

Seremban Bar, they made their way the local dance hall. The dance hall is really another Bar with a fenced off square section in the middle of the floor for the dancers. On entering tickets were bought, then it was a scrambled to get a seat at the side of the dance square.

Dave became drawn to one young very attractive dance girl, and always gave his tickets to her. As she danced for him, they would chat and giggle about all sorts of things, except going on a date, that was Taboo for these girls. Being the property of the hall owner, property in the sense that they were bought from their families at a young age and trained as dance hall hostesses.

Most were attractive young Thailand girls, and just to talk to them did a young man's moral good. Dave was told by one of the locals that once they reach about eighteen and lost a bit of their looks, they went into prostitution. Sad, he thought. His favourite girl had just turned seventeen, and must have known what her fate would be. But this he consoled himself was a different world, with different lifestyles from the one he came from.

On some of these nights out together with other mates, Mike would disappear for a while without saying, and although he wouldn't say it. Dave was sure, he was nipping off to have some Jig-a-jig with a Prostitute. Dave one night expressed to him as a pal, 'I think your attitude sucks, especially with your wife arriving soon,

Mike never denied what he was up to, and would only say in his easy oozy way, 'it's no big deal.'

The second Monday of September was a special day for Dave and his mates; they were all called on parade along with all the other units in Paroi Camp, but this time the parade took part on the Airstrip. The occasion was not because royalty was visiting, but because they were all being presented with a medal.

With the declaration of the end of the Emergency on the 31st of July 1960 this was a service Medal awarded for being in Malaya during the Emergency. In Dave's case, and a few others who had only been here a few months, he felt he did not deserve it.

The OC put their thoughts at ease when he said after the presentation, 'These are not for what time you have done out here in Malaya, but for the honour of how long and how well the Royal Signals Regiments have served during the conflict out here.'

Dave still disagreed, but over the next forty-eight hours he had a change of heart and in part accepted that maybe he did deserve his medal.

After the parade, a special dinner was laid on for them and it seemed that the army had stood still for that day, but not for Dave. That night he was on duty and Doug once more his partner. On their first trip together, he had worried what to expect from Doug, but having completed a few trips together since, He thought, *'so far I've been able to cope with him.'*

Later that night they met at the guardhouse and signed for our handguns and off they were on another trip up north. This trip it was Dave's turn to go to Sungie Petani, and Doug over to Pinang. This was what worried him, as last trip he came back after having been on a bender and was not able to carry out his duty. This time though, Dave told him, 'You work on the up trip, and I'll do the return trip.' This seemed to satisfy him.

The trip up to K.L. and the train journey up to Butterworth and beyond went smoothly. After freshening up in the Ghurkha Training camp that day, as it was a nice day, Dave walked the half mile down a rough red ash road that was flanked on either side with thick jungle, into Sungie Petani for a local meal. He had over the last few trips frequently visited a small Chinese restaurant that was situated on the side of a small river that runs past the town.

The restaurant, not much to look at by western standards, served nice Chinese food. The owner Le Ho, whom Dave got to know the more he frequented his place. Eventually allowed him to sit under the cool shade of the bamboo roof at the back, and overlooking the river that looked dark green with all the vegetation the had fallen into it. Just below the restaurant was a small waterfall, and that day as Dave watched the water cascading over the rocks, the sunlight created small rainbows which danced along the top of the falls. This day he thought could not get any better except to have Jennifer by his side, enjoying this view.

Looking out at the jungle on the other side of the river he thought of when being presented his medal and of all the young men who had had to fight in these jungles, it made him wonder if they had had time when they were here to sit and look at something as beautiful as this.

Le Ho speaking in broken English, had told him about the old days during the Emergency and the fighting that took place around this area. He said his family had always lived there and his father before him. Dave only met his wife once but his two daughters he had spoken to, as they always served him.

After a nice meal and enjoying the scenery he sighed, all good things come to an end, and it was back to camp mid-afternoon. Having still some time to spare he sat and watched the young men of the Ghurkha regiment going through their paces and was glad he hadn't had to work as hard as these lads, everything seemed to be at quick time, and he felt exhausted just looking at them. At night before leaving, he managed to grab a bite to eat in the canteen and then it was back down the twenty miles to Butterworth.

While waiting on the train for Doug, there were a lot of troops milling around the platform about to board. Dave asked one lad, 'Are you moving camp?'

'No mate,' he replied, 'we're all off back home to Blighty.'

'You lucky buggers.' Dave shouted back to him as they moved down the platform to their carriages.

Just then Doug arrived with the help of the Ausie escort, who was just about carrying him. 'Too much to drink Mate. No way he could have made it over in his state?'

Dave shook his head and grinned, 'Thanks for helping him over mate.' Looking at Doug and then at the Ausie, 'You can put your money on it he won't be back on my shift or even on the courier duty, because no one will work with him.'

Once they pushed Doug onto the train Dave with the help of the Ausie heaved Doug up onto the top bunk, and within minutes he was deep asleep. With the platform now empty of troops except for well-wishers the train rolled out of the station, while Dave settled down to sort out the mail for the stops down the line.

Work done, he ordered a coffee and a ham roll then sat back to read his book.

Chapter 30

Back to Reality

Dave was still feeling dizzy as he stood at the compartment door, his hands on his head and still trying to get over the shock of the train being derailed. Suddenly the auxiliary lights flickered and came on in the carriage, at last he could see what it was like. The passengers had stopped screaming by now and apart from the occasional whimper from some kids everything was eerily quiet for a moment, then further down the carriage he heard movement from the next compartments.

Doug by this time was on his feet asking, 'Are you all right Jock?' Then noticing blood on Dave's face. Showing concern, he said, 'Sit down and I'll see if I can get some help.'

'No,' Dave groaned, 'I'll be alright in a minute, anyway, go and see if anyone is needing help, because there might be people needing help more than me.'

'You might have concussion or something.' Doug said worriedly.

Dave stood up again and looking at him and said, 'Doug, I'll be alright, anyway we need to get this mail sorted, and if we can't go by train, we will need to get down the road somehow.'

'Well! you stay there,' he said, 'and I'll go speak to the train OC, and see what can be done.'

Dave could see Doug had snapped out of his drunken state and was reacting to the situation. While he was away Dave felt a little better, still a sore head but not as dizzy, so he started to sort the mail. It was about half an hour later when Doug returned with a nurse. It seemed there were a few nurses on their way back down to the British Military Hospital in K.L. Behind them was a Lieutenant Briggs from Royal Army Service Corp's who was the OC on the train. After the nurse treated Dave's cut head and gave him a couple of painkillers the Lieutenant asked, 'How do you feel now, are you fit to continue your duty?'

'Yes sir. I'm ok, but we have to get this mail down the line.'

'Is there anything I can do to help?' Briggs asked.

Dave was glad when Doug took over when he said, 'We need transport to get down to the next station, sir.'

Briggs was quite sharp, and seemed to know the procedure about the Couriers job. 'I'll try to arrange some transport for you.' With that he turned and left.

'How are you feeling now?' Doug asked.

'I'll live' Dave told him.'

So important that the confidential mail must be delivered, good to his word an hour later the Lieutenant came back and informed them, a Land Rover was being sent to take us down the ten miles to Ipoh Station.

He said, 'I've been informed the earlier train from Alor Setar was still standing in the Ipoh station, waiting for the up train to arrive there.' Then checking the bruise on Dave's head, he asked, 'will you be ok.' and continued, 'You'll have to make your way along to the front of the train; there is a works road there. A Land Rover will pick you up at that point.'

'What about the injured passengers, Sir?' Dave asked. His

reply put them at ease. 'We were lucky for there are only some with scratches, but unfortunately two civilians were killed, their bodies have been removed, but our priority now is to get you both on your way. We can't keep the military mail waiting.'

Dave suspected he was being evasive with the truth, but this was not the time to question more, so he replied, 'Thank you sir for everything.'

They were escorted along the line past people sitting by the side, some with bandages on their heads and various parts of their bodies, but all where mobile, so Dave supposed the Lieutenant was not that far out with his assessment.

The rain easing off considerably by this time and some soldiers were taking the opportunity to stretch their legs or stand in groups having a cigarette. The night air still hung heavy, which magnified the odours of the Jungle vegetation. The sounds of the voices, because of the humid air condition were still muted, even the sounds you normally heard coming out of the Jungle were surprisingly quiet.

Some lads from the Sherwood Forrester Regiment were busy clearing some debris away when they walked past, their eyes met, and they nodded. The Land Rover was parked up the road a piece to allow the ambulance and rescue vehicles down to the trackside. Reaching their vehicle, they climbed on board. He looked back and returned a wave to SFR lads as the Land Rover started back up the track.

The trip to Ipoh station was over in a blur and in time to catch the earlier train, which still stood in the station. The other train traveling north, because of the derailment up ahead, was sitting on the other side of the station, with nowhere to go. The couriers travelling north, when they arrive, had to take over the Land Rover Dave had vacated and travel by road to Butterworth.

Looking at the time, they were about four and half hours behind schedule. Fortunately, a compartment had quickly been made available to enable them to carry on with their duty.

Once the train was on its way south, an Army Major, who happen to be in one of the other compartments, knocked on their door. Dave slid the door open and as orders were, no one can enter their compartment while they were on duty, he blocked the Major from entering and did not salute him, which seemed to go unnoticed.

'Everything all right lads, bit of a flap was it,' the Major enquired. 'had to put some people out of this compartment when I heard you were coming, told them important people coming on board,'

'Thank you sir for your assistance,' Dave replied.

The Major turned without saying another word and went back up the passageway.

'What was that all about?' Doug asked.

Dave shrugged his shoulders and replied, 'Don't know. Probably he just wanted a pat on the back.'

With tiredness catching up on him, Doug after having enquired if Dave was all right, decided to turn in. His headache easing Dave told him, 'Get some sleep and stop worrying.'

The rest of the trip went smoothly, except for the lads at the various stations having longer, to wait for their mail. Dave assumed, *'somebody might have signalled down the line to each unit that they would be delayed.* Apparently, that did not happen.

Arriving back at Paroi camp three hours later than normal, word had travelled before them and they were treated like celebrities. Question after question were thrown at them until they ran out of fancy tales about how they fought of the commies with their bare hands, and how they saved all the damsels in distress. On a more serious note Dave told them of the two dead and a lot with minor injuries.

Their celebrity status did not last long, as they were ordered to report to the OC's office. The outcome, Doug was reprimanded for being drunk. Someone reported him being drunk and helped on to the train at Butterworth. Dave tried to put in a good word for him, telling the OC that he had been incapacitated for a while and Doug had reacted to the situation, and organized what was to be done.

'Nevertheless!' The OC said to Doug, 'I'm taken you off the Courier duty and reassigned you to cleaning up jobs in the cookhouse. More importantly, I'm docketed a month's wages, and you lose Courier money due.'

The OC turning his attention to Dave, 'You handled yourself well considering your injury, well done. I'm ordering you now to report to the MO over at Seremban Camp.' At that they both snapped salutes and left the office.

Outside Dave said to Doug, 'Sorry about your demotion. I'll speak to you later, but I could well have done without going to see the MO at this moment, as with all the problems we have had through the night I'm shattered.'

At the Infirmary, the MO examining him, 'Well Walters, how do you feel now?'

'All right sir, except a slight headache, I think I just need some sleep.'

He looked into Dave's eyes again with his scope and then said, 'I'll be the judge of that.' Pausing again, he then said, 'We'll keep you in the hospital overnight, just to keep an eye on you.'

Bang went his night out with the mates. He was thinking, this is going to be a boring night when at that moment, a very attractive nurse with beautiful blond hair entered the surgery.

Smiling at him she then escorted him to an empty ward, which had six beds.

In a very polite well-educated sexy English voice, said, 'You can use this bed at the door so I can keep an eye on you.'

Dave fell in love with her in that moment; or was it just she looked so sexy after having only been in the company of local women since arriving in Malaya. Lying on his bed watching every move of her well-rounded body as she went about her business, he thought as he closed his eyes, *this might not be a bad stay after all.*

When he woke up it was late in the afternoon, he yawned, stretched his arms, and looking up it dawned on him someone had pulled down the mosquito net around his bed. He then noticed that the beautiful blond nurse he had seen earlier had now in some way metamorphosed into a much more elderly black hair matron type, with a bit more weight on all parts of her body. He gave his eyes a rub and looked again then thought, *I must have only dreamed about the beautiful blond nurse and must have concussion after all.*

The nurse seeing him awake came over to his bed and asked in a strong Irish accent, 'How do you feel now after your sleep.'

'I'm feeling fine now, but I could do with some food, as I haven't had anything to eat since six yesterday.'

'Oh! I cannot do that for you now. You'll just need to wait another hour till you get your dinner.' She cheekily replied.

'What time is it?' He enquired.

'It's going nearly four. You have been asleep nearly six hours.

'Six hours? Dave queried, then asked, 'Bye the way what happened to the other nurse who was here when I came in this morning?'

'You mean nurse Richmond; she doesn't come on till the morning.' She replied.

He sighed inwardly; *this is going to be a very boring night after all.*

While he had been asleep that afternoon, two other lads had been wheeled into the ward, one for appendicitis and the other to be circumcised of all things. Later, he asked the lad why he wanted circumcised, he quipped, 'My unit is going on an exercise and this Op will get me out of duties for a week.

Dave jokily replied, 'After your Op you better check your dick is still there, as they tell me the surgeon here has a shaky hand,' pointing to the plaster on his head, he continued, 'I came in to have a toenail cut and look what he did to me.'

The rest of that night was passed having a good laugh about life in the army. Next morning, he was discharged before he could feast his eyes on that wonderful figure of nurse Richmond, it appeared she had a day off.

Chapter 31

First Impressions

Having been released from hospital the night before, next morning he was back in his basher after breakfast, and was sitting on his bed with his own thoughts, *Thank God no duties today. After all the excitement of my last trip up north, I hope today will be much better than yesterday.* He was still sitting on his bed thirty minutes later when Mike walked in,

'Hello mate, what are you doing today?'

With fixing out his married pad, it had been over two weeks since Dave had seen him. 'Nothing planned yet,'

'Want to come and meet Lynne and the family?' He cheerfully asked.

'Now, that's the best offer I've had today, in fact the only one.' Dave said with a chuckle.

'Before I go back home, I still have a few things to do downtown first,' Mike said, and continued. 'So, if you're ready, we can leave the now.'

Arriving at their home Dave stopped when Mike's wife came to meet them. Like in a dream, she sashayed down the path towards him, her shoulder length auburn hair bouncing in rhythm with her steps. As his eye roamed over her, he observed she was wearing a loose-fitting white blouse, a figure-hugging short pale blue Minnie skirt that revealed her figure and her wonderful legs. On her feet she wore a pair of blue strapless high heel shoes, which seemed to accentuate the way she walked towards him.

Unable to take his eyes of her, his first thoughts were, *'What on earth is Mike playing at, going out with prostitutes when he has a wife that looks this good.'*

Meeting Lynne and the children for the first time was a breath of fresh air. Her photos had not done her justices, as she was the most attractive woman he'd seen since leaving home. Her face, not to dissimilar to Jennifer's, was the kind you would never tire looking at. Deep blue eyes with a sparkle of mischiefs that shone through her wonderful smile and a perfectly shaped mouth said it all in one word, beautiful. Even at that time of day, although not wearing makeup, she looked fantastic.

Coming close, she put her arms around him, gave him a hug, and kissed him on his cheek. His senses overflowed. At that moment she smelt wonderful and made him realize what he was missing, by being apart from Jennifer.

She looked at him with her dreamy blue eyes and softly said very intimately. 'Hello David, at last! Mike has told me so much about you, and your girlfriend Jennifer. Meeting you now, I feel I've known you for a long time.'

Her mouth turned up at the corner as she playfully chirped, 'I hope we will become good friends.'

Dave, for a moment after hearing her call him David was dumb struck on what to say, feeling his face flush, he looked at Mike, winked and shyly said, 'I didn't know you were married to a film star.'

'You're a tease.' She said smiling. Taking his arm, she guided Dave up the path, and then turning her head to look at Mike. 'I think I might get to like this guy if he doesn't get too cheeky.'

At that moment, she had charmed him. The kind of girl any man would be proud to take home to meet mum. Walking up the path towards the house, he tried to control his thoughts as he speculated, *what would it be like in bed with her?* Shaking his head, he blushed as the thoughts of Lynne aroused in his loins.

After dinner Lynne quizzed him intimately, where he came from and what he did back home, what Jennifer was like and did he miss her. She was the most at ease person he had ever met or talk to, at times he felt there were only two in the conversation as Mike sat back listened.

Then Mike joined the conversation and asked him, 'What happened to your head?'

Dave filled him in about the derailment, and that took them into another long conversation about the implications and what might happen mext.

Lynne not to be left out, pried more about him personally. So, at ease in her company was he, that by the time he left that evening, she knew everything about him. Being such a pleasant person, she made him feel at home that day. He was also charmed by their children. Little Michael, and baby Virginia, who were quiet most of the time.

Saying goodnight after ten that night, and having spent a wonderful time in their company, Lynne told him, I enjoyed your company today, Mike must bring you some other time, and we can continue our conversation. He reluctantly left to catch the bus back to Camp.

All the way back to camp, Dave couldn't get it out of his head how nice Lynne had been to him, and again couldn't understand about how Mikes attitude had been before Lynne arrived here in Seremban.

Chapter 32

A New Partner

That evening sitting in the NAAFI with the rest of the lads was an anti-climax, their conversation was all about the football back home and what teams they all supported. In between the arguments, he kept thinking, '*what's wrong with Mike when he treats Lynne that way?*' Reprimanding himself to stop analysing their relationship, as he was comparing his own moral stance to how Mike should treat his own wife.

Lying in bed later, his thoughts strayed occasionally to Lynne, the sound of her voice speaking his name had left an impression on him. He felt there had been a connection between them in that instance, one that had made him very home sick and feeling guilty, he then focused his thoughts on Jennifer and what she would be doing at that moment. With home time nearly seven hours behind, he supposed she would be about to finish work.

Having been in Lynne's company, and with all that has happened since leaving home, for the first time since arriving in Malaya he thought about the night he stayed over with Jennifer in the holiday hut. A pang of missing her touched his heart and he let out a deep sigh. That night, he fell asleep with only warm thoughts of the time he spent with Jennifer as they had lain naked, enjoying the comforting warmth of each-others body.

The heavens opened early next morning, parade was cancelled as the Sarge and Cpl Duff did not want to get wet. It had been hard enough getting down to the canteen without getting wet, standing out on parade he thought would have been plain crazy, so it was with a relief that the Sarge took the roll call while they were having breakfast.

After breakfast, Cpl Duff approaching Dave inquired, 'Walters, how are you feeling now?'

'Ok Cpl,' Dave replied.

'Good,' he said, 'I need you to go out on Courier duty tonight.'

'That's all right with me Cpl,' he consented.

'Good. I want you to show the ropes to Signalman McMahon, he's to be your new partner.' He called McMahon over and introduced him. 'Bye the way, is there still a spare bed in your Basher since Higham left?'

'Yes! the one just as you go in on the left,' Dave replied.

Duff, turned to McMahon, 'Go with Walters after breakfast and he'll show you the Basher.'

McMahon sat down at Dave's table; they spent half-an-hour getting to know each other. Dave found McMahon came from the area called Anderston, in Glasgow, and had been in the army for seven years, he also found out that he had boxed for the army at amateur level. Surprised by that revelation, Dave joked, 'You don't look old enough to have been in the service that long.'

McMahon smiled as he replied, 'I went straight into the army from the Boys soldiers and that was added to my time.'

Dave felt, working with him on the courier duty would be ok, being a quite lad and didn't say much, except when talking about his boxing experience. All in, Dave found him an Ok guy. In this army he remembered being told, you have just got to get on with whoever you are thrown in with.

That night they went on their first of many trips as partners, and over the next few weeks become good mates, so much so, from no interest in boxing, Dave became a fan listening to his stories.

Chapter 33

Bad News from Home

The end of the month of September was a turning point in Dave's life, his duties were progressing without mishaps; and that month was quietly coming to an end. At this juncture things started to go wrong with everything around him and his prospective of life changed. Finishing his latest trip over the Friday 2nd October, Dave arrived back at camp on Saturday morning the looking forward to a nice break of four days before his next trip. After breakfast he decided to have another hour in bed until he was wakened by a voice.

'Come on Dave waken up we have to prepare the NAFFI for a party to night.' It was George shouting as he pulled him out of bed.

'Whose birthday is it?' Dave asked sleepily.

'Big Pete Cantrell's,' he replied.

'I thought he was over in Seremban Camp?'

'He was, but he has moved back over here yesterday.' and continued 'He's to travel over to the Signal Centre every morning, but for now, he's billeted with us. So up and get dressed.'

That night they all trooped down to the NAAFI, which

earlier with the help of some of the other lads had been decorated. Enjoying the banter, they were sitting beside Pete Cantrell, who was dressed up as a big tart and looking fabulous. Being a rugby player, he was built like a tank, which made the jokes all the funnier. With the drinks flowing and all having a good laugh, Dave was not prepared for what hit him next.

Derek entering the NAAFI walked over to him looking serious. Dave thinking, he was going to play a prank, jumped up. But Derek grabbing him by the arm and whispered in his ear 'Dave, the duty Sarge wants to see you.'

Dave looked over at the door as the duty Sarge entered and waved him over. Crossing the open floor, he could feel all eyes were on him, and in his mind, he was wondering what the hells could the Sarge want him for, and hoped it wasn't to go on duty.

At the door, the Sarge put his arm around his shoulders and escorted him outside, this friendly gesture didn't register at first. Then turning to face Dave, he looked him in the eyes a moment then said, with compassion in his voice, 'Signalman Walters. I have just received bad news from home, and I'm sorry to inform you that your Dad has just died.'

As though his feet were riveted to the ground, Dave's mind went blank, he couldn't take in what he had just heard. He looked at the Sergeant and seeing he was serious, turning his back on the Sergeant he stared along the runway. At that moment everything seemed so surreal, at the end of the runway just above the tree line, was the largest full moon in the heavens he had ever seen. Frozen in time, he could not take his eyes off it.

As though in a dream he heard the Sergeant asked 'Will you be alright?'.

Dave forced himself to turn slowly to look at him, and in that moment, everything crashed in on him and his mind went into overdrive. *Dad can't be dead; he's back home,* he told himself. *He was well when I left home. No Dad's not dead, he will be there to greet me when I return home.* His mind going round in circles, he found it hard to concentrate.

Looking at the Moon again, he answered in an involuntary way, 'Yes Sarge, I'll be alright.'

Just then George and Ron came out, Ron putting his arm around Dave's shoulder and asked stupidly 'Everything Ok mate? Will you be alright?'

As the Sarge left, they both tried to talk Dave into going back inside. Still in shock and trying to hold back the tears and unable to move his feet he managed to stutter, 'I need a minute to myself. I'll be in later.'

George not thinking, would not let it go 'Come on and have a drink mate, it will do you the world of good.'

His concentration gone, he allowed them to guide him inside, but when sat down beside them, and with all the joking going around, he was as though still in a dream and unable to take in what was going on around him, he just stared at the entrance until one lad from another table came over and said 'Sorry to hear about your Dad, mate.'

It was then it finally hit home, and he realizing they all knew what the Sarge had come to tell him, and not wanting to talk about it. Without saying a word, he stood up and walked out of the NAFFI. The steps as he climbed the hill to his Basher seemed higher and longer, and in his head, he was screaming out, *he's my Dad not theirs, so why should they know about him. It's personal to me.*

In the quietness of his Basher, he sat on his bed and with pictures of his Dad and Jennifer in his hands, and feeling as though his head would burst, he tried to cry, but no tears would come. Then for the first time in a long time, he knelt and prayed.

Later, sitting in the dark for what seemed un eternity, he switched on his bedside lamp and wrote a letter to his mother. (Weeks later his sister wrote back to say his letter had been a blessing to his mum.) The rest of that night he just wished he could have been home beside his family and Jennifer, as he knew Jennifer would have been able to take this strange feeling of loneliness away from him.

Lying on his bed, in the darkness of the night, his mind went back to the day he left home and realized that that was the last time he had seen his dad alive. The image of his dad standing waving to him as he turned the corner, brought back the feeling he had that day, and wondered, was fate trying to prepare him.

In that moment, he couldn't believe that he wouldn't see his dad again, for his dad was invincible. He had always done things for him; he even taught him to play football from an early age with a ball made of newspaper and string. Dad had always been there for him, and always would be, he thought. He just wished then that he could have shed a tear for him, but his eyes stayed dry.

Next day, time meant nothing to him, for numbness had taken over his life. That morning from the moment he raised, his mates stuck close to him and tried to help him through his grief. They arranged transport, and took Dave over to the main Seremban Camp Chapel for mass. As most of his mate's didn't go to any kind of church, this gesture left him feeling quite humble. Before mass, the padre spoke to Dave and passed on his condolence and said he would remember his dad in his prayers.

The remainder of that day was so much of a whirl wind, with his mates all around; he didn't get time to think of anything, as they arranged his whole day. He was glad because it was hard for him to make up his mind what to do. He felt in a kind of limbo, being so far from home it still hadn't really registered that his Dad had died, for in his own mind he had always thought everything was standing still back home and when he returned, everything would be the same.

The afternoon passed bye with them swimming in Seremban Camp pool, having a drink and clowning about, with the lads dragged him into their jokes.

After dinner that night, with no duties, he went into the NAAFI as he didn't feel like being alone, it would be good for him his mates kept saying, but their plans were foiled by the presence of Mike and Lynne.

Having heard about his Dad through the grape vine at the Signal centre, they decided to come over to see how he was feeling. For a while, he was in control of his emotions, that was until Lynne placed her hand on his and asked, 'How are you feeling?'

The sound of her voice and the pained expression on her face was too much for him. He abruptly stood up, brushed bye everyone as blurted, 'I'm sorry I need to go.' and walked out of the NAAFI.

Outside he felt a fool as the tears well up inside, and not wanting anyone to see him like this, he stood there a few minutes, holding his emotions together, and tried to convince himself and the world, I am a man.

He was beginning to manage his emotions, when gently he felt an arm come around his shoulder, turning around his eyes met Lynne's.

She pulled him to her, and wrapping her other arm around, embracing him. The warmth of her soft body pressing on him released the emotions that he had been desperately trying to hold back.

Patted him on the back she whispered 'Let it go David, don't try to hold it in.'

Like a burst dam, tears flowed from his eyes. They stood locked in her embrace for what seemed an eternity until his emotions subsided, and when he looked at her, he saw that she too had tears in her eyes and was sharing his grief. A long time they stood in that embrace; the silence of the night was only broken by the night noises from the jungle around the camp. The tender warmth that she showed him at that moment was what he desperately needed.

Time passed and they decided to sit down on the seat outside the NAAFI. The still night air was very balmy, and the stars twinkled brightly between the clouds. Sitting holding his hands in hers, she listened to him as he poured out his longings and his regrets. She encouraged him to talk about Jennifer and his aspirations for when he returned home. In those moments, she was like his sister.

The minutes past and he settled a little, leaning forward she surprise him by gently kissing him on his lips. Pulling apart they gazed at each other for a long moment, his mind in a daze, wondering why she did that. A thought then came into his head, *is she too searching for something*. They embraced once more, and she clung to him as if this is where she wanted to be.

The moment was only broken when she said softly, 'If you ever want to talk things over, tell Mike, and he will bring you round to our home to.' She stopped mid-sentence as thought having said too much.

Dave felt their friendship in that moment, and a close bond formed between them. They sat holding hands and eventually her presence settled him and gave him the feeling he could face the future again.

From that night on, he was often in Lynne and Mike's company, even having meals in their home. Sometimes the three of them went into town to show her the Seremban nightlife. On nights like that, she would hold both their hands and teasingly say 'This is great, I have two handsome men escorting me.'

Ten days later a letter from Jennifer arrived, Dave hurriedly opened it.

My darling,

I'm so sorry about your Dad. I wish I could have been there for you just to hold you, as I know how much your dad meant to you. My heart was breaking at the news and with you so far away I was lost just thinking about you, and how you must be feeling. I have been along to see your mother every day and she is holding up, but is worried about you as I am. Every night I go to sleep with your photo under my pillow and long for the day you come home.

Her words at that moment were what he needed to settle him, and bring his feet and emotions back down to earth. Dave spent the next hour writing a letter home to Jennifer, and his mother. He never mentioned Lynne in his letter, for in that moment he felt a little guilty.

Some weeks' later at Mike's insistence, he stayed over one night, and as time went by this soon became a regular event. These times were a great boost to Dave, and he was able to settle himself after his Dads death. Even though he liked the company of his mates, he kidded himself, there is nothing like feeling part of a family when you're so far from home.

Some of the highlights for him during this period, was the dances held in Seremban Camp on Saturday nights, he and his mates had always avoided them because it was mostly married couples that went, so it was a surprise when Mike said, 'Why don't you and George come along and join us. Lynne and I and Andy Moffatt and his wife Alison from next door will be there.'

George didn't need a second invite after Mike jokingly

said, 'There are lots of frustrated married women whose husbands are away on duty elsewhere and are always looking for dance partners.'

George accepted for both of us eagerly, 'Wild horses couldn't stop us.'

Arriving at the dance they didn't know what to expect and stood like wallflowers until their attention was drought to the table where Mike and Lynne were sitting. As they approached, Lynne said invitingly. 'David you sit here beside me.' He felt good, as her invitations felt personal. Turning to George she bossily said, 'Mike has told me you are a flirt, so you can sit over there.'

Drinks were ordered, and after some small talk Mike turned to Dave and mischievously said, 'I told Lynne she'd be alright for a dance partner, as you are a great dancer.'

Lynne gave Mike a long look and said coldly. 'It will be nice to get a dance instead of watching you drink all night.' Then turned to Dave, 'I hope it's true, that you can dance.'

'Proper Fred Astaire on ice,' Dave joked.

'Oh good, it will be nice to have a good dance partner that will whisk me round the floor,' she replied mischievously.

'Lynne, you've picked me up all wrong. I said on ice, because me feet go in the opposite direction from my body.' Dave responded jokily.

She looked at him with a steady gaze and said, 'We'll see about that once the band starts to play.'

On the dance floor he managed to please her, and said it was all down to her expert guidance. When in their company from that night on, Mike didn't like dancing, and was quite happy that Lynne was occupied, and that allowed him to hold the chair down and drank beer.

Growing closer by dancing a lot, Dave was slow to read the signs developing, but put it down to missing Jennifer, as when home, he had always enjoyed dancing with her, and they had many good times together.

It was after a few more weeks in Mike and Lynne's company, that he started to have serious doubts about their marriage. Mikes casual loftiness was not quite what it should be, and this was started to steal into his head, and saddened him, as, he was very fond of them both.

Chapter 34

Losing a Friend

Days rolled by and a few weeks before Christmas, Dave's duty was a lot heavier with the additional Christmas mail. From experience he knew it was mostly about troop movements, plus extra family mail, and trouble, he later was informed, was brewing up in Laos, not that it meant anything to Dave at that moment, but to others it might.

During this period, his life was settling down, and enjoying courier duties, while letters from Jennifer and his mum were regularly arriving. 230 Signal football team had played four matches, won two, drawn one and lost one. Dave, having a new lease of life, played in three. Their next match, being a semi-final away to BMH KL was in the inter Unit Cup and arranged for three weeks' time. Before that, though, he had three more trips to Pinang Island and two to Sungie Petani.

Pinang Island, a place Dave had grown to love because of his meeting up with Nee Nee. These days pass wonderfully until on his last trip before the big match, she was late in meeting him at their usual place. When she eventually came forward, she had her face covered. At first, he didn't think anything of it as women there sometimes cover their faces with a veil.

As they walked along the beach, he sensed something seemed to be distracting her, pressing on why she was so quiet he questioned, 'Has something happened? Are you feeling well?'

She replied softly, 'I not been well.'

'Sorry to hear that Nee Nee. Anything I can help you with?' Dave offered

'No. No. You good boy, no want you get trouble.'

Dave puzzled, but decided not to pursue more until they had walked further along the beach and her veil slipped, exposing a bruise down the left side of her face. 'Nee Nee, what's happened to you, did you have a fall?

She stayed quiet and her head went down. It was then he knew something terrible was worrying her. 'Nee Nee, you can tell me, I'm your little brother, and little brothers worry about their sisters.'

A little smile came into her eyes, but then disappeared as quickly, she took on a more worried look. 'I don't want get you in trouble, my master not like it.'

'I thought I was your best friend. Can't you even tell me what happened? Dave pleaded.

Sitting down on a rocky formation by the sea edge, she turned to look at him, tears running from her big deep dark brown eyes and her shoulders quivering, she sobbed, 'I try running away home and master catch me, when back at girls house, he punish me.' Her head went down.

Surprised by her words, Dave feeling afraid for her pulled her to him and hugged her tight as he knew deep down there was not a thing, he could do to help her, and was lost for words. He knew the army didn't take kindly to fraternizing with the locals, and if found out he had become friendly with a local girl they would have moved him on very sharply.

In this land he had learned, with their strange customs there was nothing in his power he could do, and deep down felt afraid for himself as much as for her. He knew he would be out of his depth, as her Chinese owners might not be the kind of people to mess with. That day was one of his worst days he had spent on Pinang. Before leaving her, he pleaded. 'Be careful and I'll see you next trip.'

Leaving her that day he felt he may have disappointed her for not saying he would protect her, because from that day on, he never saw her again. When visiting the Broadway Restaurant and speaking to the other girls, it was as though she never existed, and he was never able to find out what had happened to her. His trips to Pinang Island weren't the same for a while after that day, as he felt he had lost a particularly good and gentle friend.

It was fortunate his friend Gill managed to get some time off to coincide with some of his visits. Gill when back home lived by the sea, and was an excellent swimmer. During the days after Ne Ne, Gill introduced Dave to a different kind of beauty, the beauty of the sea life. Being a complete novice in deeper water, Dave learned how to snorkel off the coast among the rocky shores of Pinang and with lazing about on the beach, days past leaving him refresh for his duties ahead.

It was always moral uplifting for him getting back to Paroi Camp and have a letter from Jennifer waiting for him. Even though settled and enjoying life in the army, getting her letters it felt good she was still there for him, and he still in her thoughts. Included in her letter this time were some photos of her in a bridesmaid dress at her sister's wedding. She looked beautiful!

In the letter she wrote, *"I felt lonely that you were*

not by my side at the wedding, and I cried that
night in bed, wondering if you will still want to
marry me when you come home." And went on to
write, "I'll keep the dress on till you get home so we
can run down the aisle together."

Her words at that moment, were sweet music to his ears, as it took his all doubts away, as lately, some of his mates, hadn't been as lucky about their girlfriends. In the last month three received Dear John letters, two lads next Basher, and in his own Basher, his mate Brian Emery who came from Leeds.

Brian was a quiet lad and it had been hard watching how it affected him. All the mates rallied around him, but it was no consolation to Brian at that moment. Once he had settled down, they persuaded him to pin a photo of his now ex-girlfriend on the dartboard, and in turn threw darts at it until it was unrecognizable. That might sound cruel, but being so far away from home, there was nothing he could do about his problem.

Another blow to their moral came a few days later when Derek got word that his dad was critically ill at home. The one good thing to come out of it; was him being allowed home on compassionate leave.

After Derek left for home, Dave became a little annoyed with the army over him being allowed home, when he himself hadn't been, when his own father died. Stupidly, Dave asked to see the C.O. who was very polite about his request. However he was told that their situations were different. Derek was an only child, while he on the other hand had four brothers and a sister at home. Dave after thinking it over, understood the logic, but the decision still didn't make it any easier to take.

Life in the army during Derek's absence was now second nature to Dave and things were going along smoothly until just two days before Christmas 1961, his mate George, was hit by a bolt out of the blue, which affected them all. He had been complaining for a few days about an itch on the back of his left hand. This had spread up his arms and other parts of his body. On Christmas Eve he was admitted into Seremban hospital.

As he was being taken away, Dave jokingly said, 'You will enjoy your short stay there, as there is a blond hair nurse called Richmond, who will blow your mind.'

George in his cheeky fashion retorted back, 'Does she do any other jobs like that?'

On Speaking to the M.O. he explaining to them, 'Signalman Harris has picked up a skin disease that might turn infectious, so he was to be put into quarantine.'

Christmas dinner with the temperature around 92 degrees, was not how they were used to celebrating this special day, with the sun beating down and George in hospital, it was somewhat subdued. Their chief clown was not there and on top of that, the film lined up for their Christmas treat was the western, 'The Yellow Rose of Texas' again! Not what they were looking for. Earlier that morning Dave had taken some presents over to Lynne for her kids, but declined her offer to stay, and said, 'a group of us have decided to visit George to cheer him up.'

Borrowing a truck from the L.A.D. Dave drove them over to the hospital only to find that George's condition had deteriorated, and he had been transferred to another hospital at a place called 'The Cameron Highlands,' built back in the Colonial days they were informed, was set halfway up the mountain range in central Malaysia. A distance too far for them to travel that day, and to say they were disappointed about George's plight would have been an understatement.

Feeling down because George wasn't with them, collectively, they decided to cheer themselves up with a trip to the beach at Port Dickson, twelve miles from Paroi. Christmas forgotten, in an idyllic setting on the beach by the sea, they watched the local girls parade bye.

As Dave lay taking in the sun, his mind drifted back to what Gill taught him to look for in the sea, pointing out to his mates what it was like, he managed to get three other lads to join him to swim out to a platform tied to a buoy near a reef, some fifty yards offshore. Once out there, under water, they swam among small tropical fish, and that in part, made up for what had initially been turning out to be a sad day for all. The day was spent having a few drinks, a noisy singsong, and as the sun set below the horizon, they made their way back to camp.

Chapter 35

His Life Changes

The end of 1960 was over, and their New Year's Eve dinner celebrations were boisterous. On the morning of their dinner Dave spent catching up on letters, and then in the evening, along with two pals went over to Seremban Camp for the New Year's celebration dance, where he met up with Mike and Lynne. As the evening wore on, Lynne and Allison, Mike's mate's wife were enjoying themselves too much to notice, Mike, who had been up dancing early on, now seemed to prefer holding his seat down and drinking. At the end of the night, the dance was over. Mike, had overdone the celebrations and was in no fit state, and needed a helping hand to stay upright.

With a pleading look Lynne asked Dave to help her get him back home. Thinking nothing of it he agreed. Arriving back at their home, it was going on two in the morning. Dave told the Taxi to wait while he and Lynne struggled to settle Mike into his bed.

As he was about to leave, Lynne pointed out, 'It's quite late. Why not stay. You can sleep on the cot in the living room.' Feeling a little worse from drink himself he didn't fancy going back to the camp. It was an invitation he couldn't refuse. The taxi was paid off and as he walked back into the house, he hadn't a care in the world.

Later, the drink he had earlier started to affect him, and as he lay on his bed thinking about the wonderful time they had had, he looked out the window and caught the sight of the full moon hanging in the black sky, just like a big ball of light that was sending out beams, beams that mystically filled the room with a blue tinted glow.

Suddenly, he felt a bit nostalgic and home sick, thinking about home and what everybody would be doing. At that moment he wished that he were with Jennifer. A smile came over him when he realized, they would just be getting ready to do their own New Year celebrations. Funny old world he thought, I've just had a good time celebrating our move into 1961 and back home they were still stuck in 1960.

It had been quite a year, he pondered and wondered what this next year would bring. Would it be more drama? He hoped not. If Jennifer were still waiting for him, he knew he would get through the next year ok, and everything will turn out all right. He consoled himself with that thought.

He closed his eyes and drifted off to sleep, with thoughts only for Jennifer. Suddenly he was brought back out of his sleep by a rustling noise and surmised, Mike has managed to get his head off the pillow. Wearily he opened his eyes and was surprised to see a vision dressed in a short negligee pass across the moonlit window in front of him. For a moment, he thought he was dreaming.

The vision passed so close to him, he caught a whiff of perfume, only then he realised, it was Lynne. She had been heading to the kitchen by tiptoeing bye where he slept. Realizing she had wakened him, she stopped, and their eyes met, 'Sorry' she whispered, 'couldn't sleep, needed something cool to drink.'

Not wanting to disturb Mike who was asleep in the back bedroom, she leaned over towards him, it was then the aroma of her body filled all his senses, as she whispered again. 'Sorry, I didn't mean to wake you. just going for a cold drink of lemon,' pausing as though wanting to say more, she looked long at him then asked, 'Would you like some.'

'Yes!' He nervously said. He too was feeling hot, more so now as the night air was warm and humid.

Getting out of bed he started to follow her, without realizing he was wearing only his underpants. Stopping in his track, as normally he slept in the nude, but tonight thankfully he hadn't.

At that same moment she turned and appeared to give him a long slow look over, her gaze was more than just being inquisitive. In the glow of the moonlight filtering into the room he could see her face clearly, she was embarrassed. He smiled at the thought that in that moment she gave her feelings away.

Turning to shamelessly stand in front of him with the window behind her, showing her exquisite shape silhouetted by the moonlight, he could see through her thin negligee; she looked fantastic. Maybe, it was because they were still under the influence of the drink consumed earlier, or something that had been building up within them, he wasn't sure. All he knew was that both were showing a complete lack of discretion in front of each other.

With her eyes on him, he felt she had stripping him naked, just as he, her. With the realizing they were both staring intently at each other in a way they hadn't done before, words were not needed. They stood motionless, appreciating what they saw in each other. He wondered in that moment, is this beautiful woman as attracted to me as I to her. He felt his cheeks blush.

The spell was broken when she gave a nervous giggle then covering her mouth with her hand, she giggled again, and said nervously. 'It's all right Dave. I've seen it all before.'

Shaking his head and returning her smiles, he said in boldness 'But not on me you haven't.'

Slipping his trousers on, he fastened the top button and followed her into the kitchen. It was dark with only the fridge light casting a yellowish glow around her and shone through her nightie, silhouetting her figure perfectly, and adding a little more mystic.

She filled their drinks, he watched her every movement, from the curve of hips, her slender waist, and the gentle sway of her breasts. Turning, she handed him his glass, and as she did their hands touched momentarily. He stood captivated, encircled by the sweet aroma of her body, his senses heightened. He was speechless and didn't know what to do or say.

A tear ran out of the corner of her eyes drawing a response from him, 'What's wrong?'

'David,' she uttered with a deep sigh, then went quiet.

Dave had the feeling she wanting to say more, but not sure how. She seemed so sad at that moment, and Dave not thinking the rights or wrongs of what he was doing, put his drink down on the table and impulsively held her hand. That gesture started more tears flowing down her cheeks.

Taking her drink from her hand he placed it beside his. Instinctively putting an arm around her, he nervously whispered, 'It's all right Lynne! I'm here. It's my turn to listen to you. So, what's the Matter?'

Realizing what he had done by putting his arm around her, it was then he realised he was standing so close to her, a married woman, with only her negligee between them. He pushed her away, saying softly, 'I'm sorry.'

To his surprise, she gazed at him longingly and without hesitation, stepping closer until their bodies touched, she kissed him gently on the lips, a kiss that sent strange emotions through his body, and he could also sense her own nervousness. In that one kiss and the way she pressed closer against him, she let him know she needed him. He could feel her warm breasts through her thin negligee pressing on his bare chest; with his senses now fully aroused he wrapped his arms around her and pulling her tightly to him, kissed her again with more passion than he had ever experienced before with another woman.

His genes took over from his conscience and he could feel the blood stirring as his sexual desires starting to rise. She sensed how he was reacting to her embrace, and feeling his manhood rise between them; she took a sharp intake of breath and stepped back.

They stood looking at one another as though suspended in time, not knowing what to do next. It was Lynne who took the initiative and moved close again, this time, she threw her arms around his shoulders and pressed against him forcefully until they were locked to one another in a lover embrace.

Having abstained from sex all those months trying to be faithful to Jennifer, he found it difficult not to respond to this beautiful woman, whose body he knew could fulfil his longings and more, and who was now showing this affection to him. His resistance to her ebbed away, as she was now infecting him with her own desires. With the sensation of feeling her warm body next to his, his mind ran wild and as their kisses became more passionate his manhood, like a good soldier, was now at attention.

His inner self kept crying this is wrong, but his body kept saying I need this. As they kissed, her tongue slid into his mouth and their tongues entwined until lost in her desires. They embraced for what seemed an eternity until Lynne nervously, slowly reached her right hand down between them and fumbled to undo the button on his trousers. This done, she slid her hand inside his underpants. He flinched with anticipation. He could feel her body trembling as she took a deep breath then hesitated; she then made as though to remove her hand but hesitated.

All the while his body was saying don't stop, and as if hearing his thoughts, she continued her hand down. As she did so, he slowly brought his hand round and caressed her soft warm breasts through her negligee; at his first touch she gave off a low inner moan of pleasure.

All this time, they pressed their bodies closer as though, trying to immerse into one another, his passion rose to a level he hadn't experienced before. The more she touched him the harder it was for him to know right from wrong. It felt to him as though in their embrace they desired one another and their lips were now as one, as though trying to consume one another.

In that moment he felt he would explode, and before he could say stop, the shock, and the realization of what they were doing by touching each other, gave his conscience a jolt, pulling him back to reality.

He realized in that moment that he was afraid he wouldn't be man enough or experienced enough for her, and he reluctantly pushed her away from him. At that same moment she pulled her hand away.

Breathing heavily, she stood staring at him, her breasts still heaving under her negligee. She remained there with a look of disbelief, and frustration written all over her face. Wanting to know why he had stopped. The state of mind they were in, he was sure she thought they were about to go all the way and consummate their sexual needs, but that step would have taken them beyond where he felt, he didn't want to go.

Doing all he could to control his breathing, he looked at her, too embarrassed to say what was the real reason why he had pulled back. Shaking his head, he said, 'Lynne! This is not right? I'm sorry! I'm really sorry! This shouldn't be happening! You are beautiful, and I think the world of you.' Pausing, he looked at her, steadied his breathing more, then continued saying, 'I'm not sure how I feel at the moment. I've thought about you and how it would be with you. But as much as my body and mind wants to make love to you, I'm sorry. I can't do this!' Unable to control his erratic breathing he blurted out. 'Mike's my best mate and I don't think I could face him again. I'm sorry.'

Still breathless she had a look of disbelief, her breasts heaving rhythmically against her negligee, she gave out a sigh as she blurted out, 'I needed it. You needed it.' Shaking her head, she beat her fists on his chest in frustration, then continued, 'Why! Why, did you stop. We both needed this,' hesitating again she whispered in a softer voice, 'I too have been thinking about you since the night your dad died. I felt somehow we were meant to.' Her voice trailed off; She went quiet.

Hearing her words, he couldn't think of anything to say accept 'I'm really, really sorry. I didn't know you felt that way.'

Then realizing what she had said, and his own fear that he might disappoint her. Her words ran around in his head, and he slowly realized, his own feelings for her were deeper than he had thought. He was lost, lost for words and wasn't sure now of his own feelings. He put his arms around her and pulled her to him again, but this time their embrace was more for comfort than anything else.

After a few more tears from her, he felt both glad and

disappointed they had stopped. She, he was sure must have realised herself what was happening between them and stepped away from him. He sensed then that there would always be this feeling between them, whenever they were near each other. In that moment, his thoughts of Jennifer were deep in the back of his mind, and all he could think of was, Lynne.

They stood holding hands, their eyes searching each other's, she calmed a little. A tear rolled down her cheek as she stroked his face with her soft fingertips, and confessed, 'Oh David! I just wish.' Stopping mid-sentence, she hesitated to choose her words before expressing, 'It's a long time since I have reacted to anyone like I have with you tonight. Mike never makes me feel like this anymore, nor shows me the same kind of affection or honesty you have.' Pulling his head down, she kissed him tenderly on the brow.

His mind in turmoil, he realised he had been right, their marriage was having problems, and he was caught in the middle. Their drinks forgotten about, were left sitting on the table. Saying good night again took a little longer, but they both reluctantly went their separate ways to bed.

He watched her walk away from him with a strange feeling. And as he lay on his bed, he mused, *this was something new for me, having a beautiful woman tell me that she wanted me,* he felt elated.

As he closed his eyes, his thoughts went back to when he had been out with Mike. During those times Mike had acted more like a single man than he himself had. Even after Lynne and the kids arrived here, he had spent time with local prostitutes. Dave tried to stop questioning his action, as to him, when they were together, they always appeared a loving couple.

Now after this night, he could see that that was a false

façade for the public. He became annoyed as he should have read the signs.

Lying on his bed, he kept thinking about how he'd face them later. The rest of the that night he couldn't sleep. With his mind full of all that had happened and the feelings she had stirred up in him. Never had he felt this passionate with anyone, not even with Jennifer. His love for Jennifer, although intimate was always taken gently. Tonight though, a new feeling had sprung up in him when confronted by this beautiful woman, and it frightened him a little, as when she touched him; his body reacted too easily to her. What he felt at that moment, not even when Jennifer touched him the same way, had he experienced the surge of passion that he had had during these brief moments.

With sleep not coming, he lay there trying to convince himself what had happened was born out of the drink they had consumed earlier, and their mutual frustrations. Or was it he thought, because of the close affection they had formed over the last few months. Something had changed, and he might now find it awkward when in their company.

This encounter had left him still feeling frustrated and sexually aroused. Lying on his bed he tossed and turned so much that in the end he harkened back to what the ships doctor had told them all those months ago, and taking his advice, used his friend Palm. Satisfied only in releasing the tension but not ridding his thoughts of Lynne, who for that moment, filled him with an excitement he never felt before, pushing Jennifer further in the back of his mind?

The rest of the night he watched the moon disappear and the starry sky giving way to a brightening dawn. His thoughts were with a little regret of what might have been, had it not for him chickening out at the last moment. The vision of having sex with Lynne stayed right in the front of his feelings, and he felt guilty. Troubled at the way he thought of her, he tried to excuse himself, because of it being New Year. He turned over but sleep still wouldn't come. He was not looking forward to morning, as he knew he could not face them at breakfast time.

As soon as it was bright, he was up, dressed and quietly slipped out the door before they stirred from their sleep. Stepping out from under the porch into the cool morning air, he felt a slight drizzle of rain on his face. It didn't bother him though, as a brisk walk back the two miles to camp is what he needed. Taking a deep breath, he smiled and started down the street to the main road.

All the way back he struggled to rid his thoughts of what had happened and this strange feeling of guilt. It was with great difficulty that he tried to think again about Jennifer, would she be at a new year party or just at home The road being quiet of traffic, and with no one to bother him, he strode out.

Early morning he was thinking, just before the sun rises above the trees, is a wonderful time, especially after rain, which had now stopped. It is a time when the beasts of the jungle come alive with a dawn chorus of noises, welcoming the new day.

To Dave that morning air had a sweeter smell than he remembered. Was it just the beginning of a new day, or a new beginning to something else, he wasn't certain where it would lead him? Invigorated by the morning air and knowing he had no reveille parade, there was no need to hurry back, so he walked at a more leisurely pace along the road until the camp came into sight.

It was with a newfound confidence he entered the camp, and as he passed the guardhouse one of the lads called out. 'Been out getting some nookie, have you?'

Dave felt a blush come to his cheeks and just answered

back with a little white lie, 'A lot more than you got last night.' and smiled.

It was with a swagger he confidently continued to climb up the hill to his own bed in Basher F. Being Sunday and no duties, the rest of the lads had either decided to go down for breakfast or were having a long lie in to recover from last night's celebrations. He was glad no one was left in the Basher in a fit state to ask him embarrassing questions. While he was still feeling emotional from the events of last night, he skipped breakfast and undressed. Falling on his bed he pulled down his mosquito net. With the feeling he had changed in some way, he lay awhile until overcome with tiredness, he fell sound asleep.

Chapter 36

A New Year Dawns

In the days that followed, nothing was mentioned about where anyone had been or what they did over the New Year, so there were no surprises for Dave. Over the next few weeks, he tried to avoided Mike and his requests to come over for drinks, as he put it, 'Lynne was asking when you're coming over again.'

Dave, not wanting to get into a conversation, said, 'I've a lot on the now, and I've started playing badminton at night's between Courier duties. The club's run by the Ghurkha soldiers over in Seremban Camp.'

After that, Mike in his scheming way inquired about the club from one of his mates and that night told Lynne, 'There's a badminton club in Seremban Camp and some women most of whom were WRAC's, play there.

Lynne, having played badminton before she met Mike wondering why he mentioned it, replied, 'It would be nice to play again and get some exercise. How did you find out about it?'

'I was speaking to Dave about coming round for a drink on Wednesday night, but he said he couldn't manage as he was playing badminton.' Badminton for Mike was not his sport.

Next time they met, Mike said, 'I told Lynne about the badminton club, and she said she wouldn't mind playing again but only if you escorted her over there.' Dave was taken aback by his callous manner, as he was more or less giving him permission to chaperon Lynne out.

Feeling boxed in, Dave felt that moment, if alone with Lynne again, he wouldn't be able to control himself. That night, lying in bed, his mind going over everything, *how much more can I complicate my life? Is it because I'm missing Jennifer and feeling homesick? Maybe I should ask for a transfer,* he mused. *Staying here I know I will get involved with her.*

For four weeks, he avoided the question about Lynne and the badminton club. During that period, arriving back from Courier duties he pushed himself in training for the football team, even after that, he was still finding it extremely hard to keep her out of his mind. Writing letters to Jennifer became more difficult because of his guilt. Even up in Pinang, his trips on duty were no longer enjoyable, and it must have showed.

His Ausie mate Gill, asked, 'What's happened mate? There's a difference in you lately.'

Dave responded, 'What do you mean?'

Gill responded in his Ausie twang, 'Yir broody Mate, have you had bad words from your Sheila back home?'

At first Dave didn't say anything but after Gill's persistence He told him, 'No, everything's ok back home. It's someone back in Seremban that's bothering me.'

'Is it another woman? Is she married?' He teased.

'Yes.' Dave said shyly.

In his typical way Gill retorted, 'You bloody lucky bastard. Every young man's dream to have a married woman to jump on the side.'

Crude, Dave thought, but if his feelings for Lynne hadn't

been bothering him as they were, he might have agreed with him.

In Paroi camp, he only other light piece of nonsense they had during the month of January was, a lad called Cockney Joe, who was very upset about some Indian worker using our toilets for his own purposes. Joe had found things he didn't like to talk about, lying on the shower block floor when he went in to shower one early morning.

Really angry, his solution, he caught a snake, which are plentiful around the camp. Next night before retiring he cut the snakes head partially off, and going into the toilet, wrapped the pull chain up on the cistern so it couldn't be reached. That done, he hung the snake in its place over the flushing lever, and before leaving the block he removed the light bulbs.

Unfortunately, it wasn't one of the Indian workers who went into toilet block first, it was the Duty Sarge. The air that night was blue, and the Sarge let them all know what he thought.

When gossiping about the incident later, Dave said jokingly, 'You know, I'm sure the Sarge lost all his tan the moment he reached up for the chain and grabbed hold of the snake.' It was the topic around camp for a week.

Three other events took place to make Dave's January memorable. After the snake joke in the toilet, the Sarge had it in for some of the lads because no one had owned up. Dave, being on the Courier duty, was left out of the Sergeant's anger, but the Sarge made sure the other lads suffered. Cockney Joe, next Basher to us, thought one of the couriers had spilled the beans on him, and tried to blame one of Dave's mates Jock McMahon, maybe because Jock was a quiet lad.

This turned out to be a bad idea. Cockney Joe, who fancied himself as an Oriental martial arts specialist, having this Kit bag full of sand hanging from the roof in his Basher, which every night they all could hear him kicking and punching. He also boasted he went to a martial arts club in Seremban. All the lads took it he must be good, as when practicing he always wore his Karate gear and looked impressive.

The following week after the toilet incident, as they were leaving the NAAFI, Cockney Joe accused Jock McMahon of the toilet incident. 'Come stand your ground against me.' He challenged. Jock must have been pissed off, because he looked at him, shook his head and just said 'Ok.' and the fight was on.

Dave, knowing all about Jocks boxing experiences thought, this is all going to end in tears for someone. With the challenge on, Cockney went up to his Basher to prepare. When the lads got up to the top, he was standing outside the basher with his Karate gear on, doing his Swooshes, his grunts and practicing his kicks. All very impressive to the uninitiated, but Jock had done this before, and he was un-amused by all his antics.

Stepping up to face one another it was like something out of a western movie, but, before they could blink Jock landed a right hook to Cockney Joes jaw and he went down like a sack of potatoes, it was all over. The next five minutes was spent bringing Cockney Joe round.

When Jock was quizzed about his boxing ability, he told the lads about his boxing and that he had been junior champion at his last posting, and also held a third Dan at judo. Cockney Joe wasn't so cocky around the camp after that, and didn't say too much. Later, he was moved to a new Camp down south that was being expanded, near a place called Malacca. Later it was announced that in the near future, most of the troops would eventually be stationed there.

Chapter 37

Hospitalised

Playing Badminton can be very punishing on your feet and ankles, so Dave found out to his cost. Three nights after the big fight, he was playing badminton against two other Ghurkha lads and went over on his left ankle. Taken to the hospital, the MO at first thought he had broken a bone in his foot, and kept him in the hospital for five days, with his foot and ankle strapped up, and with pills to kill the pain the only remedy. Dave thought to himself at that moment, out of every body's sight and better still I'll be able to see more of Nurse Richmond, who was still there on duty.

On his second day in hospital, and with nothing better to do he was having a nap, suddenly he was wakened by a gentle touch on the back of his hand, before opened his eyes he wished, *please let it be nurse Blondie.* To his mixed surprise, it was Lynne. Tongue-tied at seeing her, his heart missed a beat when she touched his hand again.

'How are you,' she asked. and with nervousness in her voice, she stammered, 'Mike heard you were in hospital and asked me to visit you.' She then smiled mischievously, 'He heard you had broken your leg?'

Looking wonderful, she soon made him forget about his pain. As he looked at her, running through his thoughts was, *'Are you making Mike the excuse for this visit or was it because I had been avoiding you.'*

Thinking of their last meeting he started to try explaining how he felt, 'I'm sorry about everything that's happened between us, I don't know what.' He went quite, as he was about to say, came over him that night.

She stopped him mid-sentence by placing her fingers over his mouth, then whispered with a hint of resignation in her voice, 'I know, I know. You're missing Jennifer, and I have been feeling a bit mixed up too, that's why I had to see you.'

She sat down and taking his hand she cupped it between her hands, and he felt a warmth surge through him. He looked at her and shyly said, 'I liked your perfume.'

Their eyes met in a deep searching gaze, she smiled, but then broke the spell by asking, 'Have you heard from Jennifer, or have you written to tell her you're in hospital?'

He squinted at her again as he had a feeling she wanted to talk about what was going on between them, but could only come out with a question about Jennifer. 'No! I haven't had a letter from her for two weeks. I replied to that letter, but I haven't written since,' He told her. 'In truth, I'm finding it hard what I want to say when writing to her, and feel at this moment I wished I could see her, and speak to her.' But with Lynne there beside him at that moment, and his emotions so mixed up, he felt it wasn't the right time to say how he was feeling about Jennifer or how he had reacted to her.

She stayed an hour and talked about everything but what was happening to them both. He had the feeling as she sat there that she would have stayed longer if he hadn't said his mates were coming in to see him. When she was leaving, he sensed that there was something bothering her, as she was near to tears.

He felt down after her visit and still unsure why he should be feeling the way he does.

Nurse Richmond seeing him deep in thought, came over, sat down on his bedside, took hold of his hand, and said, 'My, your pulse has shot up, is that for me or was it for the girlfriend?' she asked playfully.

'She isn't my girlfriend,' He snapped, before realizing she was only teasing. He compounded his embarrassment, 'That's my mate's wife.'

'Oh! I see, so there is still a chance for me,' she teasingly said.

Dave's face turned beetroot red. She patted the back of his hand, laughed, and as she stood up, said. 'I won't tell if you won't tell.'

He observed how her hips oscillated as she walked away. Her white uniform skirt was so short it only covered to just below her bottom, showing of her long shapely legs. He was sure she knew he was watching her, at that moment, as blood started feeding the part of his body that had a mind of its own, he thought *'Corr! My friend Palm will have to help me tonight.'* Still watching as she slinked away, shaking his head he cursed, *'There should be a law against nurses dressing like that.'*

Lynne made one more visit to see him before he was released from hospital. She sat and held his hand and rubbed the back with her soft fingertips. He thought the whole world's eyes were on them and felt uncomfortable by the way she was unashamedly showing her feelings for him. He sensed she again wanted to converse about them, but stuck to talking about her kids.

Steering away from what was going on between them, she asked him again, 'Have you heard from Jennifer since I was last here?' before he could answer she changed the subject, 'What will you do when you get back home?'

'You know what my plans are.' He watched her for a reaction.

'Just asking? I've been wondering lately, what we would have done if we had met years ago.'

Dave looked curiously at her before saying, 'We'd be the best of friends, as we are the now.'

She stood up and squeezed his hand; her parting words were, 'Is that all we are the now, simply good friends?'

When she left that day, it was with a promise that he would go round to their home the first weekend he was off duty. He didn't keep his promise, the reason he gave them, Londoner, Derek Ellis, who had been home on compassionate leave, returned back, and they were all getting together over a few beers, to bring him up to date on camp life since he left.

One-week later his mate Derek was redeployed to the Main Signal Centre in Seremban Camp and billeted there. From then on, Dave only caught up with one him on days off. Derek still remained a good mate to Dave and one of the few he could trust. On one of their nights out, Dave told him about his problem of his feelings for Lynne, and that was the reason why he stopped going over to the Seremban Camp dances. Meeting Lynne and Mike at these dances, wasn't something he felt comfortable about. On hearing Dave's plight Derek decided he would come back over to Paroi Camp for a drink, on nights off.

Chapter 38

New Orders

Dave thought January would pass without any more problems to write home about, when on the 31st of that month posted on the order board was a notice, '**Orders of C.O. Major Hansen. All Courier duties to be transferred to Wardieburn Camp K.L. on Sunday, the 5th of February**.'

Looking down the list he found his name was one of the couriers transferred. Being away on duty that night and not due back till Thursday of that week, He knew he wouldn't have much time to do anything except get ready for his move. With only four of them transferred, that last Friday night, they all gathered in the NAAFI for a party with all his other mates who were staying behind, and as parties went, it turned out to be a real howler.

Just when the party was getting in full swing, in walked Mike and a mate and joined them at their table. and sat next to him. After exchanging a bit of chat, Dave asked. 'How'd you managed to get out without Lynne?'

He looked quizzingly at Dave, and grinned as though in disappointment, 'Lynne and Allison are with us. They'll join us shortly.'

Derek, seeing the expression on Dave's face, wanted to intervene, but decided not to when Mike said, 'Lynne was looking forward to tonight, when she heard you were being transferred to KL, she was hoping to have a chat with you before you leave.'

Dave's heart started pounding a little faster as he tried to keep his emotions in check. Mike at that moment went over to the bar to order drinks, Dave on the other hand, wanting to escape, uttered to Derek, 'I'm going to sneak out.'.

Just as he was about to rise, Lynne entered, wearing a pale flowery pink flowing dress, with a red belt round her waist, and a white chiffon scarf wrapped around her shoulders. She looked gorgeous, so much so one of the lads near the door gave her a wolf whistle

Derek leaned over and whispered, 'Is that Lynne?'

Dave looked at her and as their eyes met; she smiled a smile that would light a dark room. With his eyes glued to hers, he replied in a lovesick manner, 'Yes, isn't she beautiful?'

'Corr! Mate.' Derek growled, 'I wish she would pick on me. She's a real stunner.'

Walking straight over to their table, her eye's fixed on Dave, she paid no attention to all the cat calls that rumbled around the NAAFI. Stopping in front of him she asked seductively, 'Is there a seat for me?'

One of the lads jumped up to give her his seat, she shook her head and walked round and slid down on the seat Mike had left. Dave didn't know if his emotions were screaming out for all to see, or if he would be able to contain himself with her being so close to him. The intoxicating perfume she wore was her favourite and the same one she had on when she visited him in hospital.

He couldn't resist saying, 'I still like that perfume you have on.'

She looked at him and smiled, 'I wondered if you would remember.'

Inwardly he struggled to control himself and felt his face flush.

She leaned closer and quizzed him in a soft concerning voice. 'How have you been since you got out of hospital?' Then on a more intimate note she said softly, 'Will you write to me once you move up to K.L?'

Before he had time to answer, Derek thinking, and trying to change the mood, butted in and asked her 'how do you like it out here?'

Lynne's friends, Alison and Andy joined them, just as Mike arrived back with drinks. Squeezing in beside Lynne, he pushed her along the seat until she was so close to Dave, she was just about sitting on top of him. Feeling their legs touching, he whispered to her, 'This is not good for my blood pressure.'

She smiled and moved even more closely.

As the night wore on, some lads decided to leave, but his group continued to party a while longer. Mike asked Dave, 'Fancy a last nightcap at our house. You could stay over one last night.'

Lynne was quiet, but when they were deciding what to do next, she took hold of Dave's hand and squeezing it, whispered in a pleading voice, 'Please this once.'

He made excuses saying, he would be odd man out, but Lynne persuaded him and against his better judgment he agreed, telling himself that it was only because Allison and Andy were going to be there also.

It was around ten–thirty when they arrived at their home. After only one drink, Allison and Andy said they had to go home to let their babysitter off home. That left the three of them and mood seemed Ok. Mike in conversation, told Dave about the camp down in Malacca, saying he had been there for three months the last time he had been in Malaya.

Dave was happy the conversation was about army matters rather than personal. Lynne though, listening as they talked, changed the subject, and chipped in, 'I've asked David to write and let us know how he's getting on?'

'Good idea mate, keep in touch with us. Anyway, it will give Lynne something to look forward to.' Mike said in a mischievous way.

Dave looked at him at that moment and thought '*does he know, or does he care.*' Feeling a little uncomfortable at that moment, he wished he had stayed back at camp. But not wanting to offend them, after all he told himself, *they have been good friends to me.*

Their conversation was then more about the army, and their duties. This continued well into the night with Lynne trying to swing the conversation round to Dave by asking about Jennifer, and his hopes for when he gets home. Up till then, there had been no embarrassing moments.

Feeling more relaxed, Dave changing the subject asked Mike, 'What's your thoughts about the army now? The last time we talked about it, you said this would be your last tour as you were thinking of leaving the army and going back to your old job as a lorry driver.'

Lynne's tone told Dave, she wasn't so keen about his decision when looking at Mike, she probed 'I thought you said you were going to stay on in the army?'

Mike replied sheepishly, 'I've not made up my mind yet.'

On that note Dave sensed again that that might be part of their married problems. Trying to calm the situation he said, 'I hope I haven't put my foot in it?'

'No, you haven't mate,' Mike reacted, 'It's something we have been discussing for a while.'

It was getting late when Mike said, 'With no parade in the morning Dave, and no need to be back at camp until Saturday night, why not stay here for the night? You can bunk down in the spare room. Lynne can fix up the bed for you.'

After agreeing, they sat a little longer, then Mike went off to bed. Lynne though was hesitant, and seemed reluctant to follow him, but when Dave declared, he was feeling tired, and made to go into the spare bedroom. She dithered about a little longer before saying good night and went off to bed.

Wakening up in the morning Dave could smell sausage being fried. Looking over at his watch, it was seven-thirty-two, time to get ready before anyone came through into his room. He pulled on his trousers and was just about to put on his shirt when Lynne opened the bedroom door.

'Ah! You're awake,' she remarks, 'Breakfast will be ready in a few minutes.'

Standing in the doorway she looked great, wearing just a pair of white shorts and a green bikini top. *'What a fantastic sight to wake up to'* He thought. The expression and blush on his face gave his thoughts away. she just smiled. What she was thinking he could only guess, as her own face took on a little colour at that moment.

The silence was broken when clearing her throat, timidly she said, 'Hm hm, if you want to wash and shave you will find Mike's stuff on the shelf in the toilet.'

Touching his chin, he decided to take up that offer. Just as he had finished scraping the last bristle off his chin and felt the smooth results, Lynne entered, 'Brought you another towel in case you needed it.'

With not much room in their toilet, they stood awfully close, too close. Looking over her shoulder at the shelf behind her, he saw towels sitting on the shelf. Jokingly he kidded,

'Are you making the towel an excuse just so you can enter the toilet?'

Her face went scarlet.

'Where's Mike?' He then inquired.

'He went into the Signal Centre and said he would see you at lunch time,' she answered seductively.

They looked at each other a moment, and then playfully, she raised the towel in her hands, dried his face and then gave him a gentle kiss on his lips.

'What, what was that for?' Dave stuttered.

She just smiled, and dropping the towel she ran her hands around his face, then down on to his chest. By this time Dave's heart was pounding, making him breath heavily and unsure if he wanted this to go further. In the end, he couldn't resist her advances and pulling her closer and kissed her, this time not as before, more in a tender way. They continued embracing, and no more words were said. They just stood there, looking into each other's eyes, when suddenly they were interrupted and were brought to their senses, by a knocking on the door.

Saved by little Michael he thought. She squeezed his hand and said, 'Mind breakfast first,' turning she walked out, and Dave could hear her explaining to Michael, that he had to have his breakfast first?

Mike came home around eleven-thirty, and after dinner he proposed a trip, 'Since it might be your last time here, why don't we go into town and take the kids for a walk round the Seremban gardens.'

The grounds in Seremban Dave knew well, had a big lake with beautifully kept gardens full of exotic flowers all around. It was a nice place to be, especially as it would be his last chance he thought to go there.

The trip by local bus was surprisingly quiet, no wild fowl or vegetables, just another four customers and our group.

Walking around the garden Lynne was surprised by the number of different birds flying about.

Eventually finding a spot by the lake side, they sat watching the kids play on the grass. Looking at them as they conversed, Dave was thinking, *would it be like this if Jennifer and I had the kids we dreamed of,* but then looking at Mike and Lynne, two nice people whose marriage was in a difficult way and wondered if Jennifer and he would fare better.

Lying on his back enjoying the sun he started to look forward to his next posting, and thought, *much as I will miss Lynne, it will be better for us both when I'm far away. They can work on their marriage without any more distractions.*

When it was time to leave, walking round the grounds Lynne took both of their hands and for that short period Dave felt good that someone as beautiful as she, cared for him, and that his presence didn't seem to bother Mike,

Dave mused, *maybe it was because Mike thought he was too wrapped up in his love for Jennifer to notice or to even get involved with anyone, as wonderful as Lynne.*

His feelings for that day, were something he had struggled with since the New Year's party, even to thinking, if she had been free, he wasn't sure if he could or would be able to choose between her and Jennifer.

He consoled himself, going away to K L probably was the best thing to happen. But for the rest of that day he wallowed in her company, sharing a little bit of heaven.

Chapter 39

Wardieburn

A new camp, a new bed, and some new mates. Dave's first impression wasn't to his liking. Situated just northeast of the capital, Kuala Lumpur, it was a bustling city with majestic buildings in the centre and a sprawling ramble of buildings spreading outwards. Surrounding the city, were some open fields, and rice paddies stretching up to the jungle to the east and north. To the west, rubber tree plantations and to the south, lay one of the largest tin mines in the world, a hole so wide and so deep, it's said the whole of the city of KL, would fit into it. His new home Wardieburn Camp, lay to the north of KL and was surrounded by Rubber plantations.

More like a transit camp with comings and goings of troops all the time, it only added to his longings for his own home. There living quarters were two long Basher Huts with ten beds in each, housing eighteen Couriers, a control office for communications, all situated in its own area within the main camp, and commanded by a Sergeant Major known as Blackjack, a nick name Dave learned, he was proud of.

The Sergeant Major was Indian by birth but raised up in England. His skin was as black as coal. Secondly, he liked to gamble and drink. Dave saw him the first day he arrived, maybe because Major Dunlop was there to give then their orders. After that Blackjack was like the Scarlet Pimpernel, but no one bothered to seek him anywhere.

Out of the eighteen couriers, only three, Dave and two others who had been here for a few months, were NS. The rest were in for various lengths of tours. To start of his new duties, Jock McMahon was still his partner, but their new schedule of duties would now alternate between down south and up north. This meant one trip south then two days, one night, off, then one trip north, and so on. Dave's first trip under this new schedule was down to Singapore. The change of scenery down south, he was looking forward to.

The first mail drop point south was Seremban and by coincidence waiting on the platform when his train arrived was Mike, he was waiting to hand over mail for camps south. With no time for small talk the train was off again.

The trip was long and tiring, and after having stopped at various stations exchanging mail, they arrived in Singapore station, where they were transported to a Garrison called Minden Barracks the main far East Headquarters. It was a huge modern built garrison with admin buildings surrounding a large square parade ground.

Driven to the Signal Centre, they clocked off so to speak. This Garrison had a different environment to where he was stationed, proper brick buildings and all mod cons. One drawback though, was the number of officers and NCOs walking about. The barrack room for rest allocated to them, was in one of the New Zealand and Ausie blocks.

On that first trip they both spent their time getting to know the lay of the land. None of the NCOs bothered them, providing they kept their Courier arm bands on, so it was a lesson learned quickly when in the Garrison area.

Over time, Dave got to know a lad called Walt Chisholm, and in conversation learned Walt hailed from Christchurch in New Zealand. Dave also learned that Walt's dad owned a Motor garage and sold motorcycles. From then on, they formed a close friendship and after their first few trips, Walt showed Dave and Jock around Singapore.

Back in K.L. changes were afoot, and they were informed by Blackjack that the C.O, Major Dunlop was coming up, to explain some new procedures, and do an annual inspection on them, on the fifteenth of the month.

The C.O. arrived early that morning, his orders, to appoint a coordinator to take charge of the Couriers schedules. After they all had been interviewed, Dave was surprised when called back into Blackjacks office and informed by the C.O. 'Signalman Walters I want you to take that position. I've been going through your records, and having talked it over with the Sergent Major, I feel you are the right man for the job.'

When accepting the position, Dave asked, 'would it not have been better if one of the regular soldiers took this position, sir?

The C.O. answer dismissively, 'I want you to take on this duty because I know you will do a good job. Remember with this position comes responsibility, something most of these other soldiers don't want.'

Without knowing what his new job entailed, he was stuck for words and just replied 'Yes sir.'

All except the couriers on duty were called together and told by the Major, 'Walter's will be your new coordinator. His job will be to work out new schedules for all the couriers. On a final note, you are to treat him as you would a corporal, and that is an order.'

There was not one dissenting voice, so Dave didn't know

if he had received the chalice with good wine or the one with the poison.

With Blackjack doing his disappearing act, found Dave himself more in the office, and let the Couriers carry on as they were, until he talked to each of them in turn about any changes needed. The first thing he learned was that some wanted a change of partner, so this was Dave's priority.

They say everything happens in threes. Next day his first day in charge, he received two letters, one from Jennifer and one from Lynne. How Lynne managed to get his address, he could only guess from Mike. Reading Jennifer's letter first, she started in her usual way.

My darling David, I wish you could be by my side at this moment, as we have just learned that Gran has died. I know you liked her, and she always asked for you. I'm sorry that I should be burdening you, but I know if you were here, I would feel much better. I miss you so much. I wish I could fly to your side right now.

Her letter went on to tell him all the news about the garage and of her job there and of all his old mates, who still work there. As he read, he detected a slight difference in her writing, but put it down to the death of her Gran.

The other letter, he wasn't sure if he should open it, then thought, *if I didn't acknowledge it, it might look funny*, he carefully opened the envelope, Lynne's started,

'Hello David.

How are you? It feels as though it's been an awfully long time since we spoke, and I am missing you more than I thought I would.'

Putting down the letter he pondered, *I'm not sure who I miss the most, Jennifer or Lynne. I've had a long time to get used to not seeing Jennifer, but it's only just over fifteen days since I last saw Lynne, and I'm counting the days all ready.* He couldn't read any more of the letter and put it aside for the moment.

Later that night he lay on his bed, turned his bedside lamp on and opened Lynne's letter again. As he read, he could feel her warmth coming through to him with every word she wrote. Her words were very intimate and personal, the kind of words he really wanted to hear from Jennifer, she was saying not in words, but in expression, 'I love you.' Reading on and it wasn't until the very end that she mentioned Mike or the kids.

Putting the letter down and switching off his lamp he lay in the dark thinking about Lynne, then Jennifer, then Lynne again. Thinking about the affection they shared in her home that Saturday morning and of that night when he felt his world had changed. Such was his state of mind he fell asleep that night dreaming of lying naked between the two women in his life, making love. He woke up next morning as though he had a flu, his bed sheets where soaking with sweat. Sitting on the edge of his bed he couldn't remember his dream

Later that day, he replied to both letters and they could not have been more different. To Jennifer he sent all his love, to Lynne all his best wishes. After finishing he had a mischievous thought to himself, and smiled, *what if I put the letters in the wrong envelopes?*

Chapter 40

New Schedule

Over the next few days, he spoke to all the Couriers and with their cooperation the schedule was brought up to date. Blackjack was pleased, and that meant they hardly ever saw him, which pleased all the lads. To celebrate, some of them who had been stationed there a while, being off duty, went into K.L city Centre to look out the good spots for food and drink.

They toured the bars and for the first time Dave was tempted to go off with a very nice-looking young prostitute who sat and flirted with him most of the night, she tried her best to entice him to go with her, and just might have succeeded if he hadn't drunk so much. In his condition he wouldn't have been any good even to his dear old friend Palm.

Up early and standing in the middle of the basher next morning, he called out, 'Come on lads! Time to get up. We've a big day ahead of us. We have a jungle trip arrange.'

'What fucking clown arranged a trip into the jungle?' one of the lads cried out, having only just raised his head off the pillow and wasn't best pleased.

Dave replied sheepishly. 'I'm that fucking clown!' A barrage of pillows come flying at him, so he made his escape.

The trek into the jungle was part of training set down by the C.O. It was Dave's job to arrange the exercise for the Couriers not on duty, and this was his first attempt. The walk planned was to take them to an area fifteen miles north of K.L, dropped off and make their way back through the jungle to a rendezvous point for pick up.

The way he felt that morning he wished he hadn't arranged it, but it had been, and he had arranged with a Malay scout and sergeant Bibon, a Ghurkha soldier who was to be in charge. It wasn't until Bibon came into the basher to remind us that being wakened at six thirty in the morning suffering from sore heads was not a good start to the day, but sergeant Bibon gave them no sympathy.

After breakfast, with life still just a blur they set off in a truck and drove fifteen miles northeast of camp, into a region near a place called Bintang. From there it was all on foot, led by our guides. They set off into the jungle, which got noisier with hooting and grunts, and rustling in the trees not helping their confidence one bit.

The further they went in, the thicker and darker it became. Deeper into the undergrowth, their guide stopped occasionally to point out various animals and snakes that happened by chance to across their path. Such is the animal kingdom; they fear human's more than we fear them.

The group had been trekking the best part of two hours in the hot sticky humid heat until they finally reached their first destination, a small clearing two miles in. Dave's cloths soaking with sweat; was bushed and in need of a rest. Before they sat down though, Bibon explained about the creepy crawlies and what they should do for fear of being bitten or picking up something. He said with a smile, 'During fighting, in jungle many soldiers bitten after removing boots. They did not check to see if anything crawled into them.'

After a break of half an hour Bibon called, 'On feet, not much far to go.'

Off they set again and reaching a shallow stream, when wading over one of the lads called out, 'Crock.' He took a bit of stick to defend himself, it turned out to be a floating log. On they went, their guide clearing a trail for them until they reached a water reservoir. It was K.L's main supply they were informed. It was here while soaking their feet in the cool water Bibon pointed out to Dave the first wild elephant he'd seen. No sooner had they spotted it; it spotted them and disappeared back into the undergrowth. Such was their experience with most of the sightings they had of the wildlife.

Circling the reservoir mostly on paths, they again had to ford a couple of small streams and for their bother, burn some leeches off their legs. Dave, like the rest, was glad when they finally staggered out of the thick foliage onto a red sandy track road, which eventually took them down to their pickup point.

Their journey had taken five hours over four and a half miles through some thick jungle and had given them an idea what the Commonwealth forces had to face when driving the commies out.

Dave, feeling hot, sticky, and exhausted, was glad to see their truck was waiting at the pickup point, and that the driver had fresh water and a box of fruit for them. Once watered and fed they slithered onto the back and lay down, Dave grinned, 'This feels fantastic, no creepy crawlies or sticky leeches to bother about, and this hard floor feels like a soft bed.'

One of the other lads piped in with, 'Next time you fix up an exercise for the lads, I hope its somewhere near a beach and beer.'

'I agree,' Dave replied, 'I think we should sack the organiser.'

At that, they all pelted him with banana skins and fruit

cores. Hard though their hike had been Dave had enjoyed his day but felt much better when he collapsed onto his own bed on arrival back at camp.

The next trip Dave arranged was to the famous Batu Caves, unfortunately they couldn't enter the caves as there was a Hindu ceremony on at the time called Thaipusam. To their cost they picked the wrong day as the place was heaving with people and the celebrations went on for hours. The festival though was a spectacular sight, men were parading about carrying all sorts of ornamental designs, all painfully attached to their bodies with needles through their skin. Colourful and very noisy with hundreds of musicians blowing horns, banging on drums, and playing other weird instruments.

Their biggest disappointment that day, no alcohol on sale, so they had to settle for soft drinks. But on another time, they did manage to climb up the two hundred and seventy steps to see around the inside of the caves. That proved to be a trip worth taking, especially to see all the colourful Hindu statues around and the Hugh statue of a slumbering Buda. And seeing the Hugh Fruit Bats that hung from the roof of the caves, also was inspiring, but the stench of ammonia from their droppings, left them all desperate for a beer or two.

Back on duty again and travelling up and down the country, time passed. Letters from Jennifer and his Mum were still arriving, although not as regular, and this made him feel a little apprehensive at times but receiving the odd letter from Lynne helped pick him up his morale.

At the end of March, Blackjack informed Dave, he should have had a holiday weeks ago, but because of reorganizing the Couriers duties it had been overlooked. This came at a time when he was feeling low and was the reason, he decided to spend a week in Singapore. In writing letters home and to

Lynne he informed them, he would be on holiday the second week in April.

Two days before he was due to go on leave, having just returned from a trip up north he was handed a letter from Lynne. Impatiently, as he ripped it open he wondered, has something had happened to her.

Her letter started

'Dearest David,

How I wish I could be with you when you go on holiday. I thought I would get over you when you left for KL, but I still miss you very much.'

Reading these words, he wished he could be with her, then thought, *'should I just go to Seremban for my break,'* but in his muddled mind, wished he were away and didn't have to think like this. One minute he felt he was in love with her, then again thinking; *'it's only infatuation and feeling home sick, with me counting down the days till I go home.'*

Chapter 41

On Leave

It was a great relief to be in Singapore, away from all other distractions. Staying at the Brit Club, Dave lazed around the swimming pool, and during the daytime along with a few other lads on leave, made the most of their time sightseeing.

At night, he met up with his mate Walt and some of his Ausie mates, who had ideas of making his stay in Singapore unforgettable. This included visits to places he never knew existed. Some of the bars they went into were full to overflowing, with other lads from camps around Malaya, who were on holiday. One bar in particular that specialised with topless dancing girls, got a bit too rowdy, and had them leaving pronto, just before the Military Police arrived. Things from then on, got out of hand later that night, and after having a few drinks to many, Dave deciding he had had enough, resolved to go back to his digs.

Walt, pulling him aside said, 'Hold on mate. Wait there a minute; we'll get some transport to take you back to the Brit Club.

Dave, sat on a wall by a water fountain, feeling the world spin out of control, and wondering what they were up to. Just as he thought, he'd better start back on his own. Five minutes later, he heard a uproar coming round the corner. Turning round too quickly, he nearly fell into the fountain. In his state, he couldn't believe his eyes, Walt and the other lads were pedalling like mad, cycling Trishaws. As they came closer, one shouted to Dave, 'Quick, hop on mate, before the Choggie Bastards catch us.'

Alas they didn't quite make it to the Brit Club before being caught. After having a good laugh, Dave stood awhile, watching his friends stagger back into the town centre, singing Waltzing Matilda. He smiled at the thought, that it couldn't have been easy peddling one of those Trishaws this distance sober, never mind while under the influence of the demon brew.

After more nights out with Walt, and a few others. Dave's week in Singapore had been exciting, and hectic in the evenings, but still he managed to visit everything he wanted during the daytime. On his last day he went into a Chinese street tailor, and bought a smart new dark navy suit of fine cloth, which was tailored together in forty minutes while he supped coffee across the street.

Next morning, feeling great after having had a good time in Singapore, although it was hot, but wasn't the sticky heat of K.L. When he boarded the train at nine-thirty that morning, he wasn't looking forward to going back up country.

Once back in Wardiburn Camp, he reported back to Blackjack, and because of a change in personnel, with two couriers being re-posted to other units. He was told he had to take on a new partner, as with responsibility he was told, comes decision-making. His new partner, Will Hendon, who had been in trouble before and for some reason no one wanted to partner him.

Blackjack quietly had warned Dave the day he was put in

charge of the roster, saying, 'Keep your eye on Hendon, as this is his last chance. He was just about thrown off the couriers last time when he got drunk on duty."

Dave at that moment had thought it rich, Blackjack giving Will a hard time, and he himself, has never been seen sober. Calling Will into the office Dave asked, 'How do you feel about going out with me on duty?'

Being sober, he replied 'Cool!'

Dave then asked, 'Do you have a problem with me?'

'No, no. Everything's cool. I give you my word, you won't get any trouble from me.'

Their first few trips went Ok then on their second trip down to Singapore, Will got into a fight while in Minden Barracks. Over what, he wouldn't say. Dave was disappointed, as all the other partners confined to one another what their problems were.

When they were together back on the train, Dave asked, 'What was all the trouble about in the Singapore camp?'

Will shrugged his shoulders and muttered, 'Just put it down to a small spat that got out of hand.'

As the month wore on Dave received only a letter from Lynne, but none from home. He wondered why, and worried something might be wrong with Jennifer, but on finding the other lads were in the same position, he put it down to a hold up in the mail from home.

Having some time off he travelled to the British Military Hospital KL to get news about his mate George. George had been taken to the Cameron Highlands Hospital just before Christmas and was later transferred to BMH KL.

At the receptionist desk he explained to the nurse and asked, 'Can you tell me how he's doing? Have they found out what was wrong with him?'

After checking George's files, she said, 'Sorry, can't tell you anything about him. Signalman Harris has been transferred back up to the Cameron Highlands.' Then she advised, 'If you hurry, you can get a lift up to the Cameron Highland Hospital on a supply truck, that's leaving shortly. Tell the driver you spoke to me at the desk.'

The journey up to the hospital turned out to be a longer trip than Dave expected, as the road twisted and turned nearly back on itself many times on the way up the mountain. But what kept him cheerful was, at the end, he hoped to see George.

At the reception desk he was bitterly disappointed by the news he received. 'Signalman George Harris's condition deteriorated and was transferred back home.'

Hearing about George, the journey back to K.L. wasn't very pleasant. Started down the twisty road with sharp corners, it was monsoon rain that started pouring down heavily, that made it a hazardous journey, with the truck sliding and slithering down the road. As he hung on, the minutes seemed to slow down, and when they eventually arrived back at camp, it was long after eight that night.

Back on duty again the next night, and after what had happened their last trip south, Dave quizzed Will before their next trip, 'After last trip, how are you feeling. Do you want to miss this trip south?'

He seemed far too eager for Dave, when he said, 'Yes,' then made the excuse, 'Not because of what happened last time, just not feeling to well.'

Dave frowned, 'You'd better report to the M.O. and let Blackjack know. I'll get one of the spare couriers to take your place.'

Little did he know on the thirtieth of March that trip south would turn out to be his last, and his life was about to change again.

Chapter 42

Dreams Unravel

A letter was waiting for Dave when he arrived back at camp next day. Picking it up he looked at it for a long time, as the style of writing he didn't recognize. He opened it cautiously, only one page was inside, and it read.

'Hello Dave, you don't know me, but I feel I have to inform you, that, and there is no other way to tell you, your girlfriend has been dating another boy for some time.'

Shocked, he stared at it, but couldn't read further. Putting the letter down, it was a jolt seeing those words, that he never ever thought he would receive. He sat not knowing whether to cry or just tear up the letter.

Jock McMahon, in the basher at that time, noticed something was wrong and came over. 'Everything ok mate? Is it, bad news from home?'

Dave couldn't speak. He just handed the letter to Jock. Reading it he shook his head as he said. 'I wouldn't read too much into it. It's probably a crank that has it in for you.' Then sitting down on Dave's bed, continued, 'I had one like that and it turned out to be rubbish.'

Dave felt a little better, but later when he had settled down, he remembered Jock's girl had left him. For two days he couldn't get the letter out of his mind, then a letter from Jennifer arrived and although the content had changed a little, he convinced himself all was still Ok.

When next day he received a letter from his Mum and one from Lynne, he put all his problems to the back of his head. His Mum's letter spoke of Jennifer visiting her every week and still going to visit his brother's families, so he started to believe and dismissed that anonymous letter as just mischief.

In Lynne's letter, it seemed like he was the only person in the world, and that she wished she could be with him, even if only to speak with. He sensed in her letter that she was deeply unhappy with her situation with Mike, and again felt a jolt to his feelings when he thought about that anonymous letter. He made up his mind, not to get any more involved with her, even though he did have strong feelings for her.

It was with a strange feeling of impending doom that he left with Will, on what turned out to be his last trip as a courier. After some awkward moments of late, Will had given Dave his assurance that he was all right and not to worry.

The trip north was uneventful, and at Butterworth station, Dave decided, 'Will! You do up north to Sungie Petani, as I need to go over to Pinang Island this trip.'

Will accepted Dave's decision without question, which at the time surprised him.

Dave sat on the ferry crossing over to Pinang, and was quite pleased with himself, thinking '*Will can't get up to too much trouble up there, as there aren't many places where he can get a drink.*'

That day in Pinang, deciding he wouldn't go downtown, he spent sleeping and eating, and was fresh for the return trip back to KL. The omens were not good, at that time. While crossing back over on the ferry the heavens opened up, the wind was blowing so strong, he feared for a moment that the ferry might be sunk with all the rain that fell on deck. When it rains in Malaya, it really does pour down. When finally, the ferry reached the mainland, he had a strange feeling that something was in the offing. Glad to be off and on firmer land, he hurried across the platform and onto the train.

There was no sign of Will when he entered their compartment, only two mail bags lying on the bunk. Going through in his head, *where could he be*, he then thought he might have just slipped into the next carriage for coffee. Just then two lads arrived to hand in mail.

'Where's your mate? He wasn't here when we first arrived.' One of the lads asked.

'Don't know, just arrived myself.' Dave replied.

'There's a bit of a barney going on over in the Station Master's office, maybe he has gone over for a look.' The other lad said.

Dave with no time to think about it, got on with his job. Minutes later he looked at his watch, it was nearly thirty minutes since he had arrived and still no sign of Will. In the back of his head, he wondered if the problem in the office was because of Will. Shaking his head, he didn't want to believe it and become impatient, as it was nearing time for the train to leave. Dave leaned out the door to ask one of the porters what the problem was in the office, at that same moment the OC Sergeant of the train approached from the direction of the office.

Coming over to Dave he said. 'Your courier partner has gone off his head, and is threatening to blow the Station Masters head off.'

Before Dave could say anything, a Major from the next

carriage, overhearing said, 'You had better go and see what your partner is up to?'

'I can't do that sir,' Dave replied, 'my responsibility is to take care of this mail, and I can't leave the train once I start my duty.'

The Major's expression changed, as though he thought Dave was being insubordinate, he then snarled at Dave. 'Look soldier that is an order I'm giving you.'

Stubbornly Dave replied, 'Sir, my orders are to disregard any other officer who gives me conflicting orders, that will obstruct me, while I am on duty, unless it is given to me by a Courier officer.' Dave, wondered where he was getting this bravado from.

Just then the Station Master assistant came running over shouting, 'Quick, quick come fix out soldier.'

Dave turned to look at the Sergeant and said 'Sarge, I think it's your responsibility to fix out that problem, I can't leave his post.'

He turned and spoke with the major, words Dave couldn't make out, and then turning round said, 'You have been given an order by a superior officer. It's your duty and yours alone to fix out this mess, as he is your courier partner.'

Dave, unsure what to do at that moment thought, *should I defy an order from a superior officer, or should I break the Courier rules. Between a wall and a hard place, and in a difficult position where I can't win.* Looking at them in defiance he said, 'Sir I will carry out your order, but I must have both your names and regiments, for when I fill in my report.'

Dave was cut off. 'What do you need that for?' the Major said pompously.

'Sir, I will need to report this incident of being ordering me off the train and by doing so, breaching my C.O's. orders.'

This seemed to put them off a bit and as a compromise the

Sarge said, 'Look soldier, go over and see what the problem is. I'll watch the mail.'

Again, not sure what to do, with hindsight Dave knew he should have stood his grounds, but against his better judgment he reluctantly went over to the office. The scene that greeted him in the dimly lit office was of Will, standing with his handgun pointing at the head of a man sitting in a chair, the man was the Station Master.

Dave stopped just inside, and felt the blood draining from his head and looked around for some inspiration, as he hadn't a clue what he was supposed to do.

Chapter 43

The Lion's Den

Breaking out in a cold sweat with all sorts of questions running through his head, *'Why the hell am I here? What do I do next? What do I say and who do I speak to?'*

Never trained for a situation like this, he was a fish floundering about on the beach, in panic. As the surroundings started to focus all he could hear was swearing, shouting, and arguing in Malay, none of which he could understand. Nothing registered with him. Inside he felt numb but forced himself through the throng of people surrounding Will and the Station Master.

Trying to hide his nervousness, and show he was in control, he shouted, 'Quiet all of you, and let me speak to him.' But that didn't stop them. The noise continued. Dave then took out his handgun, held it up in the air and once more shouted louder. That got their attention.

He continued walking nearer to them and not wanting to inflame the situation more, spoke in a quieter voice, in the only language Will would understand. 'What the fuck is going on? Why are you doing this to the Station Master?'

As he spoke, he looked at the Station Master's face, who

appeared to have momentarily lost his tan, and was shaking nervously.

Without looking at Dave, Will shouted loudly, 'I'm going to kill this bastard for what he said.'

The Station Master screamed out in a frightened voice. 'Please don't! Please don't!'

'Will! Mate,' Dave said quietly, 'You are frightening him! Put the gun down and let's talk.'.

Will slurred, 'I'm going to kill this bastard. No Malay bastard is going to talk to me like that.'

It was then Dave realized he must have been drinking and possibly had taken some drugs. After a few minutes, persistently talking to him, Dave found out that all the Station Master had said was, 'Out of Office. No drunken soldier allowed in here.' Not much, but in Will's state even just to look at him would have been enough for any local to set him off.

Minutes passed by and the local police arrived and wanted to take charge, but by this time Dave, getting Will's attention, who by this time had stopped cursing the Station Master. Told the police to stay out of it until Will had quietened down more.

But just when he was beginning to feel confident of talking Will down, a soldier came running in and shouted. 'Mate! The OC told me to tell you if you're not on the train in five minutes the train will leave without you.'

With all the mail on board, thinking quickly Dave said to the police officer 'Don't approach him till I get back. I need to speak with the officer in charge of the train.' Then turning to Will, said. 'Don't do anything fucking stupid. It isn't worth hanging for a choggy.'

Will's lip turned up in an ironic smile, but never lowered the handgun. The Station Master, meanwhile, looked like he had wet himself or maybe it was just sweat.

Returning to the train Dave found the bags of mail lying

on the platform, with the Major and sergeant standing over them. 'You can't do this,' Dave shouted, and by this time he was quite angry.

The Major disregarded his tone and the situation and smugly said 'I'll be reporting you for insubordination, what's your name, number, and your unit, soldier?'

Dave supplied them his details then defiantly asked for theirs. This time they supplied them. The Major's name was Wickham from the 11th RASC. The Sergeant's name was Botham from the Pioneer Corp.

Without as much as, good luck.

Three minutes later the train pulled out of the station, leaving Dave alone with no other help. He stood a moment shaking his head, his confidence dented as he stood a lonely man on the platform. In that moment he said a little prayer of help from above that everything would sort itself out.

Picking up the mail bags he tentatively walked nervously back to the station office and hesitated before entering. Once in, with the atmosphere still volatile, he approached the police officer in charge and spoke with as much authority as he could muster, 'Please contact the nearest British army unit and have them send a vehicle, and an escort to take us in. I will place my partner under arrest and report him once I get back to camp. The police officer seemed to understand and never objected, appearing happy to wash his hands of the whole situation.

With the mail safely guarded by the police, Dave, speaking to Will calmly asked. 'What started this of Will? Surely it wasn't just what he said?'

Through the cloud that was in his head, Will replied, 'I had a run in with the baster before. I didn't like what he said then and this time things got out of hand.'

Dave shook his head, and continued speaking to him quietly, 'Will, not only have you put yourself in the shit, but you've also put me right in it too, and I'm sure you don't want to get me in any more trouble.' Dave waited for a reply, but none came. Putting his hand towards him 'Give me your weapon, let's call it a day and I will make sure no one here touches you.'

Gradually, after a few more words, the tiredness got to Will. To Dave it seemed like the incident had lasted hours, but only fifty minutes. Then, at long last, Will decided to do as Dave had asked.

Tired from standing for so long, Will sat down then handed Dave his weapon.

Once the handgun was in his hand, Dave turned to the Police officer, and with his hands shaking with relief, he nervously opened the handgun chamber to remove the live rounds, but to his and the police officers surprise, the chambers were empty. With the tension released Dave looked at the officer and he gave a wry smile of relief, and not knowing what to say, he just shook his head. and joked, 'If I had known the weapon wasn't loaded, I would have clobbered him with the mail bags.'

With everything under control Dave asked the police officer to clear the office, and with Will now sitting quietly, Dave then went over to the Station Master to apologize, who was still shaking from his ordeal, and made sure he was all right. Giving the Station master his name and unit number, he thanked him for keeping his cool while he himself had talked Will out of his weapon.

The police officer also took Dave's details and asked if he could do anything else. Dave replied 'No! Thank you. As for what happened tonight, I'll need to face what's coming to me once I get back to KL.'

Chapter 44

Race Against Time

Dave sat down for the first time in over an hour, and it seemed ages before a truck from the Australian Butterworth camp near bye, arrived at the station. When Dave thought it couldn't get any worse, it was like something out of a Keystone Cops movie. Six Ausies literally fell out the back, drunk as skunks. It took all Dave's control not to laugh, for if the situation hadn't been so serious, he might have split his sides. To make matters worse, the driver, a corporal in charge, was not much better, as he also was well liquored up.

They all strolled into the office like an invading force with rifles pointing aggressively forwards, as though ready for battle. The corporal in charge, trying to walk straight, came up to Dave and slurring his words asked, 'What's the matter here Mate, some trouble with the natives?

The police officer and Dave looked at each other, smiled and shook their heads. It was too laughable for words, at that moment, Dave felt the tension evaporate.

Before leaving Dave thanked the police officer for his patience and the policeman in turn told Dave, he would put in his report how well he had handled the situation. With that everyone piled onto the truck and drove off, heading for what camp he didn't know or care at that moment.

On arrival at Butterworth Garrison camp, he briefed the duty officer and after explaining everything, asked him to detain Will, until arrangements were made for him to be taken back to KL. He further asked the officer for a vehicle and a driver, preferably one that was sober to take him down the road, as he had to try to catch the train at Taiping.

Everything was arranged quickly and efficiently, and after a mug of tea, a Land Rover arrived with a driver and another lad who had volunteered to keep him company.

'How do mate,' The driver said and gave a little salute. 'Had a spot of bother had you. Never mind, my mate and I will get you down on time to catch your train or my name isn't Barney.'

The land Rover lurched forward and sped off down the road at break neck speed. Dave, hanging on for all he was worth and thinking, *these Ausies must train their drivers to race standard*, as they drove the seventy odd miles in the dark. Dave sat in the back, and although the driver and his mate talk all the way, he was with his own thoughts of what had gone before.

When in no time it seemed, they arrived at Taiping station and were greeted by some lads from the units near bye, still waiting. At that moment Dave thought he had been lucky, but it was not to be, for he had missed the train by fifteen minutes.

He arranged with the soldiers to distribute the mail to the other army units that had missed him. As he looked down the track his driver asked, 'What now mate.'

Dave thought a moment, then said, 'The night trains always make a long stop at Ipoh. It's possible we could catch it there, but it's another forty-five miles down the road.'

'Mate I'll drive you all the way to K.L. if need be.' Barney joked. 'After all,' he went on, 'I can stay over in K.L. and see my Sheila.'

Off they went. The time was three in the morning when they arrived at Ipoh station and as luck had it, the train was still there. Dave thanked the driver and his mate. With pleasantries and handshakes over, with a wave, they drove back up the road. His compartment had been taken with another passenger, but this time, fed up with the running around he'd had, he once again had to use his authority. This time there was no arguments.

The Major, seeing Dave's determination to carry out his duty, had had second thoughts, and was sweetness personified, and quickly arranged that Dave be given his compartment back. Settled in, he put his feet up and had a nice cup of tea and a ham roll. With having been delayed at Butterworth, and being on his own, with still a long journey left to go on the train, meant a late arrival at K.L.

The rest of the trip passed without any mishap and arrived at K.L. station two and a half hours late. Waiting to greet Dave were two MP's to escort him back to camp. It seems bad news travelled faster than the train, and the wires had been red hot throughout the night.

On the road back to Wardieburn Camp, one of the MP's told him, 'We heard you had some trouble up in Butterworth station?' Then continued, 'You appear to be in the clear by what we've heard, but the C.O. at Wardieburn Camp wants you to report to him after you have dropped the mail off.'

In the C.O.'s. office, Dave explained the incident to him. After considering what he had heard, in reply he said, 'Write a report of the events while still fresh in your mind and hand it back in here.' He then continued, 'I've spoken to Major Dunlop, and you're to report to Paroi Camp first thing Monday morning.'

Leaving the C.O's office, he went straight back to the Couriers Basher hoping to get freshened up, but was met by a very angry Blackjack. Not wanting to hear Dave's side of things, he rebuked him without knowing all the facts. Dave took his verbal abuse, as by this time he was fed up with the whole business.

Dumping his kit on his bed, he went to the cookhouse where he managed to get a cup of tea and a sandwich and just sat in the quiet of the dining hall. Going over and over everything in his head, he was tired and angry with what had happened, and fed up with being in the army. At that moment all he wanted to do was fall asleep, but before that, he had to do that report.

Chapter 45

O. C's Orders

That evening he read the last letters that he had received but they did not help his mood. Over that weekend he kept to himself and stayed in the camp. Monday morning, he was wakened early and told by the duty Sarge, 'After breakfast, there is transport travelling down to Paroi Camp, it's leaving at Eight hundred.'

Dressed in his best uniform and looking like a real soldier, he sat beside the driver of the three-ton truck on his way back to Seremban, and watched the country pass bye. He had seen all this before, but this time he felt it all didn't matter as everything was about to change. As fate would have it, he had no control over his position.

He was kept waiting for nearly thirty minutes before he was finally marched into Major Dunlop's office. He stood in front of his desk to Attention.

After reading Dave's report, the major asked him to explain further, 'What really happened up there.'

Dave again told his story again in more detail. He also gave the names and unit of the officers involved.

The major studied his report again, then said, 'You have

been through something you shouldn't have had to experience, and put in an impossible position by all concerned,' He again looked at the report before saying, 'I have never before had to reprimand a soldier before who had done, and what you have been put through, but I cannot overlook the fact that you left the train and that was against orders.' He thought a moment then said, 'As from today I am taking you off Courier duty'

Dave took a deep breath, as he really had enjoyed his duty as a courier, now his future was uncertain.

'Once you have settled your business in K.L. collected your things, and once you have completed your duties, report back down here to me at nine a.m. on Monday next week. I will reassign you then.' He then dismissed Dave.

Dave wondered why he wasn't to report back right away but surmised he would get that answer later. With no transport immediately available, it was late afternoon before he got back up to K.L.

The remainder of the week flew in but not before he and his mates decided on one last party downtown in K.L. It was a hectic night, but none the less they all got back to camp in one piece, and no one needed to see the M.O. for an injection next day.

While packing his kit Saturday morning, he received a letter from Lynne. It seems his exploits had travelled all the way to the Signal Centre in Seremban Camp. He assumed; Mike must have told her.

In her letter she said she just had to write as she had been concerned for him; obviously by her letter, they hadn't heard he was returning to Paroi Camp. Even though he felt at that moment, it would be nice to see her again, he decided not to reply to her letter.

Having settled himself while in K.L. He felt that morning,

fate was leading him once more into a position where he would have to confront his feelings again.

Sunday morning, he got a lift down to Paroi Camp. On arrival he reported to Corp Duff who arranged a place for him to bunk down. Duffy told him, 'With a lot of the NCOs away down to Malacca, and your old Basher not in use, you can bunk in one of the spare rooms near the camp shop.

Luxury, Dave thought, a room to myself.

Once settled in, he met up with the few of his mates who were still there and passed the day talking over everything that had happened since moving to K.L. The biggest discussion was about the new camp at Malacca, where he was informed, most of Paroi Camp personal would eventually be transferred there. One of the lads who had been back and forward to the new Camp said, 'It's fantastic, with all mod-cons, and to top it all off, there is a great beach there.'

'Sounds great!' Dave sighed 'Just the place to run the clock down.'

Monday morning, his interview with the C.O. was a bit of a mix bags. Firstly the C.O. put him in the picture about his partner Will, and the pending court case that will ensue. 'I'm not sure,' he said 'if Signalman Hendon will be tried in a civil court or a military one. That will be down to what further develops from the police report.' He continued, 'I'll inform you, if you will be called to give evidence, something I'm sure you will be looking forward too?'

Dave cringed inside at the thought.

The C.O. then went on to say, 'I've been looking over your record and to date, it has been exemplary, and has shown great promise till now. In the light of the other reports received, especially from the Police about this sorry mess, which I have to say, leaves you blameless. I have decided that as I need a new driver, that will be your new duty.' Hesitating before continuing on, 'You can start this afternoon by picking me up and taking me home. Report to Corp Duff and he will fill you in on what your duties entail.' Then in a more commanding voice, 'That will be all, Walters. You're dismissed.'

'Thank you sir.' Dave saluted and left his office. In the outer office Corp Duff, filling him in about the duties said, 'You're a lucky so and so, to be the C.Os. Driver, as it's a very cushy number. The only drawback is, there's no timetable for his movements, and you must keep yourself ready at all times, night and day.'

Dave thought at that moment, 'Cushy' he said, 'out of the frying pan and into the fire is more like it.'

At the LED while collecting the C.Os. Land Rover, his new charge. Corp Duff said, 'You see how clean it is. That's how it's to be kept.'

'Very smart.' Dave groaned.

The Corp seeing the way Dave looked, said, 'A wee tip. The previous driver always took it into a garage downtown and the wee Chinks cleaned it spotless. It only cost him the price of a pint of beer, so it might be worth thinking about.'

'Do you know what garage it was?' Dave asked.

In his strong Fife accent, Corp Duff said, 'Aye it's the same one I use, and tell those wee buggers, I'll kick their arses if they try to didle ye.'

He then gave Dave the keys and told him, 'Away and have a spin in the vehicle, just to get the feel of it.'

Dave drove down the hill, turned left at the guardhouse and drove a few miles up the road. Pulling into a clearing just off the road he stopped, switched off the engine and sat there. The sky was a deep blue without a cloud to be seen and the sun beat down relentlessly. All was quiet except for the sounds coming from within the jungle, a jungle that started three yards from the road on both sides of where he had stopped.

In the solitude of that moment, only broken now and then by the noise of monkeys or some other animals from within the jungle, and the occasional exotic bird flying over his head only to disappear back into the foliage. He watched and listening.

In that lonely spot deep in thought, he pondered, *I wonder what Jennifer is doing right now and then, what the heck do I do about Lynne?*

Chapter 46

Settling in Again

Over the next few weeks Dave settled into the routine of transporting the C.O. on his rounds. It was different just being his driver, and in sharing so much time together, the C.O. spoke to him more like a friend, and asked him about home and what his aspirations were, for when he left the army. He also inquired what his Dad had been like and in general made him feel at ease. For once, since joining the army, Dave felt he was being treated like a human being and not a number.

His duties consisted, collecting the C.O. at o-eight hundred, driving him into his office at Paroi Camp, then sometime later in the morning take him over to Seremban Camp, where he spent about a couple of hours in the Signal Centre, then have his lunch at the Officers Mess. Normally at this time, he would tell Dave to grab lunch in the canteen. Other times he was free and not needed till after fifteen hundred hours.

During this period, sitting in the Land Rover with time on his hands Dave once again became an avid reader of Zane Grey Westerns. While waiting for the C.O. to return, he let his imagination carry him riding over the prairies of America.

With so much time on his hands and no one to check up on him, he could just about do anything he wanted within bounds.

Since his return from KL, he had only received one letter from Jennifer, and was beginning to feel anxious that all was not well back home. He worried she was unwell, and that that was the reason she wasn't writing as much. With so much time on his hands, between reading books and thinking of home, he tried convincing himself how great it would be seeing Jennifer again. All this time he also was feeling confused about his feelings for Lynne, and wrestled hard with his anxieties, but more and more, found it harder with each day and wished for a letter from home to say all was well.

One duty he really enjoyed was taking the C.O. to KL Airport and to return two nights later to collect him. Flying to Bangkok was his trips and seemed to be happening quite a lot of late. What his trips were for; Dave was never brought into his confidence. When in KL, and with the freedom he had, by disconnecting the Speedo he could look up his mates at Wardieburn Camp, and if any questions were asked at the LED about the fuel consumption, he would just shrug his shoulders.

In the early days of being the O.C's driver he managed to keep out of Mike's way until the first week in May. While sitting in the NAAFI with a few pals, Mike and Lynne walked in. He recognised them before they were aware of him and could see that Lynne was not her happy self. She looked around the room and when their eyes finally met, she smiled and then frowned as though annoyed with him. Grabbing Mike's arm, she pointed in Dave's direction, and then together crossed over the floor and sat down at his table. There wasn't enough room at Dave's side, so Lynne sat down directly opposite, and by the way she looks at him, he felt uncomfortable.

'Hello David, how long have you been back?' She asked, and then with an inquiring expression on her face asked, 'Why didn't you let us know you were back?'

With her tone of voice, he had a strange feeling the lads sitting at the table knew what was going on between them.

'Oh!' He replied with a startle, and feeling as though he had done something wrong, quickly said, 'about three weeks.'

He could see a look of surprise on her face. It was Mike who spoke, 'I had heard you were coming back down here after the trouble you had on duty. Are you here for good?'

'Don't know' Dave replied abruptly, and continued, 'the C. O's. made me his driver the now, but I don't know for how long, or whether he will keep me here. You know the army.'

Lynne then asked in an intimate voice 'How are you.'

'I'm Ok,' he replied.

'Have you heard from Jennifer?' she asked in a considerate voice and seemed to study his face carefully trying to detect if he was going to tell her the truth.

'No. I haven't heard from her in over a month.'

Their conversation was as though they were the only two people at the table, Dave then realized that everyone had gone quiet and were all looking at them. Dave looked down at his pint hoping someone would change the subject.

One of his mates quipped in. 'I didn't know you had broken off with your girlfriend, you never said.'

Dave glared at him, and to defend Jennifer, said with a little annoyance, 'I only said I hadn't had a letter for a while not that we had split.'

He felt a bit choked at the way the conversation had gone, and when he looked at Lynne he saw concern in her eyes. At that moment he remembered again about that letter he had received from a supposed friend.

Mike thankfully changed the subject and said, 'Jock,

we would like you to come over to our house on Tuesday?'
Turning to Lynne he then said, 'Lynne here, wants to have a
small birthday party.'

'Whose birthday is it?' Dave asked.

Lynne mischievously replied, 'Someone special!'

He knew it wasn't Mike's birthday so it must be either
Lynne's or one of the kids he thought. He knew Lynne was
three years older than him but didn't know what date her
birthday was. With no real excuse, he timidly agreed to attend
the party. 'When do you want me to come over,' He asked.

'Tuesday night early,' Lynne replied.

'Wait a minute. It's my birthday on Tuesday.' He said,
surprised that one of them had the same birth date.

'Stupid!' She smiled, 'The party is for you. Mike and I
thought after all you have been through a party was what you
needed.'

He felt his face blush and was stuck for words. With
that announcement his mates joined together singing happy
birthday, then one called out 'Let's have our own celebrations
now.' The rest of the night went with a swing and the more
Dave had to drink, the weight lifted from his shoulders, and
his eyes were drawn more and more to Lynne.

Lynne, shaking her head, scolded him, 'You're drinking
too much David?'

Mike told her, 'stop harping on and let him enjoy himself.'

The more she gave a disapproving look the more he drank.
He couldn't make up his mind if he were trying to put up a
barrier between them or wanted to be with her. Mike appeared
to be enjoying what he was seeing and encouraged Dave more.
Lynne became very annoyed, stood up and while still looking
at Dave with disapproving eyes, told Mike she wanted to go
home. They left and the party continued for another hour
then with some help, Dave staggered his way back to his room.

The next few days he was kept busy running around the country taking the C.O, and the O.C to various meetings. With so much movement of troops, he knew there must be something big on the go, but what, he never found out. The next time he had to himself was the day of the party. That came about because he mentioned to the C.O. about the party while driving him home on the Friday afternoon.

'That works in fine,' he said, 'I will need you to take me to K.L. on Monday morning as I will be flying up to Bangkok for a few days.'

'What about Captain Hansen, will he need me sir?'

'No, he will be joining me on this trip. So, you can have that day off, but remember to collect us again from K.L. at twenty hundred hours on the Wednesday.' Great! Dave thought, off for nearly three days.

Monday the eighth, the plane took off on time from K.L. at o-ten hundred. Dave gave an inward whoop; he was now free to do whatever he wanted. This was when he liked this job, no one to boss him around or get him involved with anything. As the weather was nice and warm, he decided to take a detour on the road back from K.L. This took him through to a small village called Kujang. Stopping at a small restaurant by the roadside, he sat under the shade with a cool drink of fruit juice and had a specialty fruit cake to eat.

Feeling like a celebrity he was relaxing when a group of bare-footed kids came around him. At first he thought it might have been a mistake stopping, but the restaurant owner told him the kids were just inquisitive as it wasn't normal to see a British soldier stopping there. Whiling the time away he forgot about all else as he studied their houses, the street and the people.

Chapter 47

Happy Birthday

Dave hitched a lift over to the Signal Centre to meet Mike coming off duty. All the way over he was feeling a little apprehensive at first about being in Lynne's company again. When Mike came forward and shook his hand, he at first attempted to tell him he couldn't attend the party, but with Mike appearing genuinely glad to see him, he said, 'Happy birthday mate. Glad you came over early because we can have a beer before our dinner. Lynne said this morning, she was going to surprise us by making something special for tonight.'

Rather than taking the bus, they had a nice leisurely stroll the two-and -half mile to his home, giving them time to catch up on all that has happened these last few months. When they finally arrived home, Lynne was busy preparing the meal. Feeling hot and exhausted after their walk, Mike opened a couple of beers, and casting off their shoes they went outside, and sat in the shade of the veranda under a fan and cooled their feet on the tiled floor.

He still felt a little uneasy, but when Lynne came through from the kitchen, all his unease evaporated. Dressed in red shorts and a white shirt that was tied in a neat bow at her waist, showing a few inches of well-toned body, she was gorgeous. She smiled as she walked over to where they were sitting, and welcomed Dave |by placed her hands on his shoulders, and giving him a peck on the cheek. With her so close, he was momentarily overcome with the sweet fragrance of her perfume.

Softly she said, 'Happy birthday, David. How old are you now?'

'Twenty-three,' He hesitantly replied.

She cheekily said, 'Never! I thought I was more than just three years older than you.' Her face blushed when she spoke.

Dave grinned. 'Funny, I thought I was three years older than you?'

Turning to Mike, she happily said 'Hear that Mike? He thinks I'm only twenty. I wish!' Smiling she turned back to Dave, 'For that, I'll make this birthday the best you have ever had.'

By this time, the beer was loosening Dave's tongue and feeling in a cheeky mood, replied, 'Just the meal will be fine, thank you. Don't want to get Mike jealous.'

They all laughed, but when he looked at Lynne she was blushing again, fortunately Mike was preoccupied pouring another beer to notice.

Waving the towel across her face to cool herself down, and still looking at him, she said cheekily, 'It's suddenly got hot here,' Turning she went back into the kitchen, Dave's eyes following her every movement all the way.

The meal was superb and Dave complimented her saying, 'That was a wonderful meal. Mike really wasn't kidding about how good a cook you are. I hope the girl I marry is as good.'

She smiled as she flippantly replied, 'Thank you kind sir. Wait till you see what I have next for you?'

After a superb cream flan, dinner over and the kids gone

to bed, they sat talking about their lives in general, and about the army. It was then that Mike stated, 'I'm definitely not signing on again.'

For some reason, his comment seemed to make Lynne go quiet. Dave thought at first, she would have been happy about his decision; then again, he reasoned, maybe their main problem was back home.

Mike changed the subject by asking, 'What really happened up North.'

As they hadn't heard any of the details, and the drink loosening Dave's tongue, he said, 'It's a long story.'

'We've got all night.' Lynne whispered cheerfully.

Dave started telling them of how peaceful a day he had had over on Pinang Island, a place neither had been to. He then described how magical Pinang was,

Mike said, 'Don't spin it out, get to the point?'

Dave then related his experience in the station of Butterworth, He could see Lynne was quite impressed when he said jokingly, 'I strode into the station office and my presence was enough to quieten everyone down.' getting carried away with his story he went on to tell them about the police and the Major on the train ordering him off.

Impatient for more details, Lynne asked. 'Where you frightened at any time when you weren't sure if the gun was loaded or not.'

Dave said jokingly, 'I couldn't move, and no one would come near me for I had shit myself.' looking at her he tried to keep a serious expression on his face as he continued, 'The smell was so terrible, that when I tried to get away from it, everybody in the office kept moving round out of my way. It was then I started to get dizzy. Mind you the smell kept their mind off the gun.'

Lynne laughed as she cried, 'Your telling porkies.'

'No, I'm not, all the porkies were in my underpants. They all laughed again.

Mike became more serious and more interested in who was on duty with Dave. 'Who was your partner on that trip?'

'Will Hendon.'

Mike shook his head as he said, 'I know him. He's a bit into the drugs.'

Dave quizzically said, 'I wish I had known that when I was doing the rota for the Couriers.' Then continued with the rest of his story.

'What happens next?' Lynne asked.

Dave shrugged his shoulders. 'Don't know, I've been told, I may have to appear at the trial when it comes up, I suppose to give my account of what took place.'

Changing the subject, Mike asked, 'How about George, how's he doing?'.

'Again, I don't know! I went up to the Cameron Highlands Hospital where he was sent, only to find, that he had been shipped back home for treatment. I was both happy and disappointed he had, because I never got his home address, but I'll find it and look him up when I get home.'

On a brighter note, he had them both in stitches with his account of the Australians who came to his rescue at Butterworth.

As it was well into the night Mike asked if he wanted to sleep over. Having had a few beers, Dave agreed readily, and told them, 'I'm not really on duty till late afternoon,'

'That's ok, you can have a long lie then.' pointing to their spare room, 'You'll be alright in there, the kids won't bother you.'

Since the last time Dave had stayed there, they had had the spare room redecorated and a new single bed put in it.

Mike then said 'I'll be on duty all day tomorrow. If I don't see you in the morning, I'll see you at the weekend.'

Bells should have been ringing in Dave's head, but he was happy with the drink and how he had spent his birthday that he went to bed that night and slept like a log.

Chapter 48

Frustrating Dream

He was wakened around six thirty by the noise of Mike getting ready to go on duty. Turning over he went back to sleep. Some minutes later he felt someone sit on his bed, opening his eyes thinking it might be young Kenneth, but to his surprise it was Lynne.

Lying down beside him, she giggled 'Move over and give me room.'

Blinking his eyes, as he wasn't quite awake, he did as she asked, and as she slid under the cover, he thought, *I've nothing on*, and stammered 'Hey! Wait a minute. I'm not wearing anything.'

'Good,' she shrieked in delight, and reaching down wriggled about, then held up her panties and boasted, 'Neither am I.'

His resistance blown away with the warmth of her body next to his, he thought, '*what the hell.*' Turning to face her, he kissed her brow then her cheek before she kissed him on the lips. Quickly aroused, this time he didn't need any coxing for his body was ready.

Smiling cheekily, she said, 'That was quick.'

She pressed ever closer as he rolled onto his back. Her hand traced its way down his body and as they kissed, she fondled him gently, and moaned softly. moved her right leg over him. He reached down until his right hand lay between her legs. She twitched at his touch and let out a quiet moan. Pressing her body onto his hand, she grabbed hold of his manhood, and still caressing him, opened her legs further. She felt so warm and sexually aroused, he couldn't wait any longer. Pushing her onto her back, he entered her body.

They lay like that for a long moment just savouring the joining of their bodies, and he felt he was in heaven. No words were said as they locked in a passionate kiss. With time suspended, in that moment he felt her warm comforting body.

She slowly ran her nails across his back. He then felt her body start to move in a gently rhythmic way, at first encouraging his to move in the same motion. He was so oblivious to the world at that moment that he let himself go and their love making became more frantic. As he reached a climax, her face changed to that of Jennifer smiling down at him, saying, 'I love you.' Then it was Lynne's smiling face and then again, a mixture of them both. His nerve ends finally reached a crescendo of pleasure, which seemed to last for an eternity.

Lying beside him, she whispered in his ear, 'That was your birthday present from me.'

He seemed to be floating on a cloud when he heard a knock on the room door and Lynne calling, 'Dave. You awake yet,' and then 'breakfast will be ready in a few minutes.'

The morning air tasted sweet, warm, and clammy, and feeling pleased with himself, he lay on his bed satisfied. Eventually, he looked over at the clock; it was still only six forty-five. He then mused at the realization; it had only been a dream. Then he thought, had the other previous sexual encounter they had had after the New Year party, also only a dream.

The way he was feeling about Lynne at that moment, he knew he had to get away as soon as possible. With Mike going out on duty, he dared not trust himself to be alone with her and kept his hands to himself. He rose, took a long cold shower, and dressed.

Mike dressed in uniform, was still sitting at the kitchen table when he entered, 'You look like you have had a rough night Dave. Better get some breakfast down you.' He then asked, 'What's your plans for today?'

Caught by Mike's candidness, he sheepishly replied, 'Nothing much.'

Before Dave could say another word, Mike turned to Lynne, who had just come into the kitchen, and ventured. 'Dave's free today. Maybe he could go with you to the market in town, and help with your shopping.' Then looking at Dave he continued, 'If you don't mind, that is.'

Before he could answer, Lynne said with delight, 'That'll be great! I'm not too sure of myself when in Seremban, especially in the market. It's always so busy. And I'm still not very good at bantering prices.'

Stuck for an excuse to get out of it, Dave assumed, *at least it's in public, so there's no harm in that and told a little lie,* 'I don't mind, I had thought about going into town myself anyway, and it would be nice to have company.'

Mike looking at Lynne and looking pleased, said with a hint of mischief. 'That's settled then. Nanny can look after the kids for a couple of hours, while you're in town,' Mike proposed.

Chapter 49

If Truth be told

Waiting for the local bus to arrive, Dave couldn't take his eyes of her. Dressed in a very colourful floral frock, which stopped just above her knees, showed off her legs and figure exquisitely. Wearing high heeled shoes, she stood about the same height as him. Being there beside her the way she looked, made him thrilled to be in her company.

Coming close to him she took his hand and whispered, 'Thanks for coming with me this morning. When we normally went into town, Mike always disappeared leaving me on my own, and I always felt apprehensive. But I'm sure you will look after me.'

With her close, he felt a little embarrassed in this public place and tried to take his hand away, but she held on tighter and smilingly teased him, 'Oh! No, you don't, you're not getting away that easily,' and pulled him closer.

'People will see us,' He said.

Moving her head close to his, she whispered in a playful way, 'I don't care.'

He was getting hotter by the minute, even if the sun climbing higher in the sky may have contributed to his condition. He was finding it extremely hard to say no to her, and like her he was beginning to feel he couldn't care who saw them, but still asked 'But what about your next-door neighbour?'

Dave was stunned by her reply, 'She knows how I feel about things.'

He felt then, he was being drawn into a conversation that he wasn't sure they should be in, but still asked, 'What do you mean she knows how you feel?

'Alison knows how I feel about Mike,' She hesitated before continuing 'and about you.'

He looked at her, confused, and stuck for words, 'What do you mean feel about you?' It was only the bus arriving that interrupted their conversation.

Nearly full of locals going into market, the bus trundled bumpily along towards Seremban. Some passengers going into market, had cages of live chicken sitting on their laps, and one even had a live goose bound up, and lying on the bus floor. Between the din of all the people chattering and the chicken's cackling, the bus was a very noisy place.

Being the only Brits on the bus and sitting close together, they both listened quietly to all that was going on. She held tightly onto his hand, and with a look of someone stealing some precious moments, gazed at him and without speaking, they both laughed, the kind of youthful nervous laugh as though out on a first date.

The bus weaved its way along the road on that bright beautiful morning, and in no time, they were in the Centre of Seremban. Crossing over the main road they entered the market, which, by this time was heaving with locals buying their goods from the stalls. Dave pointed out, 'Think twice about buying any meat here. Vegetables and fruit are ok, because there's a large range of fresh stuff on sale each day.'

After spending an hour in the market, Lynne said, 'Let's take a walk around the gardens? It's so hot in the sun, the trees will give us a bit of shade'

Dave, not wanting to say we shouldn't, ended up agreeing, 'Yes, I don't really like these markets anyway. Too smelly.'

With plenty of cover from prying eyes they walked slowly hand in hand, not speaking, knowing something was happening between them, and weren't sure what to say or how their feelings were. Finding a nice quite place under a tree near the lake they sat down. Lynne, still quiet but looking radiant, gazed out over the lake, her face relaxed and deep in thought as though all her cares had been lifted away.

Gently Dave touched her hand and whispered, 'Penny for your thoughts!'

She turned and gazed long at him, then replied impishly, 'You wouldn't want to hear my thoughts,' and as though going to say more, stopped mid-sentence and returned her gaze back to the lake.

His curiosity aroused, 'Why wouldn't I not want to know what you were thinking?'

She turned and looked at him again, her beautiful smiling eyes now glistening slightly, and as though unsure what to say, leaned forward and playfully kissed him on the cheek, the kind of kiss you would give a child.

'What was that for?' He questioned, and knew he was being drawn into her game of teasing, so he teased her back, 'You've got another boyfriend on the side.'

By her demeanour he felt he must have struck a chord with what she was thinking because she became embarrassed and blushed. Her facial expression changed to a more concerned look, and changed the subject, 'I asked you last night if you had heard lately from Jennifer, but you never really answered me?'

Her forthright question threw him off guard. Here he

was, chatting up a married woman and hadn't thought of the consequences of his actions until Jennifer's name was mentioned. He looked at the ground between his feet as he deliberated, *Jennifer, my Jennifer, all the plans we had made*. It had now been over six weeks since receiving her last letter, and with every passing day the realization was burning in his heart that a letter from her might never come.

He gazed back at Lynne, unsure what to say.

Shaking his head, at first the words he looked for, were difficult to speak, but she had opened his Pandora box with Jennifer's name, 'No I haven't.' He chocked. 'I got a letter from somebody saying they were a friend, telling me Jennifer was seeing another bloke.

Trying to stifle the tears that was gathering in his eyes he looked down \at the ground and continued, 'I've been trying not to think about it.' Then in a boasting way, 'A letter will come when she has time to write.'

Their conversations stopped suddenly. Lynne took his hand, and showing concern, her eyes now damp with tears. In the way he was talking, she also felt his frustration, not the gentle young man she had learned to care for. Looking deeply through the tears into each other's eyes, it was as though there was some things both wanted to say, but unsure how each should respond. They sat holding hands awhile, each in their own thoughts, and time moving on.

Suddenly, snapping out of this mood he looked at his watch, stood up and feeling a little embarrassed said, 'Time to go. I need to get back to camp to prepare for duty.'

Taking her hand, he helped her onto her feet, she brushed her dress down, and as he turned to start away, she placed her hand on his shoulder. He turned and looking into her eyes saw the pain she too was feeling about their relationship.

Spontaneously she moved close to him, and their lips met, more in a comforting kiss.

Confused by her action, which impelled him to ask. 'Why are you doing this to me? You could have your pick of all the men in the army if you wanted! So why me?'

Stepping back, she looked down at the ground, then looking at him she smiled, 'Because I've been thinking about you a lot since we first met,' She hesitated 'I didn't want to say because of how you felt about Jennifer,' again pausing a moment, then taking a deep breath she finally confessed, 'I think I may be falling for you.'

Is she trying to say she loves me, he thought? Unable to take his eyes of her, his emotions more mixed up than ever, he wasn't sure at that moment what he really wanted to happen. Having tried hard to resist being drawn to her, he now was finding it was to no avail. Pulling her to him, he kissed her, and this time it had more meaning as her lips felt moist and soft. As he stared at her again, he saw the tears running from her eyes. His upbringing and his moral attitude inwardly trying to justify why he should say no to her, but the words he wanted to say wouldn't come out as he wanted them to. 'Lynne, this is wrong.'

'I know.' She whispered,

'What about Mike and the kids?' Nervously searched for the right words, he could only say, 'I don't know how I really feel at this moment, I too have been thinking about you a lot and I don't know what to do. My thoughts of you are more than just a whim, but I.'

At that moment she pressed her fingers over his lips and said quietly, 'Don't worry about it the now, everything will work out in time.' She squeezed his hand as she whispered, 'If you ever need to talk, I'll always be there for you.'

Dave looked into her eyes and thought back to when he

left home, *I'll always be there for you*. These were the same words that Jennifer had said to him, and at that moment, he wasn't sure if he could believe them.

Picking up their belongings, they made their way back to the bus station. Once on board they were in their own thoughts and sat quietly holding hands until they reached Lynne's stop. He stood up, and let her out of the seat, he then sat back down.

She looked surprised and asked, 'Not coming home with me?'

Not looking at her, he casually said, 'No, I'll stay on and go back to camp.'

Still holding his hand, she stared at him as though hoping he would change his mind, but when he made no move she then asked. 'When will I see you again?'

His answer, he just shrugged his shoulders. She let go of his hand and he watched her walk down between the seats and leave the bus. Once off, she turned to look at him as the bus pulled away and appeared to raise her hand to wipe a tear away. He was feeling very fragile at that moment himself, being with her had raised more questions than answers, about what he wanted. It was in times like this, he wished he could see Jennifer, just to settle his troubled mind for suddenly he had this feeling, everything was falling apart.

The rest of the day past him by and soon it was time to drive up to K.L. He drove along the road as though on autopilot and wasn't aware of the countryside that passed him by. As he sat in the Land Rover outside the main Airport building, he thought, *I need to snap out of this.'*

The K.L. Airport, just a long wooden and brick structure with an observation tower at one end. Not what you would call a big international Airport. Rain had started falling as the plane arrived late, just after eleven; Fortunately, he had remembered to attach the canvas roof to the vehicle before he left Seremban.

As the O.C. stepped down from the plane. Dave saluted him and taking his luggage, said, 'Good evening Sir, is Captain Hansen still to come off yet?'

'No! He replied, 'He won't be back for another two days You will be informed what flight he is coming back on later.'

Travelling back to Seremban with the road quiet, the O.C. passed the time asking Dave about his home life and what he will do when he gets home. He also chatted about his own home movie hobby. Arriving at his residence, the O.C. stepped out of the Land Rover, Dave walked behind him, carried his luggage like a porter, up to the front door, and laid the cases down.

The O.C. in conversations with him, knew Dave was also keen on photography, and just before they parted he suggested, 'Some time when I have a spare moment I'll let you see some the films I've taken.' With that he said, 'Goodnight Walters, I'll see you in the morning.'

'Good night Sir.'

The road on the way back to camp with no moonlight, was very dark and on top of that the rain was getting heavier, not the kind of night or place to break down. After parking his charge in the L.E.D, he had to run the few hundred yards in the rain to his quarters. One consolation he mused, there will be no mosquitos.

Once inside and out of the rain he shed his wet cloths, sat down on the only chair in his room and dried himself. The soaking hadn't dampened his emotion of today's events though, and in the quiet of his room he sat awhile until tiredness caught up with him, he then decided bed and sleep, for tomorrow will be another day.

Chapter 50

Dreams End

May, normally Dave's favourite month, became the one he would dislike for a long time. On Friday, the twenty-sixth he received three letters, two from Jennifer and one from his mother. His spirits lifted when he opened the first post-dated letter from Jennifer and all seemed to be Ok, she told of her visits to his brothers and his mother and all the news about the Garage and friends who worked there. She then went on to tell him about friends that were asking for him. All nice but there was something different about her writing, as there wasn't much about how she was missing him, or more intimate things that normally were in her letters. But, because he was so pleased just to get a letter from her he was blinded by his love for her.

The next letter he opened hit him as though a dagger had been plunged into his heart, as it started,

'*Dear David,*

I'm sorry, and I don't know how to say this without upsetting you, I have been struggling with this for some time, and I feel I have to tell you, I have been dating another boy for a few months. I'm

sorry, but I can't go on living this lie and keeping your hopes up for when you come home. I think we should stop writing to each other. I have returned your ring to your mother, and have explained to her what has happened, etc, etc. Please forgive me.' signed just Jennifer.

Dave had never been sure how he would have reacted to getting a letter like this. Now he knew. The world stopped turning and nothing was important anymore. This letter had taken his breath away, and he felt every muscle in his body tauten. Unable to move he felt his legs wouldn't support him; he sat down.

Why? He asked himself.

Anger took over and throwing the letter down he hurried out of the room and kept walking up to the top of the hill, over the parade ground, through no man's land until he reached the perimeter fence near the jungle edge. He would have continued on into the jungle if he could, and get lost, but he just stood there hanging on to the fence, staring into the jungle, looking for what, he had no idea.

Overwhelmed, he then raised his head up at the sky asking himself and God, *'Why? Why is she doing this to me? She said she would wait forever for me.'*

All his dreams and ambitions he had held onto these last years passed before him; with only the stroke of a pen they had all disappeared. Jennifer's face grew stronger in his mind and the love he had for her burned strong at that moment, but with nothing he could do about it, he felt his life had ended.

In that moment, feeling abandoned, no noise entered his ears from the rustling of the trees, as they swayed in the breeze, only the swirl of green filled his eyes. His senses now frozen in time, his world crashed down around him, and he stood struggling for breath.

Falling to his knees he kept thinking; *I still love her!* But after that letter from a friend, deep down he was in denial, and had shielded his feelings from the truth, by refusing to contemplate that it would ever end this way.

Even when reading the last few letters from Jennifer, he had convinced himself there wasn't a problem. Guilt then spread through him as he accused himself for unwittingly giving her the feeling in his own letters that he hadn't cared for her, and again blamed what was going on between Lynne and himself. In his mixed-up state, he accused everything and everyone, including Lynne.

Trying to find some sense to it all, something to hold onto, tears burst from his eyes as he could no longer contain them. With his emotional state so distort and no one there he could talk to, he felt he was the last person on earth.

A self-destruct button pressed in his brain, and without thinking of the consequences, he found himself in the NAAFI having a drink, then another, and another, something he'd never done before. But now, with no one to stop him, he drank and drank until the world was a better place in his head, and he couldn't remember where he was, or more importantly, he was on duty later.

Chapter 51

Back to Reality

When he finally re-joined the human race, he didn't know that it was Corp Duff that was standing over him, or that he was lying in the guardhouse cell, with a lump on the back of his throbbing head. He tried to raise his head from the pillow to get off the bed but felt there were weights keeping him down.

'Stay where you are,' He heard this voice ordering, and trying to turn round to see who it was, only made the room spin around. 'Everything is going to be Ok,' the voice said again.'

Dave managed to mumble, 'What, whaall will be alright?'

The voice spoke again 'I covered for you with the C.O., and I understand what you're going through.'

Corp Duff must have thought Dave was aware of what was going on, even though he didn't know what the voice was talking about, or if the voice was only in his head. All he knew, he felt extremely ill.

The next time he opened his eyes, his mate Brian, who had been unlucky to cop some guard duty, was beside him. Seeing that Dave was awake, he came into the cell, sat down on the bed, and with a little bewilderment in his voice said, 'That must have been some bender you had yesterday, you even had Corp Duff flapping.'

Dave swung his legs round until they touched the floor and then tried to sit upright, but as he did, he felt sick again and lay back down. For something to say, through a cloud he asked, 'What time is it?'

'It's five in the afternoon.' Brian said.

The last positive thing Dave remembered was that it was just going on lunchtime, so he mumbled, 'That's alright. I must have been exhausted, to have slept for four hours.'

'What do you mean, four hours?' Brian asked, 'You have been asleep since yesterday since Corp Duff brought you down to the Guardhouse.'

It was then, Dave realized he wasn't in his own room, but in the Guardhouse cell. He covered his face with his hands, slowly it all came flooding back to him, and he couldn't hold back the tears. He then remembered reading Jennifer's letter, after that his mind was a blank, and as to why he was here in the guardhouse he didn't understand.

'Why am I here?' He asked.

'Corp Duff said he will speak to you later.' Brian explained.

Just then one of the other guards brought him a mug of tea, which he drank gladly. His stomach though was groaning, but at that moment, he felt he couldn't look at food again. All because his world had turned against him. He spent that Saturday night in the cell with only coffee to drink, and all he could think about was Jennifer.

On Sunday morning Corp Duff came in to see him. 'How are you feeling now?' He asked.

'I'm feeling a bit better, except for a sore head.' Dave groaned.

Duffy explained, 'I'm sorry I had to hit you,' and

continued, 'In the NAAFI, no one would go near you the way you were swinging your fists about, and the only way I could stop you, was to knock you out. Sorry about that.'

That answered how he had a lump on his head.

Sitting down on the bed beside him, he said, 'When you hadn't reported to me for the C.Os. duty, I went looking for you. I found your room door wide open, and went in, your letters were scattered about. I hope you don't mind but I looked at the letter on your bed and knew right away what the problem was.'

He went on to say, 'I searched around the camp, until I heard there was a commotion in the NAAFI, so I headed down there.' He went on, 'when I entered, you were throwing things about and in general, making a nuisance of yourself, and weren't in a mood to listen to anyone. The only action you left me with was to knock you out.'

After a chat about Jennifer's letter, Duffy said he had experienced the same thing himself a long time ago and knew exactly how he was feeling. After exhausting the reasons for and against he said, 'Grab yer gear together, let's go to the NAFFI and get some grub down Ye.'

The rest of that day Corp Duff was like his shadow and made sure he didn't cause any more trouble. The anger that was still inside him, and the realization that his life was over with Jennifer, it wasn't food he craved, but alcohol. To get drunk again he felt was the only way he could release the pain of rejection.

Because Duffy refused to let him have a drink, he tried to sneak out of the camp to go into town. Where no one knew him, or cared less what happened to him. The guards having been told not to let him past, stopped and held him till Corp Duff arrived.

Taking Dave into the Guard room cell, Duffy sat him

down and said, 'Look Walters! I told you I know what you're going through but what you want to do won't solve a thing, it will only make things worse for you.'

Dave heard what he had to say but was in no mood to heed his advice, all he wanted was to get the hurt out of his head. When Duffy saw Dave was determined he gave up trying to persuade him. 'Come on then. I'll go with you over to the NAAFI, if that's what you want?'

Chapter 52

Words Not Enough

Sitting in the NAAFI, Dave looked into a pint of beer that lay before him. All he could see was destruction as the froth swirled around, matching his mood of thought. Having not eaten a decent meal since Friday morning, except the few sandwiches, his stomach at that minute was feeling rather tender. *'This is what I really want,'* he told himself, but was finding it hard to start drinking.

Later some mates gathered around, and trying to keep his mind off his sorrows, joked about how he had once said he would never let a letter affect him.

An hour past, and even though he still thought it was what he wanted, he was finding it hard to work up enthusiasm to drink his pint. The lads though, in trying to help, wouldn't let him out of it and by the time he had drunk about half, it had gone flat and put a sour taste in his mouth. His mates, thinking it was what he needed, another drink was put before him. He tried to focus on what was going on around him, but couldn't, and as he struggled with his problems, he didn't notice Mike and Lynne entering the NAAFI.

Seeing Dave surrounded by all the lads, it would have

looked to them, that he was having a good time? They sat down at a table over in the far corner and were joined by their friends Alison and her husband Andy.

After a few minutes, Mike approached and spoke to Corp Duff, who was still orchestrating the proceeds. They talked quietly for a few minutes, then Mike came round to where Dave was sitting, and tapped him on the shoulder. That was when Dave first realised, they were there.

Leaning over to him, Mike quietly said, 'Come on Dave. Come over and join us for a while, mate'

At first Dave didn't want to move, for in some twisted way he felt Lynne was responsible for his condition, and it wasn't until his eyes caught Lynne waving him to join them, Corp Duff leaned over to him and said, 'Go on Walters. That's the kind of company you need at this minute.'

Dave looked again at Lynne; in her eyes she had a despairing look. His heart skipped a beat as he thought about their last meeting, and thought, '*what the hell! Out of the frying pan and into the fire. I couldn't care less what happens to me from here on in.*'

As he joined them at their table, Lynne made space for him between her and Alison. He hesitated, but drawn to her he sat down. Both women took a hand in each of theirs, and Mike and Andy retired over to the Bar.

Lynne and Alison in turn asked Dave how he was feeling, and that he should talk about his letter. He tried to tell them, but felt just numbness and anger in his heart, for all the injustices that were happening to him.

He sat awhile just listening to their comforting counsel and feeling their hands in his, he calmed down a little. Listening to their advice though, only brought the realization of what they were talking about. He felt the hurt rise again and tears well up in his eyes.

Putting his hand up to stop them talking, he said defiantly, 'I have to get out of here. I need time alone to think.' He stood up and leaving them sitting, walked out.

Mike seeing Dave leave, hurried over to Lynne, and asked, 'Where's he going?'

'I don't know. He just got up and left. I hope he doesn't do anything to himself?' Lynne said, holding a tear back.

Mike consoling her offered. 'I'll nip down to the Guard house and stop him from leaving, as he has tried a few times already.'

All the while, Dave outside, stopped a few paces from the NAAFI entrance and tried to hold back the tears he didn't want them to see. Looking around he thought he'd nowhere to go. There seemed no escape from the feelings he had, as he wasn't allowed to leave the camp.

Looking into the darkness that was trying to overcome the small landing lights which were spaced every twenty-five yards along the Airstrip, he set off in the only direction he felt he could and started walking aimlessly along the runway.

By this time Mike was outside, but never thought about looking along the Airstrip, having already decided to head in the opposite direction down to the main gate.

Dave had walked about fifty yards when he stopped. Realizing it was no use; and unable to contain his grief, he raised his arms above his head in defiance and shouted, 'If there's a God, why have you done this to me? first Dad and now Jennifer!' At that moment what faith he had left him.'

Lynne, having followed Mike out, had been standing there a few seconds when she heard his cries of despair. Following the direction from where his voice came, she saw the faint glow of his white shirt illuminated by one of the runway lights, and started towards him.

He stood, his arms raised, and his fists clenched, trying to make sense of his life. All his good times and experiences in the past seemed to have all been stripped away from him, and he felt naked of everything he had ever cared for. Alone in the stillness of the night that seemed to last an eternity, he felt the darkness close in on him. That was until from behind he felt a gentle hand rest on his shoulder. At first he didn't react to the touch for his mind was detached from his surroundings.

'David,' a sweet gentle voice called. At first he thought it was Jennifer's voice, but when he turned round, it was Lynne who was standing before him. Her hair was hanging down straight like a curtain framing her beautiful face, and her dress clung to her body with the heat of the night.

Softly with a touch of awkwardness and sadness in her voice she said. 'We've been looking everywhere for you. I thought you might try to leave the camp, but I'm glad you didn't.'

He looked at her, but all he could see was Jennifer's face and wished it were her standing there, but it wasn't. Through his tears he could see in Lynne's expression, she cared for him and the tears in her eyes spoke volumes.

With arms held wide he asked, 'What do you want from me Lynne? I've nothing left to give. She's taken it all away from me and left me with nothing but pain and anger, I don't know what?' His voice tailed off.

Pressing closer to him, she put her arms around his waist and kissed him tenderly, he stood motionless with no feelings in his body, her kiss could have been on someone dead. She then held his face with both hands and said, 'David, you have lots of love left in you to give to others.' Then she sniffled before sensitively whispering, 'Let me help you to get over how you feel.'

Realizing what she had said, she sensed maybe he wasn't ready for that kind of affection. Still with her hands on his face, she tried to wipe the tears from his eyes as she softly said with concern in her voice, 'I told you once before. I would be here for you if you wanted to talk. I'm here now.'

Confusion reigned in his head, and he tried to think through all what she was saying, and the muddle of what was left of his life. With her standing so close, and his head clearing a little, he angrily replied. 'She said those same words to me. Why should I believe them now?' he paused, 'Anyway, What will Mike think about you coming out like this?'

In the insipidness of the night, she looked long into his eyes and softly said, 'I'm sure he knows.'

Chapter 53

Comforting Arms

Dave in his state, didn't quite understand what she meant, as in that moment things were still so surreal, and he was thinking more of his own problems than anybody else. Even though both were unsure what to say or do.

At that moment the moon was drifted from behind the clouds, lighting up the runway ahead. She looked up at the glowing light in the heavens and for the first time that night he saw Lynne and not Jennifer.

When she turned to look at him again, she saw his pain had eased and suggested. 'Let's just walk and talk awhile, or if you want, just walk, and hold hands?'

The night air was clammy as they silently continued down the strip. Further along, she slipped her arm around his waist, and feeling her comfort, he was grateful she was by his side. At that moment she was probably the only other person in the world who understood him. Ever step he took he could feel himself relax out of his foul mood.

'Thanks for being here for me. I don't know what I should or shouldn't do,' he sighed, 'I'm lost.' Shaking his head, 'I don't know where to go from here?' His voice faded away.

Lynne tightened her arm around him, 'It will all work itself out over time, and who knows, she might regret what's she's done and change her mind.'

He mulled over what she said, but somehow, he knew in his heart it was over, and life wouldn't be the same knowing Jennifer wasn't waiting for him. It was only then that he felt the light rain that was falling, and not wanting to say anything more about Jennifer, putting his hand out to feel the rain he muttered, 'What are we doing in the rain? You're getting wet.' He said apologetically.

'Ah!' She said mischievously pointed to his heart, 'You do still have a wee soft spot in there for me.'

With the light-hearted way she spoke, the tension in his body began to ease. By this time, they had nearly reached the end of the strip. Turning to face him, she said calmly, 'Well matey, the only way back for you now, is on your own two feet,' and playfully dug him in the ribs, 'I'm sure,' pulling him closer she whispered in his ear, 'There is a special girl out there waiting for you, one that deserves a nice boy like you.'

He looked at her long when she said that, and was about to ask her, could you be that girl? But something tugged at the back of his mind telling him, '*you've been hurt by Jennifer so be careful with Lynne.*' He moved close and kissed her, this time their kiss felt sweeter.

The rain started to come down a little heavier and in the eerie glow from the perimeter lights, a faint shape of an open fronted shed over to one side could be seen. Taking her hand, he pulled her towards it. Suddenly they were undercover and standing with his arms around her, they looked out over the airstrip as the rain bounced on contact with the ground.

Shivering, and snuggling closer, she playfully asked, 'Aren't you going to keep me warm?'

Shrugging his shoulders, he replied. 'I don't have a jacket or anything to cover you with.'

'Yes, you have?' Even though semi dark, he could still see her mischievous smile as she continued, 'You have your lips,' she kissed him gently, and whispered. 'And the passion we had that first night when we.'

She kissed him again with more passion. Her words tailing off at that moment were what he needed to hear. Even though, he still wished it were Jennifer that was saying them, and not Lynne. He tried to let his emotions go as he had that night they got carried on a sea of longing, but now was not the right time, so it was not as lovers but as intimate friends they kissed.

Staying in that embrace until the rain eased off, the deep dark hole that he had fallen into was now beginning to open, and he felt that night he had started on his way to climb back out. The rain stopped, and the muggy heat raised a mist over the ground as they walked back giving the feeling, they were walking on the clouds. The heat drying the tarmac of the runway also dried their clothes as they walked slowly hand in hand back to the NAAFI. Stopping outside the entrance, she asked for his comb to tidy her hair. One of the NAAFI assistants standing by the back door gave them a towel to dry themselves. Once presentable, they walked into the hall.

Mike seeing them enter came over and asked, 'Are you alright Mate.'

'Yes. Yes thanks. I feel a whole lot bit better now, and it's all thanks to Lynne being a good listener.'

Dave looked in Lynne's direction; she was deep in a conversation with Alison. Mike never asked where they had been even though they had been missing over an hour.

At that moment Dave wasn't in the mood to be in his company, after what Lynne had expressed to him. He quietly said, 'If you don't mind Mike, I'll join the lads, because I've taken up enough of your night,' Not waiting for an answer Dave turned and walked over to where his mates were all sitting.

Once sat down, one mate put his arm around his shoulder in a brotherly fashion and teased, 'That must have been some walk, you look a bit more settled.'

'It wasn't the walk that helped. It was having someone who was a good listener.' He didn't mean it to come out and sound the way it did, but the lads all laughed and together called out, 'Oooooh.'

Dave could feel for all to see, a blush warmed his face. Just at that moment another mate said, 'Look at him, he's blushing.'

Dave squinted over to see if Lynne was looking, only to find all four at the table were looking across at the lads teasing him. At that moment he didn't mind, as the wonderful smile on Lynne's face had made his night.

Chapter 54

Life goes on

Days after DJ letter day, as the lads referred to call it. He settled into his new life with no real ambitions, no future, and with no plans, he just got on with his daily duties. Occasionally he slipped into depression and felt it wasn't worth living. Life was not the same even knowing how Lynne felt about him. There was still this emptiness inside him, but as the days wore on, these pangs of times got fewer, and not so hard to bear.

Sometimes while sitting waiting for the C.O., he didn't know if he were deluding himself that it was all just a bad dream and once home, he would walk up to Jennifer, she would say she was sorry, and they would be back together again.

Time, he convinced himself had stood still and everything back home would be as it had been before. With these thoughts in mind, he was able to function and face each day, and with Lynne and Mike's friendship being great pillars of support for him, occasionally he spent Saturday night in their home after dances at Seremban Camp.

Knowing the feelings they had for each other, when in her company, it was becoming more difficult to keep that friendship just platonic, especially whenever they were near one another, and she would tease him. For all that, she stayed in the background at times, allowing him space to work things out for himself, but always there if he needed to talk.

His duties driving the C.O. gave him plenty of time to think things through. During these moments, he started to realize his feelings for Lynne were, if she were free and felt the same way as he, that life might not be so bad after all. The feelings underneath were really focused one day while driving the O.C. when he asked innocently, 'Are you feeling alright now, that you are over your problems with your old girlfriend?'

'Not really, sir.' He replied automatically, 'I think it will take a while to get over losing her.'

The O.C. then said, 'I've come across your situation many times before with other lads. All I can say to you is that all the lads came through it and went on to make a good life for themselves.' He then gave Dave some advice, 'Keep busy and get involved with more sports. In general try not to leave any time to think about her.'

Keeping as active as he could and in Lynne's company at times, certainly helped, but it was a struggle and he knew in himself it would be a long time before he got over Jennifer, if ever.

Having seen the back of May, the pain was easing a little, and now well into June, the C.O. had him on call regularly. One day he said in a casual way, 'I have another job for you, Walters. My daughter has arrived from England for the school holiday term. I want you to escort her when she wants to go into town, just to make sure she's safe.'

As he didn't say much more about how old his daughter was, apart from, 'Come round to the house later tonight, and I'll show you some of my movies. You can meet her then.'

Dropping the C.O. off at home that night, as he stepped

out of the Land Rover, he reaffirmed, 'Remember, seven thirty sharp and just dress casual.'

Dave wasn't sure what he was getting into, as he was thinking his daughter might be a screaming thirteen-year-old.

After dinner in the canteen, Dave just wore a white shirt, tan trousers and at the last moment put on a brown tie. Over at the LED having convinced the Sarge he was on duty at the C.O.'s house, he signed out his Land Rover.

Arriving at the C.O.'s house with some trepidations, which was in a leafy part of town set among beautiful parkland, he nervously walked up to the door. As the C.O. liked punctuality, it was around seven twenty when he knocked on their door.

The door swung open and there before him stood an attractive nineteen-year-old woman. 'Hello,' she said in a very posh voice, 'you must be Walters? I'm Sandra. Please come in, Daddy is waiting for you in the lounge,' and pointing, 'It's through there.' Then calling out 'Daddy, David, I mean Walters is here,'

Walking into the lounge, Dave was greeted by Mildred, his wife, who made him feel at home. Right away Dave could tell she was a very down to earth woman, and not as posh as her daughter. She had been sitting with a glass of cool fruit juice, patiently waiting to see his latest epidemic as she called them.

As the films rolled both Sandra and her mum lost interest, much to the C.O.'s annoyance, and turning to Dave, asked questions about his life. The C.O. kept telling them not to pry and let Dave enjoy the films.

'Films.' Mildred cried out in laughter 'They are more like a beauty parade with all those young things you keep taking films of.'

The films only lasted half an hour, and by the end of his visit, Mildred in her motherly way had pried out just about all there was to know about Dave's life. Leaving their home that night he couldn't have imagined that he would spend a few more nights visiting their home.

Once back in camp and in his own room, it was here he felt the world closing in on him again. The photos of Jennifer that he had put out of sight were drawing him to have another look at them, and once looked at, he wished he could turn back the clock. With his emotions overcoming him, he wondered, *when again will I ever see and feel the way I had, when with Jennifer?* With his mind deep in that dark place, he found it difficult to sleep unless he had had a drink, or when he forced Jennifer out of his mind to let the images of Lynne come in. Even then, sleep still never came until the early morning.

Collecting the C.O. in the mornings, he always asked, 'How are you feeling this morning, are you getting enough sleep,'

Dave always replied, 'Yes sir.' But was sure the C.O. had noticed that his attitude had changed and knew he was lying. He was letting himself go and wasn't as presentable as he used to be. He knew it himself, when looking in a mirror, that he had let his demeanour go. This ritual went on for a few days, then one morning the C.O. told Dave to smarten himself up or he would be looking for another driver.

During this spell, Daves trips into Seremban at nights became more frequent and feeling sorry for himself he abandoned his inhabitations. On one night out with the lads, after having a good time, Mike and Lynne who also had been in town with friends spotted Dave, the worse of the wear, rescued him for his own good, so they told him later.

On another occasions he found himself wakening up on the cot in their spare room. Lynne's attitude to him, seemed changed, more annoyed, and scolded him. 'David you've got to get a grip of yourself, if you don't, you won't have any friends at all.' Then she said softly to him. 'I can only help you if you help yourself.'

For a spell her scoldings seemed to work, but when one early morning he fell back into that deep black hole he woke up in a room with a young Chinese woman lying beside him, and no recollection how he got there. The last time Mike and Lynne found him in this state, they took him back to their place, and plied him with coffee until he couldn't drink any more. He became violently sick then feel asleep.

When he awoke in the early morning, Lynne was sitting by his side watching over him, her eyes damp from crying.

Through a misty veil he looked at her and asked, 'Why were you crying?'

Snivelling she replied, 'I'm worried you're going to let things slip to far, and won't be able to get back to us.'

Dave didn't know what to say or think what she meant, but instead asked, 'Where's Mike?'

'He's gone off to bed now, as he thought you were going to be alright.' She answered, 'But I told him I wasn't so sure you were.' Then looking at him she pleaded, 'Are you going to be alright now, for I can't stand to see you like this.'

Dave sat up and swung his feet on to the floor. At that moment Mike, hearing their voices came back through from the bedroom. 'Ah! Back in the land of the living are you mate.' Then sitting down beside him and asked, 'How are you feeling?'

Dave unable to look them in the eyes, searched for something to say. Eventually he confessed, 'Sore, stupid, feeling confused, and grateful for having good friends like you.'

Lynne rose from her seat, went over, and sat at the other side of him. Putting her arm around his shoulders she gave him a hug and said, 'Dave, if you don't snap out of it and try to forget Jennifer, you are going to lose more than just our friendship.'

Her words stung, and his life flashed before him. Realizing that their friendship meant more to him than anything else at that moment, his emotions got the better of him and with the comfort of her arms around him, he wept. Those tears were the last to flow from his eyes, over his loss of Jennifer.

Managing to catch a few hours sleep, early that morning before they both were awake, he was dressed and was out the door. The walk back to camp was what he really needed, just to blow the remnants of his past out of his system. It was a nice morning, and the sun was just beginning to rise over the treetops. and it was the first time in a long time, he was noticing the things that he loved about this country. The damp sweet smell that comes out of the Jungle after it had been raining and the calls of the wildlife, as they too greeted the new dawn of a new day. *'What a great morning,'* He mused*, 'I hope this day will be the dawn of a new time for me, and I can learn to live with my past.'*

Arriving back at camp, he still had just enough time to have a shower, a shave and put on his best uniform. Going into the dining hall he found most of his mates already there. To some he must have looked different after the way he had been acting these past weeks, as he confidently walked in. One of his mates called him over to sit beside them and seeing he was more like his old self, slapped him on the back, and cheerfully said, 'Welcome back mate.'

He did feel a little different and knew at that moment, it was time to start putting his life back together again.

Collecting the OC that morning, Mrs Dunlop, who was having her breakfast with her daughter Sandra, invited him in, declaring. 'Major Dunlop will be a little late. Would you like a cup of tea while you wait?' Then smiling at him, she then said, 'You're looking well this morning.'

'Thanks, I do feel quite good this morning, and I wouldn't mind some tea if it's no bother.' Dave replied.

The morning had started well and considering he had had so little sleep the night before he did feel full of life. Sitting supping his tea while looking out their kitchen window, he smiled inwardly as he thought, *maybe, just maybe, there is more in life to come for me.* With this positivity attitude he had one of the best days in a while.

Chapter 55

On The Move

The remainder of June came and went and most of July followed. Life during this period was all about doing his duty and trying to enjoy what he could when he could. One day near the end of the month, over at the Signal Centre he bumped into Mike, who cheerfully inquired, 'Hi Mate, what are you doing over here?'

'Brought the C.O., apparently he's here for a meeting about the lads who will be moving down to the new camp at Malacca.'

Mike retorted. 'We were told about that when we came in this morning. It looks like I'm in the group selected to go to Malacca in a week's time.'

'Not much time to prepare,' Dave acknowledged. Thinking about Lynne, if she would also move with him, 'What about Lynne and the kids are they moving down as well?'

He shrugged his shoulders 'No, not at the moment, as the married quarters won't be ready for another two months or so.' Then hesitating he continued, 'While I'm away will you make sure Lynne, and the kids are all right?'

Dave, taken aback by his candour, looked at him, then replied, 'I'll drop in now and then if you like.'

'That would be great mate. And if Lynne ever wants to go to the dances with Jock and Alison, would you accompany her? Save her from wearying.'

Dave gave a little inward sigh of relief at the news Lynne would be here a while longer, but was still surprised in the manner Mike had asked him to take care of them. Dave knew their marriage was a bit shaky but, was still taken aback. 'Don't you think you are leaving Lynne open to gossip if I do that?' Dave intimated.

Mike just shrugged his shoulders, and in his usual callous manner, replied, 'I don't think so. She can handle herself! Anyway, everyone knows you are my mate.'

Dave wasn't sure what to think and considered, I know we've been good mates since first we met, but that's an insensitive attitude to take even for him.

After their brief talk, he had the feeling Mike was looking forward to being away for a while, and by now, Dave felt he shouldn't have been shocked about anything Mike might say.

Monday, six days later, at O-eight hundred hours, eighteen Signalmen left from Seremban Camp and ten from Proi along with quite a few RASC lads from the LED, making Proi Camp quieter still.

For the first few days of that week, Dave hung about with his mates that were left and managed to play some badminton over in Seremban Camp. Then one night, Andy, Mike's next-door neighbour came into the NAAFI and handed him a message from Lynne.

The message read, 'Dear David can you call in to see me tomorrow after dropping the C.O. off.'

After reading it Dave with a look of surprise asked Andy, 'Do you know what is in this note?'

Andy replied, 'Only that she said she needed to speak to you.'

Dave looking for an expression on his face, then said, 'I don't know what to do, as this puts me in an awkward situation.'

Andy stared at Dave with an uninterested expression as he replied, 'I wouldn't worry about it. I think most of their friends have enough of their own plate, to be bothered with other people's problems. Anyway, most have an idea of the situation between Lynne and Mike.'

Dave wondered at that moment if this callous attitude was prevalent in most army marriages.

Next day after dropping the C.O off at his home, he was in two minds whether to stop at Lynne's house or just carry on back to camp. He hesitated as he approached the entrance to her housing estate then passed by. All the while trying to convince himself he was doing the right thing, but a few hundred yards further up the road he pulled the vehicle off the road and stopped, got out and stood looking around him.

'You're a bloody fool to go to her house,' He said out loud. After a few moments standing there, he climbed back into the Land Rover and in the end became that fool. Turning around he drove up to her house. Stopped outside and hesitated, looked at the house for a while longer, then went up to the door and knocked.

The door opened and Lynne, looking pleased to see him, said, 'Hi! Dave, glad you could make it. Come in for a minute?'

She stood holding the door, on entering he brushed past her and could smell the sweet fresh fragrance that shrouded her as thought having just come out from having a shower.

Turning to look at him she asked, 'Have you got time for a coffee?'

Dave for some unknown reason, feeling uneasy and

having difficulty focusing on how he should react to her, timidly mumbled, 'I have to get back to the camp. ..... There's something wrong with the vehicle.'

Giving him an inquisitive look, 'A cup of coffee won't take that long.'

Still feeling uneasy, he agreed, 'Ok, but I have to get back before the LED closes.

As she was making the coffee, she asked right out, 'Would you accompany me over to the film show in Paroi Camp on Saturday night?'

He was lost for words, then tried to get out of it by saying, 'All the lads might talk, and we might be storing trouble up for ourselves.'

Before he could say more, she stopped him, 'It won't be like we will be by ourselves, Alison will be with us.'

'What about Andy, will he be going? Thinking at least he would be some support.

'Andy's on duty that night. She replied, 'So, you won't have to worry what anyone says. Any way you will be escorting the two of us.'

Seeing Dave was still not sure she came close and put her arms around him, then snuggling up, said, 'Let them say what they want anyway, I don't care anymore, as long as I have you by my side and back to your old self.'

That Saturday night, Dave arranged a taxi to collect Lynne and Alison, but still felt uneasy when escorted them into the cinema. Once the film started, he left Lynne sitting beside Alison and went to the toilet.

Corp Duff, seeing Dave come in, chided him 'I see you have two married women in tow? Watch yourself mate, as there are a lot of married soldiers who might take exception to you being with them, especially with Mike being away.'

Dave glared at him, 'Don't you think I haven't thought

about that, but first they should ask Mike, why he asked me to bring her over to the pictures.'

'Alright son,' he growled. 'Just be careful. That's all I'm saying.'

Sounded like a warning to Dave, which only made him more annoyed, probably because he was feeling embarrassed. As he left to join the ladies he was defiantly thinking, 'To hell with the lot of them, I'm doing what I want, and no one will stop me.'

The picture finished at nine-thirty and Dave invited them over to the NAAFI for a drink. 'No, I think we'd better get home and let our babysitters away,' Lynne said, then continued, 'You're going to escort us home Aren't you?' then coyly speaking. 'Just to make sure we get home safely.'

Cornered, he agreed.

Chapter 56

Two Lost Souls

Outside the Guardhouse, while waiting for their taxi, they had to take some banter from the lads on duty that would have made their grannies blush. Dave felt red under his collar but was sure the girls, being army wives had heard it all before. Fortunately, within minutes the taxi arrived.

Alison, who hadn't seemed to mind Dave escorting them, was first to alight at her house. They said good night and as she left them. Dave said loudly more for Alison's benefit than his own, 'I'll just see Lynne off at her house then get back to the NAAFI for a drink with the mates.'

Just round the corner they arrived at Lynne's house, she leaned forward and told the driver to go down the road a little and stop. Dave slow to think about it at the time and like Sir Galahad he jumped out and opened the door for her and as she got out she leaned close and asked, 'Coming home with me for a night cap. You can get a taxi later.'

'No. I'd better not. I think I'd better get back,' Dave mumbled.

She caught hold of his hand and said 'Please, just for a little while.'

Her longing gaze took all his objections away. He paid the taxi driver off. Walking back round to her house. It was then he realised why she had stopped the taxi round the corner, it was out of sight of the neighbours. Entering her house they were greeted by her Chinese babysitter, who, was already waiting to go home.

Once the babysitter was out the door, Lynne took her shoulder wrap off and asked, 'Would you like a coffee or something stronger to drink?'

'A glass of beer would go down well' He replied, and sat down in one of the single chairs. His mind strayed back to the last time they let their emotions take over.

She poured a glass of beer and a soft drink for herself. Carrying them over to where he was sitting, she put them down on the table then sat down on the two-seater opposite. Patting the seat next to her, she said in a sultry voice, 'Come sit over here beside me so we can talk.'

He hesitated, took a drink of beer. Put the glass down and looked at her, she had the look of someone who was troubled and wanted to talk. She held out her hand and insisted 'Come sit beside me.'

In the end he gave in, musing, *it's what I really wanted anyway, and she knows it.* He got up and walked round the table and took her hand in his, just the soft touch of her skin sent a warm feeling through him. 'Are you sure you want me here?' He whispered as he sat down.

She didn't answer his question, just smiled, 'Thanks for accompanying me to the movie, it was good to get out for a change.

'The pleasure was all mine.'

'When is the next movie to be shown at your camp? Will you take me again?' She inquired.

He responded, 'Don't know when the next film show is, and I'm not sure if we should!'

'Did you not like being with me?' Curtly she asked

He looked at her, her face glowed slightly, as though mischief was on her mind. He nervously replied, 'I like being with you, but I don't like sharing you with all the others.'

She leaned close and gave him a peck on his cheek, and then as she inclined backwards, her hair spread over the back of the seat. Looking very composed she asked, 'How are you feeling now?' Hesitating for his reaction and before he could answer she continued, 'What about your feelings for Jennifer now that?' Stopping short of what she was about to say.

She Looked at him intently, and Dave sensed she was trying to find the right words to asked him, 'Do you think you will ever get over her?' she finally asked.

He shrugged his shoulders and studied her face, looking for a hint of why she is asking, 'I'm not sure. I still feel I love her at times, then at others I get so angry with her. I've pushed it all to the back of my mind, so I won't really know until I see her again.'

She went quite at that moment and the expression on her face changed.

'What's the matter, are you feeling alright,' He asked her.

She stared at her drink as though not knowing what to say. He himself was also stuck for words for he felt there was something she desperate wanted to tell him, but his perceptions of how he felt about her were now becoming entangle and his instincts were, just hold her, but he was afraid to.

'David I' she stammered, 'I'm not sure if Mike's concerned whether our marriage fails or not.'

Stunned by her words, he considered at that moment, being with her wasn't going to help matters. Even with his own emotions mixed up as they were, he dismissively asked. 'What makes you think that?'

Having had his suspicions, still he was a surprise, and it saddened him to hear her put it into words,.

As they gazed at each other, her beautiful eyes fill with tears, and as though she wanted to get everything out in the open, she suddenly blurted, 'Mike hasn't touched me for nearly a year, and I know he has been writing to an old girlfriend back home.'

Everything started to fall into place, Dave contemplated, the way she had come on to him after the New Year party, and the way she has been treating him over these months since they first met. The question running around in his head was, *has she been using me just to get back at Mike? or had she just been searching for a friend to comfort her?*

He put his hand on hers and with no words of wisdom to say, he hesitantly enquired, 'How do you know that? ... It might be a pal he was writing to.'

She studied his face, but didn't answer, and then as though finally knowing it to be true, she blurted out, 'Because I found some letters from her in his pocket.'

Stuck for words, nevertheless there was something in the way she spoke and looked at him that pulled the strings of his emotions and wouldn't let go. Unable to resist the frailness of her in that moment, and as she had done for him when in the depth of despair, he put his arm around her shoulder to comfort her.

Before he realised what was happening, she cuddled in and wrapped her arms around his neck. She started sobbing with tears of resignation that her marriage was failing. He ran his hand through her smooth hair and tried to console her, but her dismay engulfed him. His only thought at that moment was to protect her in any way he could.

After what seemed an eternity, she lifted her head and poured out her story of her fears and aspirations for her marriage. 'It had been a whirlwind affair, and we got married not long after that, he joined the army for the second time. I became pregnant with young Mike almost right away.' She then went on to say, 'it wasn't until two years later I found out from one of my own girlfriends that Mike had broken off with a girl months before we married,' And this she continued, 'Is the same girl he is writing to now.

'Are you sure it's not a relative he's writing to?' Dave stupidly inquired.

She shook he head, 'Looking back over our married life, I now realize, with some of the things he has done he probably never loved me.' She then went quiet

He stayed silent, there was nothing he could say, for who was he to give advice, when he had been on the receiving end as well. He realized then, that this was what was bringing them together and why they have these strong feelings for one another. Looking at her still sobbing, her shoulders hunched, he wondered. These feelings we have for one another will just have to burn themselves out in their own good time, if they ever will. But for now, the feeling's they had for one another was what both needed at that moment.

As though drawn to her plight, he kissed her at first on her brow, then on both eyes, they tasted sweet from the dampness of her tears. He then kissed her nose, cheeks and then her lips, lips that were waiting eagerly for him to reach. This kiss opened both their hearts and set off a reaction they couldn't hold back. From that moment Dave knew he wouldn't be able to resist her ever again, being with her he forgot all else.

Not wanting the magic of that moment to end, they kissed passionately and let their hands explore until they lost control of where the moment was taking them. Suddenly, she pushed away from him a little and breathing heavily looked long into his eyes, as though trying to fathom what he was thinking.

Easing herself away from his embrace she stood up looking flushed but glowing. With a wave of her hand across her face, smiling, she said, 'Whooo! I need to check the children and change out of these clothes.' She then disappeared into the bedroom.

He sat back into the soft cushions and sipped his drink, and went over in his mind all she had confided to him. In the quietness of the room, he felt his heart pounding in anticipation, not knowing what to expect. The last time he felt like this, he told himself, was because of the influence of the drink. But now sober, his feelings were much stronger than he had dared admit, and that in some way he felt he loved her. His blood by this time was pumping hard through his veins, raising his expectations.

This time, he convinced himself, there will be no turning back, after all, she's a beautiful woman. He then thought about all the hurt he had felt over the last few months and all that hurt mixed up with his own needs.

Like a young schoolboy waiting for his first taste of sex. He thought impatiently. *What is taking her so long? Has she taken the time to rethink what's happening and has decided we shouldn't go any further?'*

All the time his frustrations were building, he convinced himself, *I'll show you Jennifer; you played about behind my back before dumping me, even after I had kept myself for you. So why shouldn't I do the same?*

With his impatience about to burst Lynne walked back into the room wearing a bright yellow housecoat, which she held together with her left hand. His mind stopped playing games and all he could see in front of him was someone he was falling in love with. Coming round the table and sitting back down beside him, she folded her legs up under herself and said, 'That's better, I feel a lot cooler now.'

Sipping her drink, she looked at him and asked mischievously, 'What were you thinking about when I came back into the room.'

He blushed, and embarrassed about what he had been thinking, clumsily replied, 'I was thinking, you're the most beautiful woman I've ever known.'

She leaned forward and kissed him, as she did, she forgot to hold onto her housecoat and one side dropped open. Undaunted she said, 'Flatterer, I bet you say that to all your girlfriends.' Then realizing she had exposed a little of herself to him, giggling said, 'Ooops.'

Dave couldn't help but notice that all she was wearing under her housecoat was panties and that her breasts were partially exposed. She raised her hand as if to pull her housecoat to cover her body.

Without words and gaining in confidence, he put his hand up and stopped her. They both put our drinks down, and looking intently at each other, slowly but nervously moved their heads closer until they kissed, gently at first then with more passion. As he drew her to him, they slowly slid down until they were lying full out on the settee. He wanted to say something, like I love you, but he was so overwhelmed by the feel and the sweet smell of her body, that all thoughts went out of his head and all he wanted to do was make love to her.

Time seemed to slow down, and it was as though they had become oblivious to their surroundings, and could have been on a deserted island, so engrossed were they in each other. She started to undo the buttons of his shirt with her slim fingers, he winched at the coolness of her touch. As she was occupied with his shirt, he slid his hand under her housecoat and felt her silky-smooth warm flesh.

Shirt open, she impatiently tugged it aside and pressed her body onto him. At that moment feeling her bare breasts press against his chest, his hormones took over, and their kissing become more eager to be satisfied. Their hands began to explore each other's bodies when suddenly she stopped and stood up.

For an instant he thought, *what now, has she changed her mind again, or is she teasing me?*

She stood a moment looking down at him, by this time her housecoat was hanging open revealing her magnificent, curved body in all her glory, to him.

Reaching out her hand she said softly, 'Let's get comfortable.'

Chapter 57

Bed of Dreams

Taking his hand, she led him through to the spare room, as they entered she switched on the lamp, and the ceiling fan started turning slowly, cooling the room. Leading Dave over to the bed, she pushed him backwards until he was sitting on the edge.

Taking a step back she stood a moment, then ever so slowly let her housecoat slide slowly onto the floor. Standing legs astride she stared at him brazenly, as though saying, look at me, I'm yours. Then with her fingertips slipped under her knickers, wiggling her hips as she slipped them over her thighs and down her shapely legs until they lay on the floor. Stepping out she caught her toes on them and flicked them over to him. He caught them and sat mesmerized not able to break his gaze, as he took in all her beauty.

Never had he ever had a woman stand confidently in front of him displaying all her charms and letting him know how she felt about him in this way. His eyes remained on her, he could see by the manner she was smiling; she was enjoying his embarrassment, as he looked at her. She slowly came over to him and with mischief in her eyes, took his hands and said, 'It's your turn.'

Pulled him up off the bed, he stood embarrassed, 'I've never done this in front of a woman before, not even with Jennifer,' He felt his face heating up and turn scarlet.

Giggling mischievously, Lynne articulated as she sat down on the bed, 'Move back I want to see all of you.'

At first he felt awkward but with her smiling at him, he started nervously by kicking off his shoes and socks then removed his shirt. At this point she raised her hand and cried out like an excited schoolgirl, 'Slowly, slowly, slowly'

He proceeded slowly to remove his trousers until he stood with only his underpants on, and not sure what to do next. She again with her mischievous smile, growling playfully, 'Everything! I want to see all you've got.'

Slipping off his underpants, he stood for the first time in his life in front of a woman, completely naked, and feeling awkward. That could not be said about his manhood, which was rising to the occasion.

She gave a little smile as her gaze stopped at his growing prospects and yelled 'Wow!' Covering her mouth with the corner of the bed sheet like a veil, she giggled.

Now over his own embarrassment he stood for a moment and looked at her. Suddenly she stood up, hesitated, then quickly crossed the few paces over to him, threw her arms around his neck and embraced him. When her naked body pressed against him, his mind went into overdrive and by wriggling closer, his blood raced down to feed his sexual desires.

They kissed, and still in each other's embrace they somehow shovelled over to the bed and fell onto it. At that moment he thought he was in heaven, just lying there with this beautiful woman, who was caressing and stroking him as though wanting to keep him for herself. Letting his mind drift, he wondered. *If this is what true love is like. I like it.*

They explored each other's bodies until they knew them intimately. Arousing each other the way they were, his blood became inflamed. Their emotions and expectations increasing, their breathing became nervously erratic. He became inpatient and when Lynne whispered in his ear 'Love me David! love me!'

At that moment, he wasn't thinking of Lynne or of anyone else, except himself. Their lovemaking was frantic and didn't last as long as she may have wanted. As they lay, their bodies joined together, it was then he realized how selfish he had been, in his haste to satisfy his own needs, he hadn't worn anything to protect Lynne.

Raising his head and as he steadied his breathing, he said apologetically, 'I'm Sorry,'

'Why! Why should you be sorry?' she asked.

By this time with his nervousness gone, speaking calmly he said, 'I've been selfish and was not thinking of you. I was too busy thinking of myself, and I didn't wear anything to protect you. I'm sorry, for not thinking about your needs.'

She stroked his face and said with sympathy, 'I know. I know, but you have been through a lot lately.' Hesitating, she then kissed him gently and said, 'it's alright for I needed you too! So don't worry about it, I understand.' She then kissed him long and tenderly.

Lying there close enjoying the warmth they shared, they whispered loving words to each other. After a few more minutes holding onto his head, she looked deep into his eyes and kissed him again and whispered, 'next time it's my turn.'

Giggling she started caressing him in a way that started to make him aroused again. Putting her lips close to his ear, she bit his ear lobe softly and cheekily whispered, 'My we are impatient aren't we. But this time make it last longer.'

Smiling he looked at her, gave her a peck of a kiss and showing off, said, 'As long as you like, for I've got months of intense longings to catch up on.'

To this she replied, 'Oh! Goody,' and snuggled into him.

They then made love again but this time a gentler love than the first time, she guided him through all that she wanted him to do and where to touch her until their bodies moved together. All her moans of ecstasy only increased their lovemaking, and at that moment he was in heaven, and lost in her body.

How long they made love, he had no idea. All he knew was all those months of longing were being drawn from his body. Only after she gave a deep groan and let out a soft involuntary moan like scream, and he felt satisfied himself; did they lie still.

Sleep was far from their minds and after a time she aroused his expectations, and they made love once more until all their energies were spent, and then wrapped in each other's arms they fell asleep.

That night he slept soundly for the first time in a long time, and it was only a voice singing that wakened him. He looked out the window; it was still dark, and unable to see a clock he surmised it was still only around five in the morning. It was then he heard the shower running and heard Lynne humming to herself. That was the first time he had heard her sound so happy.

Rising from the bed, naked, he stood listening a few moments, then went to investigate. Entering the toilet, through the screen he could see she was standing under the shower with her back to him. Creeping over he pulled the screen back, stepped inside the shower and slipped his hands around her waist. She wriggled her hips, stopped singing, turning round to face him she beamed a smile that said, your mine. Jokingly she declared 'Your just in time. You wash my back, and I'll wash yours.'

That early morning, they made love again standing under the shower, with water cascaded down over them. In the quiet of the early morning the only sounds that could be heard apart from rhythmic noise of their bodies coming together, was Lynne's pleasurable moans, and this heightened their climax.

Once dressed and ready to leave, he gave her a long lingering kiss at the door and stood quietly gazing into her eyes, knowing what they had started, might be hard to stop. Before it was daylight, and the neighbours were out of their beds. He walked down the road with a newfound confidence. He feared nothing and his experience of the sex they had shared, made him feel that he had finally become a man, and knew then, this experience would stay with him always.

It was with a spring in his step that he marched quick time back to camp. Smitten was he, all the way back to camp his head was full of when he would see her again.

From that day on they met as often as they could. After dropped off the C.O. he occasionally met Lynne at a spot near her home when she was able, to arrange a babysitter to wait behind. Driving to a quiet place in the country, they spent an hour or two, talked and walked with arms entwined. Other times they just sat holding hands and observed the oriental scenes, women in the rice paddy fields, and the men ploughing the field with bullocks. Their best times though, were when he called later at night at her home, and they made love.

Growing close to one another, their conversations became more intimate, with Lynne confiding more of her feelings. One day, they took a room in a hotel in Seremban, but this proved not a romantic place, and they had to settle for the only way they could be together, was in her home. All this time he was more relaxed when seeing her and wanted to know all about her.

With all that was happening to them emotionally, he was still unsure where their affair was leading. He always felt Lynne was holding something back from him, and knowing that Mike was due home in a few days, this intensified their stolen moments. During this period, he started to feel a unease between them, that it might be their last time together.

Chapter 58

Mike's Back

Mike, having been away for over four weeks without a visit home to see his kids, finally returned. Even though it had been hard for Lynne and Dave, they agreed not to see one another. On the Saturday night of that week Mike brought Lynne along to Paroi NAAFI. As fate would have it Dave had to collect the C.O. from K.L. Airport, and because of delays he didn't get back until they had all gone home.

When he entered the NAFFI, his mates were still sitting having a beer. Standing at the bar being served, Derek joined him and said, 'Your lady friend was asking where you were? She didn't look too pleased when I told her you were away on duty, but Mike said he would catch you later in the week.'

With what Dave knew, he wasn't too worried seeing Mike again, and joked, 'Great, it will be nice to have a beer with a better class of bloke for a change.'

The next time he saw Mike was Wednesday, he was driving a Land Rover, and Dave's newfound confidence; when speaking to Mike, for once, he didn't feel guilty, as Lynne's name was only mentioned briefly in their conversation. Then he stated, 'I thought we might have met up with you last Saturday for a drink, but you were away.'

'I had to collect the C.O. from K.L. and didn't get back until after ten.' Dave said, and then asked, 'What's the position with Malacca?'

'It will be a few weeks before it's all finished. In the meantime, I'm back for spell, although I may be sent down from time to time,' Mike replied.

'Great then we can get together for a drink when you have time off,' Dave declared.

'Oh! Before I forget, thanks for looking in on the family to see they were alright,' he said casually, 'Lynne told me if I saw you to thank you for being the perfect gentleman when you escorted her and Alison over to the movie.'

Dave knew he was being sarcastic, so responded 'To be honest I felt a bit awkward, and a touch embarrassed with the comments I got from some of the lads,' and thinking of having a dig at him, he continued, 'next time make sure you bring her over yourself. Not that I didn't mind their company. But you know what I mean.'

'I know mate.' He replied, 'We were thinking about coming over this Friday night to see the Doris Day film, Lynne loves Doris Day movies so we might see you if your around.'

'Should make Friday ok! as the C.O. is going away for a week starting from tomorrow and I'll just have Captain Hansen to ferry about.'

'Good till then, must go.' He called out as he drove off.

Taking the C.O. up to K.L. next day, they had the company of his daughter Sandra, who had asked her Daddy as she called him, if Dave could show her some of the sights in K.L. So, after dropping Daddy at the Airport, he was driving around K.L. stopping and pointing out the sights, he then took her to Lee Chung's street side restaurant in China town, a place he had frequented when stationed at Wardieburn Camp.

Launch over, she asked, 'This has been the most exciting day I have had in a long time. What else can we see?'

'We should be getting back home.'

'It's still early and there must be lots to see?'

Dave thought a moment, 'We could go for a stroll in the Lake gardens. The flowers thrive nearly all year round in this tropical heat, and the gardens will be in full bloom. But after that, we must head back.' He insisted.

Before he had finished, she grabbed his hand and asked pleadingly, 'Can we? I love flowers.'

The drive to the gardens took a few minutes. Parking just outside the main entrance, Sandra like a little schoolgirl ran ahead the stopped. Her eyes were wide, filled with the wonder of the display of colours and at the number of different birds that flew around. That afternoon with no strings attached, Dave was thinking this is ok, and she's nice company. Letting her lead, he followed like a Coolly servant and seeing she was enjoying herself, he himself relaxed. After an hour, their walk over, they returned to their transport.

As he drove around the busy street heading to join the main road to Seremban, gushing at having had a nice day she expressed, 'I've had a wonderful day, I never ever thought I'd get to see as much of K.L. as you have shown me today.'

She then went and spoilt it all by saying, 'I bet you wished your girlfriend Jennifer was here and not me.'

Annoyed at her comment Dave stayed quiet.

Undaunted she went on 'Daddy, told me you loved her very much and now you have' she hesitated when he made no reply, then asked, 'Will you try to get back with her when you get back home?'

Trying to concentrate on the road and listen to her, he

shook his head, and still looking straight ahead answered indignantly 'If you don't mind, I don't want to talk about it,'

Annoyed that she had sked the question, and surprised at himself, how the question had hit deep down, their conversation dried up. By the time they were well on the road to Seremban, words spoken were mostly about the countryside.

Dropping her off at her home, nothing was said, she just ran into the house. It was another two days later that he had to take Mildred the C.O.'s; wife into town and Sandra accompanied them that morning. Conversation quiet to start, with only Mildred asking how he was, but then, Sandra sitting in the rear shouted over the noise of the engine, 'I forgot to thank you for the wonderful day I had in K.L. and I'm sorry for having brought up the subject of your girlfriend.'

Mildred scolded her, 'I told you not to be nosey.' then turning to Dave, 'I hope she didn't upset you?'

'It's all right, she was just being friendly, but I took it the wrong way.' After that, they got on ok.

With the C.O. away for a while, Dave's duties were few and one good thing he thought, '*I don't need to listen to Sandra's questions.*'

Chapter 59

In Limbo

Captain Hansen only needing a lift to Paroi Camp and back to his home, Dave with no other duties except to wait on his call the days stretched and with nothing to keep him occupied except skive, this gave him plenty time to idly think of Lynne.

With Mike back home and unable to see Lynne on her own, he restricted meeting them only if they were together, but even then, that didn't stop him catching her sneaking looks at him, or purposely brushing her hand against his as they passed each other. He stopped staying at their house over the Saturday nights for he couldn't lie next room, knowing that they were lying together.

A little jealousy was creeping into him, and he didn't like what was happening, and it must have started to show, for one day Mike asked, 'what's with you Mate, you seem to be avoiding us. Lynne keeps on asking me if we have had a disagreement.'

Shrugging his shoulders, 'Nothing's the matter.' He lied, and then trying not to give away his true feelings, 'sometimes things get on top of me, and I just retreat into my shell.' He couldn't say what he wanted, *'my body was craving to make love to your wife again, could he.'* He told himself.

On Friday just before launch he arrived back to camp after having dropped the O.C. off. A quick dinner, then decided to have a kip for a while as he didn't feel like company after yesterday. He was still unsure of himself after the way he had reacted to Sandra questions. He felt the torch for Jennifer was still burns inside him. Looking at her photos it all came back again. Slipping them into his bedside drawer he wondered, *'how long am I going to feel like this?'* He closed his eyes and drifted off, sleep he desperately needed as the last few nights he had been having trouble sleeping.

It was Derek rattling on his door that woke him up, looking at the room clock he realised he must have been sleeping for over three hours. 'Teatime Dave,' Derek said as he shook him.

'Yip! I'm getting up,' he replied.

Derek was a good mate and had stood by him even when he had turned his back on everyone. Of all the lads in the camp Derek knew him best and knew what he had been through and what he was still going through.

Walked down to the canteen Derek asked, 'Going to the pic's the night?'

'Na. I don't feel like it,' Dave said, 'I think I'll just go for a drink, or the way I feel right now, I might just go into town.'

'Oh, no you won't, not this time, you're going to the pics, then the NAAFI for a nightcap,' retorted Derek. Then continuing he said, 'Dave you have to let go or it's going to drive you round the bend.' Then trying to cheer him up, 'Anyway Lynne's coming over, so Mike tells me. I know how you two get on, so let's forget about everything and have a good time tonight.'

'If only Derek knew what was going on between Lynne and I,' Dave thought.

The cinema was nearly full by the time Mike and Lynne arrived, spotting Dave near the back, they crossed over and asked, 'No seats left for us?'

With only one seat left beside him, Dave was about to stand up, but Derek jumped up first, 'Here take mine, I'll stand at the back.'

Lynne sat down first leaving the seat beside Dave empty, making out she wants Mike to sit there, but Mike growled, 'Move along, you sit next to Dave.'

She looked at Dave with the kind of look he had grown to love; she then slid along until very close, so close he could feel his body tense as she moved her leg, brushing against his. Earlier he was thinking about Jennifer, now sitting here beside Lynne, all he could think of, was getting into bed with her.

Once the lights dimmed, moving her hand she brushed over his leg until she held his hand. As they stole that moment he couldn't care less if anyone saw what they were doing. All during the movie she kept moving her leg against his, watched the film was far from their thoughts and sat stealing the pleasure of each other's touch, until the movie was over, and the lights came on

Rain was streaming down when they came out of the cinema, this meant a mad rush over to the NAAFI. which was about fifty yards away.

Dave decided to stick to soft drinks while in Lynne's company. Mike seeing what he was drinking challenged him, 'What's this, lemonade? No beer tonight?'

'No,' Dave countered, and remembering their next football match, lied, 'I'm in training again for the team, we have an important match coming up and Duffy is struggling for players, with some of the lads have moved away. I need to get fit'

'Quite right David,' Lynne butted in.

'Come on, a pint won't hurt you.' Mike sarcastically teased.

'No, I'm sticking to my guns, and if I get drunk tonight it will be because somebody' pointing at Mike, 'has put something in my drink.' Dave said decisively in a voice of bluster, and knowing Lynne was looking on, it was more to impress her!

At the end of the night Mike asked, 'Coming back to our place for a chat, you could stay overnight.'

Lynne stood behind Mike nodding her head in agreement, but Dave felt tonight he just wanted to stay there, 'Maybe tomorrow night if you don't have any other plans.'

Lynne out of ear shot of the other lads she whispered, 'Why not come around in the afternoon and have tea with us.' She gave him the kind of look he couldn't resist and then to cover herself she continued with, 'Young Michael will be glad to see you, he keeps asking when you are coming to visit him.'

'Ok'! Dave exclaimed, and was going to say more, but decided not to.

'That's settled then, we'll expect you tomorrow afternoon.' Mike confirmed, and seemed pleased. As they parted, knowing Dave, Lynne made him promise he definitely would be at their house next day.

Chapter 60

Family Time

The afternoon started with Dave playing on the grass with young Michael, and little Virginia, now walking on her own couldn't resist joining in. As Dave played with the kids, Lynne was sitting watching them rolling about the grass. Mike meanwhile disappeared into the house. Lying on his back looking up at the sky, Dave felt relaxed. Lynne, unable to resist joining in the fun came over and knelt beside him. With a glint in her eyes she said with some contentment, 'I don't think I've seen you this happy before. A family life suits you.'

Mike came out from the house at that moment and joined them, seeing Dave was quite cheerful, said, 'This is what you have been needing Dave, just getting away from army life for a while.'

Obviously not aware what Lynne and he had been up to while he had been away, Dave went along with him saying, 'It's been awhile since I've felt this contented.' Seeing young Michael was still full of beans, Dave jumped up and changing the subject asked, 'Who wants to go for a walk?'

'Me, me, me,' called the kids,

'What about you two?' Dave asked.

'Not me,' groaned Mike, 'you all go! I'll just sit here with my beer.'

'Come on, the walk will do you good, get rid of the beer belly your starting to put on.' Dave chided unconvincingly, and tried again to talk him into coming, but he was stubborn, even after being told, 'It's only for half an hour.'

'Take your time I've got plenty beer here since you have stopped drinking.' He countered.

Dave carried Michael on his shoulders, while Lynne carried Virginia. They set off down the road until they reached the main road. Walking beside her he couldn't take his eyes off her, and catching him observing her, she smiled, gave him a reassuring look, and said, 'I'm happy you came. I've missed your company.'

Further along the road he pointed out to the kids some brightly coloured birds, green pigeons, Bee-eaters, parrots, Sultan tit and Flycatchers that are abundant in these parts. He was waiting for Lynne to say something, but she stayed quiet. He thought maybe she's just enjoying their time together as her relaxed look, said it all. Further along the road they came to a dirt track path about eight feet wide that travelled into the woods.

'Who wants to go into the jungle?' He asked,

'Me,' shouted Michael,

Lynne shivered as she said, 'I'm not sure, you never know what you will find in there. There might be creepy, crawly things.'

'Mummy's frightened,' Dave said to Michael, 'What do you think we should do?'

'I want to go into the Jungle,' he cried out.

'Ok. We'll explore this big Jungle.' Dave winked at Lynne and went along the path for about thirty yards, stopped, and said, 'Listen and tell me what you hear?'

It was cool in the shade, and they could hear all sorts of noises from Crickets, frogs, and hooting from some monkeys in the distance and some rustling in the undergrowth. As they neared a thick bush, a flock of Fruit Doves took flight, rustling as their wings brushed the leaves. They stood quietly and little Michael's mouth opened wide as he stared at what he saw. Lynne, having seen they were just a short distance in, plucked up courage and joined them just as the last Dove disappeared. Coming closer, she grabbed his arm.

Michael's attention now back with them, seeing his mum had ventured in, shouted, 'Mummy I'm in the jungle.'

Lynne slipped closer and taking Dave's hand said, 'I'm very frightened in here, so I'll need to hold Uncle David's hand.'

Little Michael giggled, enjoying being braver than his mum. Virginia being too young was much quieter and hardly made a noise. They all stood, Lynne close beside him holding his hand tightly, listening to the sounds all around them and let their imaginations fly with the doves. In that tranquil moment Dave leaned close to Lynne and unexpectedly whispered. 'I love you.'

She looked long at him, taking in what he had said, and with eyes smiling brightly, she whispered, 'I love you too.' At that they gazed into each other's eyes and the jungle noises disappeared.

Back at the house Michael excitedly told his dad about the walk, and of how he had been in the Jungle. Dave felt good hearing him so happy, and it rubbed off on them all. As it was still warm, Lynne took the kids away for a nap leaving Mike and Dave sitting outside reminiscing the good times they had together, during the last fourteen months.

Dave, listening to Mike talking, realized that their friendship had stuck firm even with all the things he had done in the past, which he disagreed with, especially his treatment of Lynne. Mike, never at any time, told him to mind his own business. But now, he wasn't sure if he was being used as a means of breaking up their marriage, which he felt was inevitable. But even though their marriage hadn't turned out how they had wanted, seeing them together now, and staying together because of the kids, they outwardly look good friends, and still help each other.

All the time they were sitting outside, Lynne was in the kitchen preparing the food for dinner. As Dave didn't have a glass in his hand, Mike said, 'I made up some orange juice for you, it's in the Fridge if you want some.'

'Good idea! It's thirsty work sitting out here'

Lynne smiled as he entered, then queried, 'You seem different today. Is it because of playing with the kids and being here, or have you at last got back to your old self, and over your problems?'

'A bit of both, I think. Seeing you looking happy has helped me to see there's more to life than worrying about things I've no control over.' he replied.

She put the plates she had in her hand down and walked over to him, and with a sigh whispered, 'Right now,' she hesitated, 'I wish I was going to be the one you will settle down with, as when I'm with you I lose all my inhibitions. I've never felt this relaxed in anyone's company as I am in yours. But I fear!' Her eyes glazed over, 'I won't be the one you'll stay with, as we both know what is happening between us.'

Mike, sitting outside during this time, and being out of sight, she pressed close to Dave, put her arms around his neck and kissed him tenderly. At that moment he couldn't care less if Mike walked in and caught them, for he just loved having her in his arms and feeling her body next to his.

She whispered playfully in his ear, 'You know I could grow

to love you if you stuck around long enough.' Then looking into his eyes she continued, 'but I've a feeling that we only have this short time together, and I wish it could be longer!'

Surprised by what she had implied, he gazed into her eyes, and understood the wisdom in what she said. He replied, 'You've been my guardian angel. If it hadn't been for you, I don't think I would have sorted myself out and back to as I am now,' he choked, 'For that, I'll always love you for being there for me......Whatever happens from now on, I'll remember you for the rest of my life, especially this moment, when we mean so much to each other.' Then hesitating he smiled, and then teasingly said, 'Anyway what do you mean, grow to love me. I thought you did?'

A tear came into her eyes, and he kissed them away. She then kissed him with such tenderness that he wanted to hold onto her forever, and with a knowing smile she then said in a gentle intimate voice. 'I do love you.'

Standing in that embrace a moment longer he gave her a hug and they laughed, a little louder than they thought they had.

Going back outside, Mike turned to look at him as he asked, 'What was that all about?'

Dave quickly thought, and replied, 'Oh! Lynne was fixing the salad and I told her there was a big green worm swimming about the bowl and she dropped everything.'

With a touch of sarcasm Mike rasped, 'Hope she only dropped the knife and fork and nothing else?' He then smiled when he saw the guilt look and blush on Dave's face.

It was with comments like that, that made Dave wonder, if he was playing a game with them. He shrugged his shoulders, as he couldn't care less what Mike thought.

Minutes later, Lynne joined them outside, having tidied herself up and looked her beautiful self, Dave winked at her. She blushed and sat down beside Mike who started the conversation about when they move down to Malacca. 'The O.C. said that everybody may be transferred down there eventually. You might be as well?'

Seeing this subject was not to Lynne's taste, Dave changed the subject, 'You never know, I might be.' Then lying back he confided, 'It's been a long time since I felt as good as I feel the now, and I can finally get on with my life, so I intend to enjoy the remainder of my time in Malaya, wherever I'm posted.'

Mike asked, 'Now you've settled down, what are your plans for the rest of your time here?'

Dave, lay on his back, and looking up at the clear blue sky, said, 'Up until a few months ago I used to enjoy travelling around taking photos of the old temples, and places I've visited. I think I'll get back to that again, as there is still a lot to see out here, and I may never get an opportunity like this again.' He paused before finally saying, 'I'm now beginning to see this country in a different light'

When Dave turned his head to look at them, they were both smiling. Mike leaned forward and stuck his hand out in friendship saying, 'Welcome back mate.'

Chapter 61

Mike Leaves Again

On the twenty-fourth of September, Mike and Andy both moved down to Malacca Camp leaving Paroi Camp, Seremban, and their families. Mike's last words to Dave were, 'Look after Lynne and the kids for me will you? I don't know when or how often I'll get back up, as it's over sixty miles away, and it will depend on what transport is available.'

They shook hands, 'Don't worry Mike. I'll, look in on them from time to time to see how they are coping.'

Lynne and the kids, along with Alison and her son, were in Paroi camp to see Mike and Andy off. As the trucks moved away from the camp, it was like they were going for good. The kids cried, but there were no tears in Lynne's eyes. Dave invited them all into the NAAFI for a cool drink, and while Lynne and Dave sat drinking theirs, Alison offered to take the kids for Ice cream. As she walked away, she grinned as if to say, 'I know what's going on?'

Seeing Dave was uncomfortable, Lynne patted his hand, 'It's alright Dave, Alison won't tell?'

'How much does she know about us?'

She didn't answer his question directly, just said, 'She's been a good friend to me, that's all I will say.'

When it was time for them to go, Lynne asked if he could take them home, with the C.O's. permission he got them all into the Land Rover and drove them back to the married quarters. Alison and her son got out first and then he drove round to Lynne's house. As they got out of the Land Rover, wee Michael grabbed Dave's hand and pulled at him shouting, 'Come see my pet lizard.'

Dave tried to say he hadn't time but Lynne pleaded, 'He's been wanting to show you his pet lizard for ages.' So, he gave in to him and followed him up to the house. As he did, he couldn't help feeling Lynne had planned this.

Once inside and he had seen his pet lizard, which turned out to be one of the many little Chitchats that run all over the walls. Lynne joined them and touching his arm said with a little nervousness in her voice, 'Are you coming over tonight for a drink or a coffee or.' She stopped and just looked at him.

He wanted to say yes, but instead asked without thinking, 'What's going on between you and Mike? I feel like the pig in the middle with my strings being pulled.' He observed her and saw her smile disappear, then continued, 'Lynne, are you using me to get back at Mike or is something else going on?' Why he asked, he didn't quite know, but he struck something within her.

Stepping back from him she said in a petulant voice, 'Don't come then if you don't want to,' and turned her back on him. It seemed so final, he turned and was walking out when he heard wee Michael asking, 'Why are you crying mummy?

Dave, unsure what had just happened, continued out of the house, and drove off wondering, *Why is she so upset*? They had never had a cross word before, but her tone of voice was something new to him, and made him think, *I don't need this again*. Putting his foot down on the accelerator, he continued his journey back to the camp.

That night, after dropping the O.C. off, as he passed the entrance to the married quarters he hesitated, but stubbornly drove past, and with fewer troops left in the camp now, he spent a miserable night back in the NAAFI, but settled for a soft drink instead of beer.

Derek sitting beside him teased, 'You're quiet tonight. Hope you are not going to go through all that again.'

'No!' He went quiet a few minutes, 'Just taking stock and trying to work out where I go from here,' Dave replied.

'Ha! Heard that somewhere before. Have you had any word from home recently?' Derek asked.

'Yes. But mums letter didn't make very good reading, so I didn't finish it,' He paused, 'At times I don't know where I'm going and now even out here I seem to get myself into position that only confuse me.'

'Are you talking about, you know who?'

'Yes, I suppose you could say I'm a bit confused over her,' Dave mumbled. 'After I received that letter from Jennifer, I just wanted to take it out at the world and didn't want to get attached to anyone again?' Hesitating, he shook his head, 'I really don't know how I feel about Lynne. I only know she is married and I'm not sure how I've got myself into this situation.'

Derek clapped his back in a buddy fashion and said philosophically, 'Mate, I wished I had your kind of problem, for there aren't many women as beautiful as Lynne out here,' Then jokingly, 'All I think about is getting back home to where all the real women are. London!'

After a period of silence supping their drinks, they changed the subject. Some of the other lads joined them and the atmosphere took on a different meaning for the rest of the night.

Chapter 62

Some R. and R.

Over the next two days and nights, Dave conveyed the C.O. to various places to organize the rundown of the 230 Signal Squadron. Those nights he was either sitting outside some officer's mess, or some other office, waiting to ferry the C.O. to his next appointment.

Because of these late nights, the C.O's wife Mildred organized a late supper for him before returning to camp. At the end of the third day, having been on call on what seemed nonstop running about for twelve hours. The C.O, in a quieter moment, confided in him that he and his family would be returning home to England in ten days' time.

Three nights before the C.O. was due to leave, he expressed to Dave, 'I'm having a bit of a party tonight, and I want you to come round to my home.'

An order is an order, and as Dave thought he might be needed to take some of the guests home afterwards, he duly found himself attending in body only, as his mind was elsewhere.

As the evening progressed, with so many brass officers there. In between helping to serve drinks to the guests, he found himself sitting out on the porch most of the night with Sandra, Dave felt that that was the only reason he had been asked round, to keep Sandra company. She herself was also returning home, in her case, to study medicine at University.

Their conversations centred around her time here in Malaya, and the day he spent with her in K.L.

She apologized again for that day, 'I'm very sorry I ruined it when I mentioned Jennifer's name that day. It was stupid and I hope you have forgiven me?'

'It's all in the past now, so don't worry about it.' He responded.

'I'm glad! Daddy said he had noticed a change in you, and Mum and Daddy were worried for you for a while. How are you feeling now?'

He gave a wry smile, 'It's all right now, as I've got over it.'

She relaxed. 'I'm glad for you, that your settled in your own mind. We all noticed a difference in you from the first time I net you, but after you got that letter you changed a lot, you were quieter, and didn't smile as much.'

Dave went quiet, as he didn't know what to say, he hadn't thought what other people had thought of him, as he had been in a destructive mood, during those days, and knew he wasn't good company for anyone. For her part she just sat looking at him thinking she had said too much.

Dave thought to make excuses, but just said, 'Sorry if I offended you at any time, I know things got a little out of hand and I did and said things, that I regret now, but I have come to accept that it's all over between Jennifer and myself. I just have to move on.'

After listening, she asked, 'What are your plans for when you leave the army?'

With no definite plans he replied, 'I may come back out this way to New Zealand, I've had an offer of a job and a place to stay. But first I have to go home and face my demons and see if I might settle back home.'

That night before leaving to go back to camp, he said goodbye to Sandra and wished her all the best in her studies.

The party finished very late, and after taking a few of the guests home Dave arrived back at camp around 3 a.m.

With the C.O. now away and Captain Hansen not needing him as much, he was informed he had some leave coming to him. He thought about staying there in camp and trying to see Lynne again, but decided that it might be better taking a holiday and cooling off a bit. Singapore seemed the logical place, so without informing anyone, or his mates, he set off by train down to Singapore.

On arrival his New Zealand mate Walt fix him up for four nights at Minden Barracks. As he couldn't stay there any longer than four, he booked in for three nights at the Britannia Club where he could laze around the swimming pool.

The first four days he went sightseeing, and the nights, along with Walt and two of his mates were hectic. culminating in being thrown out of the Raffles Hotel, not from inside, because they only managed to get their feet into reception hall before being thrown out again.

On his last night in Singapore, out with the lads and with too much drink they ended down at a notorious place called Boogie Street, the street of Brothels. A street of a thousand smells where even the rats are trying to fleece you. Dave at first was very reluctant to enter, but with having had too much alcohol, plus his three mates egging him on, they entered one of the brothels.

It was dark, fusty, and smelt like to much cooking or other things had taken place. The smell of fried rice and Oriental spices drifted along passageways that were narrow throughout the building. They were ushered into a big room, where sitting on big cushions in front of them where all the girls that didn't have a client at that moment. Even with all the drink they had had, it seemed to them that all the best-looking girls were on holiday or had been picked first. As they joked, 'a brown paper bag can make an ugly girl into a princess.'

They joked again about who would get lumbered with the ugly one. At that time, Dave believed they were all identical twins. Picking his partner Dave was ushered along the corridor and into a very narrow cubicle. Looking through his beer filled eyes, the girl he had chosen had a fine sturdy body.

Draping her sort of housecoat over a chair, she lay on the bed on her back like a big slice of meat and opening her legs wide and tried to say very romantically, 'Me velly beautiful no, You hurry, you quickie time jigjig. I velly busy girl.'

Dave tried to focus on the prostitute lying there exposing all her charms to him, and all he could think of was, *this is like a pigsty,* and then looking at her again, *god you are ugly,* and that was with him drunk. Trying to strip he fumbled with his buttons, laughed and the more he tried to drop his trousers the more he giggled at the thought of what he was trying to do.

She became annoyed and kept shouting at him. 'You hurry, hurry. Me velly busy girl?'

His trousers dropped to the floor, and as he took his underpants down. He looked down at his limp Willie, and tried to bring life into it with his friend Palm, but it was to no avail, having had too much to drink his best endeavours could not get Willie up from his slumber. All he could hear was her screaming, trying to hurry him on. With the sounds of whoever was next cubical grunting and groaning, again he had visions of big fat pigs copulating. It all seemed to be too much of a effort.

She called him over, grabbing hold of his Willie and tried to speed things up, but all he could do was laugh as she pulled and pushed, but her best efforts were to no avail. Willie was not for playing, and this made her angry knowing all her beauty had failed to make Willie stand to attention. She let loose a tirade of words in Cantonese, then threw his clothes at him.

As he struggled to put his clothes on, he couldn't stop himself laughing, and staggered out the room still fixing his clothes, the only words he could make out as he left were. 'You boyar, You boyar.'

He left that prostitute having failed in her duty still shouting at him as he stumbled his way to the exit where the others joined him outside. None of them were about to tell the truth what had happened in the brothel, so the talk was all about how they had ridden those prostitutes silly.

Walking, or should be said, staggering up the street they were all having a good laugh when Walt asked. 'What was your Sheila like Dave?'

'Not bad if you were blind and desperate.' Dave giggled.

'But we were desperate mate,' Walt slurred.

Dave couldn't stop laughing, and not wanting to admit that he couldn't raise his manhood, he mumbled, 'Well I was desperate, and she was ugly as sin, but she liked me so much she kept shouting you Boyar, you Boyar, all the time I jumped her.'

One of the other lads put his arm around Dave's shoulder. Mate, she wasn't complimenting you on your sexual proficiency. She was shouting, you big baby, you big baby.'

At that Dave came clean and told them what really happened, and the air filled with their laughter as they staggered out of Boogie Street.

Before that night, the last few days had been spent mostly wandering around Singapore and with time on his hands tried to put his life into perspective. He felt quite at ease within himself and confident that whatever twists happen in his life, from then on, he would be able to live with it. The only other thing on his mind during that time, he missed Lynne, and wished she and the kids were with him visiting The Tiger Balm Gardens and sights around Singapore.

On his last full day before catching the night train, lying by the Britannia Club poolside soaking up the sun, he wondered what Lynne would think of him for not telling her he was going away?

The holiday over, he travelled back up overnight to Seremban. That Long journey up country turned out to be his last time he would travel on the night train up north, as his time here was wearing on, and the days left on his calendar were getting fewer by the day, and it wouldn't be long till he was going home.

Chapter 63

Resistance is Low

Arriving back at Paroi Camp early next morning, tired, hungry, and desperately in need of a cool shower, only to find the place like a ghost town, as more lads had left the camp during his absence. Entering his Basher room things had been changed, new curtains for the windows, probably taken from some of the other NCO rooms, he thought, *very homely, wonder who was responsible?*

As his eyes grew accustomed to the dull interior, an envelope lying on the top of his bed caught his attention. The note was from Lynne, in it, she was asking why he hadn't been round to see how they were doing. She sounded a bit apprehensive with the way she had written her note. Having another two days before going back on duty, he decided he'd better go see her later.

After lunch he walked to the married quarters, not knowing what to expect. *Maybe she has cooled on me* he thought. Arriving at her house it was quiet, and with most of the husbands having already been transferred, it was a ghost estate. Moving up to her front door he imagined, *maybe they have moved down to Malacca while I was away.* Knock, knock, his heartbeat faster. It seemed forever before the door opened, and once their eyes meet, whatever problem there had been, vanished when they saw one another.

'David!' She said in surprise, then paused and looked at him with a quizzical expression.

'Aren't you going to ask me in?' He asked.

'Come in, come in!' She said delightfully.

He was no sooner in the door when she took his hands and kissed him casually on the cheek, then hesitated another moment, looked into his eyes as though uncertain what next. Instinctively he pulled her to him, kissed her lips gently, still she felt hesitant. He then with more passion kissed her again. This time it was as though they hadn't seen each other for years, and her lips were warm and ready to meet his.

'The kids,' He panted.

'They are in bed having their afternoon nap,' she whispered in his ear.

They kissed again then she stood back, shook her head, then with a hint of annoyance in her voice asked, 'Where have you been? I was worried about you, for no one had seen you for ages.' Then giving him a sober look, continued, 'Why has it taken you so long to come to see me?' she paused again, 'I thought you had grown tired of me.'

Sensing frustration and anger in her voice he apologised, 'I'm sorry! After that last night I needed some time to think.' Feeling she wasn't satisfied, he reasoned, 'I know, I should have let you know.' Still trying to justify himself to her he hesitated before saying. 'I had some leave due to me and went to Singapore for the week, and I had also promised my mate stationed in Singapore that I would see him before he went home to New Zealand.'

Looking into her eyes he could see that she wasn't accepting his reason, 'It was a spur of the moment thing, he's offered

331

me a job beside him and I just might take up his offer, and immigrate out to New Zealand later.' Shrugging his shoulders, 'I just took the chance when I had it.'

She took his hand and led him into the living room where they both sat down on the settee. He could see what he had said, had made her think, but what he couldn't work out. He then thought, maybe she's just lonely and wanted some company.

'What are you doing for the rest of today,' she asked.

'I'm here and have nowhere else to go, so what do you want to do?' He asked.

She smiled and leaned nearer, and their lips met. When he was with her like this, he felt like a thief, the excitement of stealing these moments, it seemed to be a turn on for them both. Before long, they were into heavy petting and getting excited by the second, 'what if the kids.'

Before he could finish saying, 'walks in,' she planted a kiss on his lips so he couldn't continue. Pulled back from her he giggled, 'Is this how it's always going to be whenever we get together?'

Cheekily she replied, 'If you want it to be.'

Her answer had him thinking, *'Heaven. Just heaven.'*

After some more petting like two lovebirds, she asked, 'How long can you stay? Can you stay for tea?'

'There's no way you could get me to leave,' He replied with a smile.

Playfully she then said, 'Even if I said that I didn't want you to stay.'

He stood up, and kidding he was leaving saying with a hint off playful resignation, 'If that's what you want?' then with a touch of melodrama he continued, 'I will get out of your life forever.'

She grabbed his hand and pulled him back down and said

boastfully, 'After all we have been through? You're mine till you return home.'

He smiled, 'Will I be in a fit state to go home if we continue like this.'

She playfully punch him, the bruise took days to disappear. After a little more larking about, they collapsed together in laughter. That afternoon while the kids slept, they lay on their love bed explored each other's bodies, made love, and let the world pass bye.

The next six weeks, the attraction for one another that was pulling them together seemed to intensify, and they couldn't be together without having sex. Often, he sneaked into her house without the neighbours seeing him, even thought by now most of Lynne's neighbours knew all about their marriage, and it consoled him with the fact that some were happy for Lynne. Each moment spent together, she filled his heart more and Jennifer was pushed further away.

When Mike did manage to get home, nothing was said, and they still got on well as mates, even going out in a threesome. If any rumours got to him, he never let on. Dave felt for Lynne, but he was beginning to think that Mike had his plans well made out before he came on the scene.

Dave and Lynne continued their relationships as often as they could. On his days off, they took the kids to Port Dickson on the local bus, to play on the beach. Other times they just went site seeing and just being together was all that seem to matter. They knew the day was fast approaching when she and the kids would have to move down to Malacca, but that was never mentioned. It seemed in their own world they were happy, and were both living for the day and not thinking about tomorrow.

Chapter 64

Fleeting Moments

On Mike's next trip home on the twentieth of October, they were both sitting outside having a beer when he said as though in a passing thought, 'The houses down in Malacca will be finished in the next ten days. I'll then come back here to help Lynne and the kids move down.'

His comment struck a blow, but Dave did his best not to let on it bothered him in case he was being tested. Dave, looking sympathetically, said, 'It should be good having the family beside you, as I'm sure you have been missing the kids.'

'I suppose so! But it won't be much fun for Lynne though, as my duties will take me away for days at a time.'

Still the same old Mike, Dave thought, and glancing at him as he replied. 'But at least they will see more of you than they have over these last few months?

Mike was less than enthusiastic in his reply, 'I suppose there is that.'

Dave stared at him, and wanted to say more but thought better of it. He then pondered, *now I know why Lynne has been so quiet and distant when I arrived today.* Time has caught up with them, and it didn't appear she was looking forward to leaving.

After dinner Dave, not having a chance to speak to Lynne on her own, made the excuse that he had to collect the O.C. later that night, and left.

Mike only stayed that day and went back down to Malacca early next morning.

Knowing he had left, that night, Dave wasn't sure if he should go to see her. In the end he didn't need to. Being movie night in the camp she and Alison arrived at Paroi camp to see the movie.

The movie was of no interest to Dave as his attention kept sliding towards Lynne, who was sitting across from him. Unable to take his eyes off her, and for her part she kept looking over at him as though trying to say something, it was obvious they both wanted to be somewhere else. Making the excuse he had to collect the O.C., he slipped out the side door and stood awhile outside. Moments later Lynne came out and crossed over to join him.

As he took her hand, the way she spoke he knew she was feeling anxious, 'David, I'm so mixed up, I don't know what to think now. I thought I would be able to just move away, and all would be alright, but now that day is nearly here, I'm not so sure it's what I want to do.'

Her remarks baffled him as it was she who always seemed to be in control, and he was the one that wasn't sure of himself. Now though it would seem she was just as emotionally mixed up as he was.

Looking at each other, he could see by her uneasiness that it may not be that easy to break apart, and he sensitively said. 'We knew this day would come. I know it's going to be hard for us, but I wan't you to know you have done so much for me, and I hope that when we part, we will always remember this time with only good memories.' He wasn't sure if what he had said was the right thing or not.

Tears formed in her eyes as she whispered sadly, 'I'm going to miss you an awful lot. I just wish we.'

This time it was Dave who put his finger over her mouth to stop the words he was afraid to hear. In his own head he hadn't made up his mind what he'd really like to happen. 'What did Alison say? Is she alright in there?'

Lynne shook her head and replied, 'She is sitting with two of your mates enjoying the movie.'

With the camp being so quiet, and without another word he took her hand, and not thinking of the consequences led her to his Basher room, that was only a short distance. Standing in the centre, she had tears in her eyes, they kissed in a nervous way, comforting each other. Nervously he disrobed her and holding her hand, led her over to his bed.

She lay down on the fresh cool sheets and watched him undress. Once on the bed he pulled the Mosquito net down around them. Feeling the warmth of her body close to his and wanting to hold on to what they had, they made love, a love that at first was tender but became more desperate with each passing minute.

So engrossed were they in each other, they forgot the time. It was the knock on the door that reminded them where they were.

A voice softly called from outside. It was Derek 'The movies over Dave...... Alison's waiting for Lynne.'.

As they reluctantly dressed, he said, 'We still have at least another week before we have to stop seeing each other.'

Tears flowed down her face, 'Can't you come with me to my place tonight?'

'I can't, not with all the camp watching.'

'Later then.' She urged.

'I can't. Maybe tomorrow night.' He insisted.

She seemed resigned, and their kiss before leaving his room was brief but tender. He took her hand and led her the long way around the camp to avoid being seen.

Alison was waiting impatiently by the Guardhouse. In the darkness of the night, they kissed again, and parted a distance from the Guard house so as not to cause any suspicion. He watched her walk down the last few yards and found himself thinking, *what a fantastic woman and she has been mine these past weeks.*

Chapter 65

We Say Good-bye

The next five days flew in, and he couldn't meet her as often as he would have liked, then before they knew it, the last night had arrived. He finished early that day as he wasn't needed to drive. Making the excuse that he was helping them pack, on arrival, he learned that Mike wasn't coming back for another two days, and it would be another few days after that before they left. So, it was more of what time they could get to themselves rather than what belongings they could pack.

He stayed those extra nights with her, but sleep was far from their minds. Into the early morning, they talked of each other's aspirations and of what life might bring them, they promised not to forget one another and to write to each other. After the kids were in bed, they lay together exploring each other's bodies. As she said, 'Once we part, all we have to do, is close our eyes to feel their presence? They then made love together as though, the world was about to end. Then exhausted they lay together till sunrise.

One early morning before leaving her to walk back to camp, holding her in his arms, he said, 'If love has two faces then you would be both, as you have been my world these last few months and the reason I am, who I am today. I'll always treasure our time together, and I hope we will always be able to see each other again.'

Tears were flowing from her eyes that morning as she said to him before he left, 'David, I hope you will always remember me.' Then continuing she softly whispered in his ear, 'you will always be here in my heart.' As she spoke she crossed both hands over her chest. He looked at her breasts and wondered, *will I ever find the same comfort again as she has given me.*

'I'll see you again, I know in my heart I will.' He promised.

The long walk back to camp that early morning was hard going. Having expended so much of his energy through the night, he wished he had had the day off to catch up on lost sleep. But for his sins, he would only have two and half hours before he had to collect the O.C., only enough time to freshen up, change cloths and have a bit of breakfast before going on duty.

His thoughts at that moment as he willed his weary legs on, were all of Lynne, but not in any way that it would break his heart when they said goodbye. He was his own man now and had more command of his feelings. His thoughts were more in hope she will find real happiness wherever she goes, for she had been so good for him over the most difficult time in his life.

The O.C, kept him busy with all the coming and goings. During that time Dave had to hang around, sometimes in the blazing heat for ages, then travel to other camps. It was a hectic time for everyone concerned, and in the end, he only managed to be in her company for no more than a few minutes.

On the day they were to leave, he put a request into the O.C to have time off to see them before they left. As luck would have it, as he wasn't needed on that day, the O.C kindly gave him permission.

He arrived about two hours before they were due to leave, and to say it was awkward, is like asking how his life had been over the last year. Lynne's face lit up and even Mike seemed glad Dave had come to wish them off.

Their time was passed, reminiscing over their time together and of how they had been glad to help Dave over his dark days. After exhausting their conversation Lynne said. 'I've got something for you.'

'For me,' Dave said jokily.

Just then their neighbour came to the door and Mike left to speak to him. Lynne seeing this said in a loud voice, 'Will you give me a hand with this David,' and waved to him to come through to the kitchen. Once in the kitchen she took hold of him and pulled him to her and said cheekily, 'This is to last us until we meet again someday.'

Giggling like a naughty schoolgirl, she slipped her hand down the front of his shorts and fondling his manhood saying, 'I wish I could take this and you with me.' she kiss him so tenderly that he remembered it for days.

Embarrassed, he grabbed hold of her hand and groaned, 'I won't be able to hide how glad I am to see you if you continue doing that.'

Giggling as she removed her hand. She kissed him again and said quietly, 'Be happy, and I hope you find that special girl wherever your travels take you.' She smiled, and then said, 'Thanks for everything you have given me and all the love you have shared with me. I'll always cherish these times we stole together and wished we had had more time to….....'

He stopped her saying more. 'Shssss. It's me who should thank you, as you are the one who is responsible for making the man you see before you. I know I'll miss you, and might never get over you, as you've given me the faith to stand on my own two feet, and for that I'll love you always.'

Tears rolled down her face, as they held hands and quietly stood looking intently into each other's eyes. He smiled at her, and she settled. Wiping away the tears with his handkerchief. He said softly 'I really hope things work out between you and Mike. If it doesn't, I hope you find the right man to make you happy, as you deserve to be. Who knows what's the future holds? We might meet again.'

'I pray we will.' She whispered.

With Mike still outside Dave pulled her to him and with one last kiss they said goodbye. Before going back outside she gave him a photo of the family, and underneath she had hidden a photo of herself in a swimsuit and one with the two of them in each other's arms taken by young Michael, when at the beach. His last words to her were, 'I'll keep in touch.'

Watching them as a family drive away to catch the train that day, he knew life would not be the same again around there, but consoled himself with the thought, that his own time was drawing near to the day when he himself would be leaving.

With Lynne going out of his life and only her photo to console him, life took on a more humdrum way, and with more soldiers leaving every day for Malacca, he too wished, he were joining them.

With all the reconnaissance planes and staff having left earlier and being the driver to O.C. who would be the last to leave here, there were now only a dozen NS soldiers left in the camp, probably Dave thought, *because they were all going home in two months' time.*

Chapter 66

New Girl in Town

The NAAFI at nights, now the only Centre of entertainment, but even there it was quiet, and with more empty Bashers the place really felt like a ghost town. With no roll call each morning and more time to himself between driving the O.C about, Dave's days dragged. Now his every minute was spent thinking about going home, that was, until a new young girl started helping in the camp shop owned by an Indian man called Bapoo. Why he needed an assistant when the camp was almost empty, Dave could only guess.

Dave's, who's Basher room being across from the shop, was first to notice her the morning she started. From a distance his first impressions were, she was tall for an Indian girl, but attractive looking. When speaking to Derek he joked, 'Wonder who'll be first to chat her up for a date?'

A few days later, and with so much time doing nothing between duties and only a Sergeant Hamilton from the RASC and a Corporal left to keep them in place. One morning after dropping the C.O off at his office, he was informed he wouldn't be needed that day. So here he was lying on his bed reading when, Bapoo shouted to him for assistance, 'Can you give hand to me, lift box?'

With nothing better to do Dave responded, 'Yes, where do you want it?'

'You bring in back shop, please.'

Good! Dave thought, *I might get to meet his new assistant*, Entering the back shop the assistant was still there, and Bapoo asked him 'Have you met new girl yet? She very nice girl.'

Dave eagerly replied, 'No, only seen her from a distance when she arrived.'

'Philo, please to come meet good friend,' he waved her over.

As she slowly walked over, he was surprised by her looks. Up close she was gorgeous for an local girl, had a fantastic smile that lit her face up, showing her pearly white teeth against her golden tan and all set against her striking long black hair. Crossing over the floor towards him she seemed to glide above the ground. A very graceful young lady he thought, and much nicer to look at than first seen.

Bapoo introduced Dave, 'Philo, this Dave. He very good bloke and nice customer.'

She replied in perfect English, 'Hello, I'm pleased to meet you.' and held out her hand.

Dave took her hand in his, her touch felt silky soft and cool. He held onto her hand as he replied with a glint in his eye 'I'm pleased to meet you Philo.'

Even under her tan, she blushed, but never let go of his hand.

'Philo, is that your full name?' He asked.

'No!' she said bashfully with a slight orient accent. 'It's Philomena Egbert.' then continued, 'My fader's name was William Edberg. He was born in Belgium;' and went on, 'He was manager of a rubber plantation near Seremban.'

'So, you're not Indian by birth then?' he pried.

'No! I was born here in Seremban. My mother is from India. She met father when she worked in plantations my father was governor of.'

Dave decided at that time not to pursue further as he felt it was getting too deep and personal. Over the next few days, when not on duty, he spent his spare time chatting with her outside the shop, learning more about her family. Trying to find out how long ago her father died he asked, 'Has your dad been long dead?'

She replied unashamedly, 'He died in nineteen forty-seven, when I was just, I'm seventeen now, but will be eighteen in two months.'

'Can you remember your father? Dave asked.

Her head went down, and she replied softly, 'Only from photos...... He was killed during the Emergency in nineteen forty-seven. I was only four at the time.'

Feelings of sorrow stirring Dave, and he changed the subject, 'You speak nice English? Did you learn it at school?'

'No, my mum and Grandmother who raised me, taught me to speak proper English.' She went on to say, 'We all still stay in my father's home on the other side of Seremban.'

The more they talked the more he liked her, and always wanting to learn, she asked lots of questions about Britain, where his hometown was, and what he'll be doing when he gets back home. Their friendship blossomed over the next few weeks, into a brother, sister relationship.

He for his part, had no inclinations of taking their friendship further. Anyway, he told himself, *I'm going home soon,* in their conversations one day, he mentioned how he liked to visit the old temples that are scattered around the area.

'Have you seen the Seremban Hindu Karma Temple?' she asked.

'No. Where is that about?'

'Not far, if you like I show you.'

He thought for a moment, 'I can only go on Saturdays or Sundays.'

'If you want, I can show you place on Saturday, as I not working in the shop.' She said shyly, 'but you will have to come to my home to meet my mother first.'

He thought, *no harm in that, it's probably only a custom.* 'That would be great, as long as your parents say it's alright.'

That became the start of other trips whenever he was off duty and filled the weeks of his time left. He treated her as he would his own sister and felt it was all harmless, and as was the custom between friends in Malaya, when going anywhere she held his hand.

As he got to know Philo more, he was invited home to have a meal with her mum and Granny. They treated him very respectfully, and made him feel like he was a suitor to Philo. With Philo being Eurasian and not being full blood Indian, her own race hardly spoke to her; such was the class distinction among them.

When arriving at her home that day, in his honour a traditional Indian meal was prepared, and the family could not have been more pleasant to him.

He should have seen what was coming; like an animal caught in the headlights of a car he was walking into a problem of his own making. But he thought he was just a young soldier far from home enjoying the company of a nice girl with no strings attached. There is nothing like an old fool and he was innocently beginning to fall into that category.

Chapter 67

Malacca

Over the period since Lynne had left, he had been exchanging letters with her, but his feelings were, that they should tone down their wording, as it was not helping either of them. He himself by this time was starting to live his life without her. That was until Captain Hansen told him to drive him down to Malacca.

After that trip, he had to go down to Malacca Camp on other occasions taking Captain Hansen there on business. The first time he only had time to say hello and goodbye to Mike, but on other occasions, Captain Hansen had to stay the night, and Dave, billeted overnight in one of the new Barrack rooms.

On these overnight stops, he spent some time with Lynne and Mike. Their talk was strictly about old times, and how it was at Paroi Camp. The first occasion, when left on his own with Lynne, they managed to sneak a kiss.

'She tormented him, 'I'm missing you terribly and I dream about you every night.' Then she joked playfully, 'Do you dreamed about me as you lie on your bed?'

He teased her back, and said, 'I go to sleep each night with your photo under my pillow, and you in my thoughts.' That pleased her.

The second time he was in their company he told them about his new friend Philo. Mike was all ears, but Lynne was more inquisitive and asked, 'How do you feel about her?'

Dave said, 'She nice, but our relationship is no more just friends.'

Lynne teased him like she always did, then when they had a few moments alone she said, 'Remember we always thought our relationship was supposed to be like just friends and look where that led us.'

Dave said quietly so that Mike, who had left the room couldn't hear. 'But you're special to me and you know why we became so close.' He looked for a reaction, then said in matter-of-fact way, 'Philo is a nice girl and anyway her traditions wouldn't let her act the way we did.'

Lynne smiled, and playfully whispered, 'I'd scratch her eyes out if I could see her the now.' Then smiling, 'I think I'm jealous of her, so you watch yourself.'

Then in a more serious tone, 'Remember, keep in touch with me and let me know where you are, how you're getting on, and how you are feeling,' She hesitated, 'As I missed you, these last few weeks,' then with a playful dig she said, 'I may be losing you in person, but I'm not ready to give up the thoughts I have about you.'

At that moment he wished that he weren't there, for speaking to her unsettled him more than he thought it would. If she had asked him to run away with her at that moment, he would have. It was then that he felt, although they would be far apart, they would always stay more than good friends, even if they learned to live with their feelings.

On Dave's next trip down to Malacca, The O.C, told him that would be their last trip. That day Mike was on duty, and he was left alone for two hours with Lynne. Before Mike had left, he said to him. 'I never got the chance to thank you mate, for looking after Lynne and the kids. By what they have told me they enjoyed being taking to the beach and the other trips.'

Mike grabbed his hand in a handshake like two good mates that day and he left. That was the last time Dave spoke to Mike in Malaya.

During those two hours alone, Lynne told Dave, 'Things haven't changed much between us, as he still spends a lot of his time, with his mates. Although lately, he has spent a bit more time with us.'

'Well. Is that not a good sign?' Dave flippantly asked.

'I'm not sure. Since spending those time with you I feel I have changed.' She replied.

'What do you mean, you have changed....... In what way?'

Quietly she paused, then looking at him said, 'His attitude now, doesn't bother me as much as it used to,' She hesitated, 'but I will only keep going for the sake of the children.'

Dave turned his head away and with a pang of regret, felt he had in some way made their marriage worse.

Sensing his mood, she touched his hand and quietly said, 'Being with you has made me feel different and that there should be much more to loving a person than just having children.'

That day, being so close together, and alone he knew he could not resist her, and making love for the last time was in the front of his mind. In the past, she had always been the first to make the move, but this time it was he who move close to her and kissed her gently, that moment told him what he was missing. Her lips felt soft and her lipstick sweet, she responded and before long they were lying in each other's arms making love. Their lovemaking that sunny afternoon, although over quickly, was much more tender than they had had before.

Afterwards he decided to leave before Mike got back. They lingered long at the door as they kissed goodbye, but there wasn't any feeling of the end of the world now, more like two good friends who will miss one another's company for a long time to come. He looked deeply into her eyes and drank in all the love that was radiating from them, and smiled, knowing at the thought, that they had shared something few people in their lifetime get the chance to feel.

Her last words that day to him were 'Be happy, and remember I love you.'

Dave said goodbye to Lynne that day physically, and moved out of her life, not knowing if their paths would ever cross again. Stopping outside, as he waved to her, the same feeling he had had that day he waved goodbye to his dad came to him, and he felt a deep sense of regret.

Chapter 68

A Heartbroken

Life was much slower in camp now, and Dave started his countdown to Christmas again, and to the day he would be going home. The day was the thirteenth of December and another day marked off his calendar, leaving just thirty-five days to demob. From that day, life went along it's merry way.

Philo took Dave to visit a local Dayak village who's people still survived in the old way, and were still fearsome looking warriors. Some of the tribe's men he was informed had been guides for the Commonwealth troops during the fighting in the jungle. They were a proud race, There language was different from the local Malays, but Philo managed to interpret for Dave, who enjoyed spending his afternoon with them.

The days past, and on the eighteenth of December, Bapoo called him over to his shop, and asked, 'When you go home, you take Philo with you?'

Surprised by what he was asking, Dave replied curtly, 'No! I have other plans and they don't include taking Philo home with me.'

Dave didn't see Philo at the back of the shop, and on

hearing his reply, she came running out of the shop crying, and hurried down the road towards the camp entrance.

'What's all that about,' Dave asked Bapoo,

'Philo thinks you her boyfriend, and take her as wife back home with you since you no girl to go home to.' He replied.

Suddenly it donned on him, and Dave realized what a fool he had been. By telling Philo he didn't have a girl back home, she had surmised, by going out together, he would take her back to Britain with him.

The sergeant on duty who had seen what had happened, told him, 'That is the dream of a lot of young Malay girls, to get a British passport, a cherished prize they wanted, so they could leave Malaya and escape the poor conditions they lived in.'

With the picture in his head of Philo crying as she had brushed by him, Dave shook his head thought, *I'm a stupid selfish bastard, thinking about me again and not what others think.*' He had hurt Philo who did not deserve to be.

Once again, he had lived his life and never thought of the consequences of his actions, and had mucked things up for someone else. This time thought he was not sure how he could make it right.

That night as he sat in the quiet NAAFI, with a couple of mates, he took stock of his life, He had discarded all the things that he had held dear to him before joining the army, like treating people with respect, and decency.

He sat quietly thinking, *how far I've travelled from the kind of person dad brought me up to be. I could blame the army, but these things,* he supposed, *are in us all just waiting for the right moment to come to the fore. It's time to get back to how I was before all the events of the last two years overtook me. I need to straighten myself out before I get back home.*

Sitting alone in his room that night, he looked at his

photos of Jennifer for the last time and tore up most of them but could not bring himself to discard them all and held onto two. After viewing them for a long moment he put them away, never to be looked at again. Lynne's photo now had the place where all the other photos used to be. As he looked at them, he thought, *someday it might be the turn of Lynne's photo to go the way of the others, but not at this moment.*

Next day Philo did not appear at the shop and after dropping Captain Hansen off, Dave told him he was taking the vehicle to be cleaned and was given the Ok. With the vehicle cleaned and shining, he did what he thought was the decent thing and drove straight to Philo's home.

On arrival he was met by her mother. She looked solemn as he asked, 'Is it possible to speak to Philo?

'She no want speak you.' She said in broken English.

'I'm sorry for being so stupid. I didn't mean to hurt Philo or give her the impression that my intentions where more than just friendship. I think of Philo more as a young sister and nothing more.' Dave said with remorse.

'She cried when come home' Here mother stung.

Dave feeling a little guilty, could only shrug his shoulders as he replied, 'I'm sorry if I've hurt her. I tried to treat her with the nothing but respect.'

Her mother's expression changed when she heard his apology, and said, 'You wait here, I call Philo out of room and you explained her.'

Ten minutes passed and thinking she was not coming out he was about to leave when Philo came to the gate. 'Can we go for a walk? I want to explain my actions to you.' He said sincerely.

'There is nothing to explain, I thought you liked me.' Philo countered.

'I do, but I still think I owe you an explanation to why it

would never work out if I took you home with me.' Dave said with honesty.

Her mother, standing near spoke to her quietly in Punjab and reluctantly she agreed to go for a walk. A little way down a path they sat by a little stream that flows near her home and for over half an hour they talked. Dave explained again that he had not meant to give her the impression that they were anything other than friends. She cried as he spoke, and he felt, she was not taking in what he had said.

Back at her home, he said goodbye to her family and at her garden gate he took her hand and said, 'Philo I am deeply sorry for not having thought about how you felt. I liked you as a sister not as a future wife. Someday I hope you will look back and remember me as a good friend and see that this was all about nothing, and by that time you will be happily married with a family of your own.'

Tears rolled from her eyes as he promised, 'I'll write to you if you want?'

She did not answer, as she still appeared too upset to think straight. With nothing more he could say to appease her, he gave her a brotherly kiss on her forehead, and as he jumped into the Land Rover, with one last look at her, he called out 'Bye Philo,' and sped off.

Dave drove along the road, his mind in disarray thinking; *it has taken how Philo had reacted to me, to show me that over the past two years I haven't taken other people's feelings into account, when making friends.* Since receiving Jennifer's last letter, he had submerged his true feelings to everyone, even Lynne, for he didn't want to get hurt again, and consequently, he has taken, but not given much. Seeing Philo hurt the way she was, he felt a pang of guilt as he realised, he had shattered her dreams.

Philo never returned to the camp shop again, and Dave was sorry for that, for he never really said goodbye properly, and after that day, never saw or heard from her again.

Chapter 69

Thinking of Home

During the week before Christmas, the C.O. tried to talk Dave into signing on for another year, telling him, once the rest of the lads left for home, he would be transferred down to Malacca with him. Dave was tempted, at that time, as his thoughts were, *what have I at home to look forward to*, and in that moment, was unsure whether to sign on or not.

Having settled into army life, he felt comfortable in it, also going down to Malacca he would be close to Lynne again and kidded himself, who knows what might develop.

He expressed to the C.O. 'Can I give you my decision after Christmas,' even though he knew he had a deep desire to return home, even if only to finalize things and to finally bury his past.

Another hot Christmas, and still in Malaya, but not for much longer, he mused. Christmas dinner wasn't as noisy as previous ones, and the dining hall wasn't as decorative as last year. By this time all the other troops had moved down to Malacca, leaving only twenty soldiers in Paroi camp and another fifteen N.S. who joined them from the main Seremban camp, as they too were going home at the same time.

354

This Christmas, the celebrations were more about going home, in Dave's case, after they were informed they wouldn't be going home by ship, but by plane. Having never flown before, it was with some trepidations felt by Dave. Their flight was scheduled for the third or fourth of January 1962. Only another ten days to go

Dinner over it was a scramble to the NAAFI for a few beers. During the high jinks, a plot was hatched to play a prank on the chef, a grumpy old man. He had given abuse to everyone when serving them and this Christmas was no different. Somehow two lads caught a Hugh Fruit Spider, how no one knows, and decided to hide it in the food waste bucket, as one lad said, 'If no one let's it out it can stuff itself to death till morning.'

Back in the NAAFI, and some more beer. With so much to drink, Dave thought, *if the OC asked me now to sign on again, he could have Shanghaied me to any part of the world, and I wouldn't have cared.*

When the party ended, how they all got to their beds no one knows, but Dave heard next morning that some didn't make it, and spent the night lying outside being bitten by the mosquitoes. You could tell which ones, by all the red blotch marks over their bodies and the queue at the M.O.'s.

Next morning late, Dave crawled out of bed, his head thumping, he somehow made his way down to breakfast. Things cannot get any worse he thought, being so late, it could have been mid-morning dinner, not breakfast!

With sore heads he and his mates staggered into the canteen, only to find that the Chef had done the bunk, and breakfast was off. Not thinking straight, they all thought he was drunk again, as he mostly was.

The duty Sergeant entered the canteen and with no sympathy, in an extra loud voice shouted, 'Chef's gone, there will be no breakfast.' He then broke into a fit of laughter and still shouted out loud, 'Chef went to put some scraps of food into the bucket and got the fright of his life when he lifted the lid.'

Innocently, Daves mate Brian, asked. 'Sergeant, what happened?'

The Sergeant burst out laughing again as he spluttered, 'Some bastards put a great big fuckin Fruit Spider in the bucket, and it was bloody annoyed when Chef lifted the lid.'

Trying to contain his glee, Brian chuckled, and asked, 'They don't bite do they sergeant?'

'I don't think so. But it was angry enough to fly out onto him, and the last anyone saw of Chef, he was running down the road trying to get that hairy thing off his back. So, breakfast is off this morning except for toast and coffee.'

By the time he had finished telling them, no one could contain their laughter at the thought of Chef running down the road, swearing at the spider, 'get off my F-n back.'

The next few days with no duties for the lads, after roll call it was do as you please, except for Dave that is, who still had to run the O.C. about to tie up all the loose ends before he too, was due to be departed.

With no one bossing them about duties, they all hung about camp playing snooker, darts, or cards, just winding down time.

During that period, Dave gave a lot of thought to what he wanted to do and made up his mind not to sign on again. He was sure now, he had to try home for a few months before making his way out to New Zealand. He also planned when home, to go back to work for a while, then again wondered how he would feel when meeting Jennifer, if she was still there.

The last few days dragged bye, and most of the lads with no duties spend most of the time talking about taking up where they left off once back home, until one of the regular lads said something that made them all think.

'When back home,' he said, 'don't look for anything to be the same, as everything has moved on while you have been out here.'

Derek asked, 'What do you mean, moved on?'

The lad replied, 'I did my NS and when I got back home my ex-girlfriend was married, most of my mates were married and the young girls that were at school when I joined the army were now the only girls available to date, and they all thought I was too old. I lasted six months and joined the army again, for that's where all my mates were.' He left them with something to mull over.

The O.C. left for Malacca Camp two days before New Year's Day, but before going, he asked, 'Have you given a thought to signing on for another year?'

Dave, more in control of himself these days told him, 'Yes sir I have, but I won't be joining the now, as I want to go home first and see what awaits me there?'

That day after Dave had driven the O.C. for the last time, the O.C. shook his hand and thanked him for driving him about and wished him well. He then gave Dave an address to contact if he should change his mind about signing on again and said he would still be able to get him back out there, and driving him again.

New Year's Day, they celebrated the turn of the year for the last time in Malaya, and like all other New Year's Day, with a certain amount of regrets of what has passed in the year gone bye. But this New Year was different, as all their thoughts were of what life would be like back home. Some still had wives or girlfriends to go home to. Others like himself, were facing going home to an uncertain future. In general, all were glad to be going home, however, sad that they might not see one another again once demobbed. This New Year was a time for them to make pledges they knew they may never keep.

The pace picked up and the last few days were taken up getting jabs for some thing or another, and packing up their gear into their kitbags. As he stashed his possessions into his kitbag, he was amazed the rubbish he had gather around him, just to make the Basher room feel like home. It was a time to give, and he gave most of his things not wanted, to the lads that were staying for a few days to clear out Paroi Camp before they too would be moving down to Malacca.

It was on Wednesday the third of January they all boarded the train for their last journey in Malaya, and it was with some sadness that Dave felt leaving all his local friends behind. Friends like Philo, whom he hoped had forgiven him. Nee Nee Than, a good friend, he hoped she was all right and had managed to get home. Mike, a good mate, he hoped he would understand if he ever found out about Lynne and him, and little Mike and Victoria, whom he thought the world of.

As the train picked up speed his thoughts strayed to the lads who had moved on to other destinations whom he had spent some good times with. Most of all he thought about Lynne, the one person who had been there for him when he was in most need. He knew he loved her in a special way, but also knew they had to move on, as the train was, taking him away from what had been his life for the last nineteen months.

The journey south was long and monotonous; Dave slept a lot, as the thought of all that had happened to him was making him think back too much. The sun had set by the time they arrived in Singapore and leaving the train they climbed onto the waiting trucks. Passing over the same road they had taken on their first journey here. It was around 1900 hours when they arrived back at the same Transit Camp.

On entering the camp, the first thing Dave noticed was

the number of young new pale N.S. soldiers that had arrived and were waiting their turn to travel up into Malaya to start their adventure, or to continue the same one he was leaving. Silently he wished them luck.

The next day they handed in their tropical kit and receiving kit made for Britain, but as they were travelling home by plane they were to wear civilian clothes, and the army kit was stored away to be loaded into the planes' hold. In the NAFFI that night before the new lads left, his mates spoke to them, and as always with having done their own time, they let the new lads know it by teasing, 'Get some time in.'

They were smug, they were veterans, and had done their time, and Dave felt quite proud of himself in those moments. They were all brought back down to earth, when they found out that, back home they had suffered some of the heaviest snowfalls for years. But by this time they had met up with all the other lads they had done training with at Catterick and Ripon, and all had a different adventure to talk about, so much in fact all their sadness about leaving mates behind were all wiped away. That last night there, the Transit Camp NAAFI appeared to be the only place to be.

Chapter 70

Fly Away

It was seven-thirty on a warm, balmy Thursday morning in January 1962, the plane raced down the Singapore Changi Airport runway, and took off. By Dave's reckoning, around midnight back home. As the plane rose off the runway into the sky, the sun was climbing fast in the east as though trying to catch up with them. Once in the air the four-prop engines of the plane roared away, climbing higher and higher until the pilot levelled out, and banked northward. To their right and still in shadow, ran the west coast of Malaya.

Following the coast all the way north, the sun by this time was showing how beautiful from the air Malaya was. With a clear sky, Dave could make out K.L. and as they flew further north the beautiful island of Pinang, where he had spent many good times. Then in no time at all he had his final view of the Malaysian Peninsula. It was at that point, that he said a silent farewell, as the plane banked north-west out over the sea, and Malaya was only a memory.

The lad sitting next to Derek and Dave asked, 'Have you flown before?'

Derek replied instantly, 'Yes. I have.'

Dave could only say. 'No, this is my first time.'

The lad must have thought this was his cue to wind Dave up as he went on about the wings, 'Look at them, they're flapping up and down like a bird's wing.'

Dave, being a mechanic, was relaxed and had been listening to the steady throb of the engines, coolly said, 'Well as long as they're flapping and not falling off, I think we'll stay in the air.'

Two hours into the flight the intercom buzzed, and the stewardess said in a very posh voice, 'Please fasten your safety belts please. The Captain has informed me that we are about to enter some turbulence. Thank you.'

The lad next to us said, 'If he knows we're entering turbulence, why doesn't he go round it.'

Derek responded to him, 'Because crossing over the Indian Ocean the area is full of turbulence.'

For the next hour it was a white-knuckle ride as the plane went up and down like an elevator and was shaken about with all the air pockets.

Dave Thought, *my first ever flight, not a good advert for flying.*

Eventually the cabin signal lights came on and a voice said, 'You can remove our belts now, and thank you for your patience.'

From then on, they had a smooth flight over the remainder of the Indian Ocean, and then the mainland of India was below them, until touching down a few hours later in Bombay Airport.

Allowed only to disembark into the terminal to stretch their legs for an hour, and although having had a pack lunch with them, Dave decided to buy some food from the cafeteria. The selection on display though, was not very appetizing, only sandwiches of various sorts. What was on then he wasn't sure, but so hungry was he, he would have eaten anything even Rat meat, which were plentiful in supply, scurrying around all over the Airport passages.

After their short stay, he was glad to get back on the plane. Then with a change of pilot and crew, and the plane all refuelled up they took off again, and headed northward. By this time, the sun was now catching the plane up as it flew over the remainder of India.

To the east his view in the distance, and majestically rising above the clouds were the snow-covered peaks of the Himalayans bathed in sunshine. The plane hummed on, and Past over Pakistan and then Iran.

Looking down, Dave could now see the land changing colour to brown shades, and mountaintops covered in glistening snow, a complete contrast to the lush green of Malaya. For the first time in two years seeing the snow he started wondering what it would be like in Blighty. Then he thought of the Ochil hills back home with snow covering the peaks, making him nostalgic to be there now. Before that, the plane had another stop to make at Constantinople Airport, Turkey.

Once more only time was given to stretch their legs, and grab a bite to eat. Before long the plane was back up in the air and racing the sun through the skies on the last leg of their journey. The sun by this time had passed overhead and was now travelling ahead of them and the lands below were now darkening quickly. Further north pinpoints of lights sparkled, as though pointing the way to their destination, and by the time they had flown over France, the sun had long since set. As they crossed the Channel, only the lights of London let them know that they were at last home.

After twenty-one hours in flight and allowing for the time difference, the plane touched down at Stansted Airport around eight in the evening. Dave looking out the window as the plane taxed along the runway, it was a great feeling just knowing he was at last back and not far from his own home. That thought lasted only as they taxied to the disembark point.

Excitedly he grabbed his personal belongs and was along with his mates, ushered to the door. It was here that he had second thoughts about leaving the plane. A blast of cold air hit him as he stepped out to walk down to the tarmac; the wind he felt, went right through into his bones and he wished for the heat of Malaya again.

Buses ferried them to the customs' shed. Dave with nothing to declare, having previously sent home all his presents bought weeks before, was passed through customs. Boarding the bus again, they were driven to an old army camp just outside the Airport, where they were then herded like cattle by a Sergeant into old round corrugated covered barrack building, and then with a smile told, 'Welcome home to Blighty lads. Grab any bed, it's only for the night.' He watched them all trying to get as near as they could to the central fire. 'Once you are all settled, I'll take you over to the canteen for a meal.'

Half hour later, crossing over to the canteen was like walking in the Artic, but once inside the canteen the odour of British grub caught his nostrils, and the cold was forgotten.

Fortified with warm food and drink, it was back outside and a race over to the barracks. But before leaving them for the night the Sergeant said, 'I'll give you all a call in the morning,' and closed the door.

To stave off the cold the only redeeming feature for them was a big cast iron heater in the Centre of the room. Dave had managed to bag a bed near the fire in the Centre, and stood close trying to heat himself, but to no avail. He felt so cold, he wished his bed were on top of the fire. A few minutes later the Sergeant came back in as they were all fighting to get closer to the heater and threw some extra blankets on the floor and smiling said, 'You picked the wrong time to come home, for the weather has been like this for days.'

After an extremely uncomfortable night, Friday morning, the breakfast was nice and hot, but still Dave felt very cold. Breakfast over, they were ferried by truck to the Railway Station and boarded a train that would take them North to the Transit Camp in Chester. With the civilian passengers having their coats off, Dave and his mates surmised the train heating must have been on full, but to them it was still perishing cold.

Derek more annoyed than most, was only a few miles from his London home, but still had to travel to Chester to be demobbed, then travel back to London.

Arriving at the Transit Camp in Chester around one-thirty, a late lunch was laid on for them. Afterwards they had signed some forms and handed in their kit. They were then assembled again, and informed, 'Most of the officers are off home for the weekend, so if anyone wants a pass to go home on a week's demarcation leave, speak to the duty officer.' It seemed the army had no more use for them.

Chapter 71

Going Home

It was a short goodbye to Derek, and most of his mates before setting off. With two mates travelling north with him, they arrived at the station just in time to catch the train. Looking at the timetable, Dave saw the train was due to arrive in Edinburgh with time to spare to catch his train to Falkirk. Sitting back as the train chugged north, their conversation was about what they might find once home. An hour up the line his two mates got off the train, and he was then alone with his own thoughts.

As the train clicky clacked nearer Scotland, he started feeling nervous and wished he had had the company of Lynne to give him courage, but in his heart, he knew he needed to face this on his own. In many ways he thought, these were the same feelings he had when going into the army. He got through that, he told himself, *so I'll get through this as well.*

At Carlisle Dave had to change trains to travel further north and that was a start of problems to come. Because of the weather the train was belayed, and when he finally arriving in Edinburgh at eleven-thirty that night, it was too late for his connection to Falkirk.

Having only his army rail pass and no time to get British money, he sat on the cold platform feeling miserable and wishing that this journey was over. All he could do was hope another train might be going in his way. With no late buses running because of the weather, he felt he could be stranded there.

The station was near empty and with no kind Samaritan to help him. he explained everything to the Station Master, and told him, 'If I could even get to my sister's home in Kincardine, she would help me.'

'There's a train due to leave in a few minutes, going over the Forth Bridge and stopping in Dunfermline,' the Station Master advised, 'from there you might be able to get a late bus to Kincardine.'

Dave knew it was the long way round, but with no other option he boarded the train and crossed over the Forth Bridge to Dunfermline. As he stepped from the train there was a bitter wind blowing, and walking up to the bus depot through the dark streets that were deserted of human life, and with only the whistling of the wind to keep him company, he trudged on through the snow covered streets. Worse was still to come for him, on arrival at the bus stop, no buses were running.

He felt cold, miserable, and thought at that moment, *what a place to come home to, nobody seems to want to go out of their way to help me.* After all the pleading to people he met, telling them he had just arrived home from Malaya. He thought, maybe his problem was, *he's dressed in civvies.*

Just when he thought all was lost, he was standing shivering in the cold night air, when a policeman approached him and suspiciously asked, 'Why are you waiting at the bus stop.'

Dave explained his ordeal, and the policeman helpfully said, 'Come with me and I'll see what I can do.'

Dave followed him to the Police station where the PC

phoned a taxi for him. When the taxi arrived thirty minutes later, Dave explained to the driver his financial position and explained, 'I'll be able to get the fare from my sister to pay you, once there.'

Even though the Taxi driver had finished for the night, after talking to the policeman, he agreed. Dave still feeling desperately cold, thought at that moment, *That since arriving home only the driver, and the policeman, were the only people prepared to go out of their way to help me get that last nine and a half miles to Kincardine.*

By the time he reached his sister's home it was well after one in the morning, and they were all in bed. Dave knocked on the door gently, not wanting to wake up the neighbours. It seemed ages before the door opened and there stood with gaping mouths were his Brother-In-law Bill and his sister Helen. The moment he set eyes on them his emotions gave way and a tear of joy rolled from his eyes.

'David'! She shouted in surprise as tears of joy streamed from her eyes. She threw her arms around his neck and held on so tightly he thought her arms would need to be cut off, to free him. Still holding onto him, he was ushered into the house. All the while, his brother in-law took care of the driver. When Bill came back in, Helen, still holding onto Dave's hands, exclaimed, 'My wee baby brother is home at last.'

All the tiredness left him, and the excitement of seeing them again, brought the realisation to him, he was finally home.

When he had been courting Jennifer, they had visited here regularly, and his sister had always been his confidant as he grew up. They sat up that morning for ages talking over everything and everybody, even to how he was feeling about Jennifer.

Helen, a good listener, went silent, then said, 'You both

seemed so much in love. I was shocked when I heard what had happened. Jennefer used to come to see us when you were away, but I haven't seen her since you both broke up.'

Then, looking at him she changed the subject, 'You look wonderful with your tan, and you look so healthy.'

Dave replied, 'I feel great but it's bleeding cold here. I left what seems a week ago, around ninety-eight degrees temperature and come home to these freezing temperatures. I think I'll need to sleep on the fire to get some heat into me.'

Leaving him in peace on their settee to try to catch some sleep she left extra sheets for cover. He lay, sleep still far away, and thought, *just yesterday I was in Singapore and a week ago I was in my own Basher room in Seremban. How small the world is becoming?* When sleep did come, it was sound and deep.

Bill, an early riser, was up and away to work by the time he woke. It was the chatter from the kitchen that wakened him. Helen, had a place set at the breakfast table beside his two nieces, waiting for him when he entered. 'This is your uncle David. He's been away in the army for a long time.' She told them.

Looking at them Dave shook his head, 'They were toddlers when I left, and now look at them! They're both at school.' He sighed, 'That's the one thing I will find hard to get used to,'

'What's that?' She asked.

'Seeing all the people I knew before and seeing how different they will be,' He said in resignation.

Helen touched his hand, 'Bill said the same thing when he came home from Korea. He found it difficult at the beginning, but said, gradually it got better the longer he was home.'

'I hope so, I hope so,' Dave said with a hint of despair in his voice.

After breakfast, the two girls went to play and Helen sat him down on the sofa, and holding his hand asked, 'Do you want to talk?'

Dave looked at her, knowing that all his life she had always known what he was thinking before he said it. Over the next two hours they talked about his disappointment about Jennifer and all his other aspirations for what he would like to do and of all his mixed-up feelings. She then asked him, 'Is there something else you want to talk about?'

A little embarrassed at her prying, he whispered,'It's nothing, just something I have to work out for myself.'

'Come on out with it, you know I will find out what is bothering you, before you leave this house, so what's the problem?'

Dave thought a moment then said softly, 'I met a married woman out there and got involved with her.'

'Oh!' She went silent a moment, then enquired, 'Was she nice?'

'Yes. Very.'

'Well then, tell me all about her, for you know I'll keep pestering you.'

He looked at her and knew there was no escape, so he told her all about Lynne and how she had been the only good thing out in Malaya that had kept him from going overboard and making a real mess of his life.

Helen watched him silently before asking, 'Do you love her?' Then she paused as though not wanting to pry more, 'how did she feel about you?'

'Yes, I think I do. As for Lynne, she said she felt the same about me,' He said with a silent sigh.

'Are you going to keep in touch with one another?' She asked.

Dave was silent for a moment and with Lynne's face in his thoughts, he then said, 'Yes, we'll keep in contact, but she thought it might not work out for us, as she said, I'd come home meet someone else and forget her. I told her I would never forget her, so in the end we parted good friends.' Then hesitating for a moment, he then said, 'but who knows what might happen if she gets a divorce.'

'What was she like? By what you have told me, she sounds like she was a wonderful person.'

He took her photos from his wallet and handed them to Helen. The first photo was of them together, and the other of her in her swimsuit. Helen had a good long look at them then said, 'You both look good together. I can see why you cared so much for her. She is beautiful.' Still looking at him, she then said, 'I can tell in your voice you miss her right now. Do you?'

'Yes, more than I thought I would.' He replied softly.

They went quiet, and no more was said about all that had been spoken of, as it was time for him to make the final part of his journey.

Chapter 72

Familiar Ground

Crossing over the Kincardine Bridge that day, for the first time in nineteen months he looked at the Ochil hills, mountains some would say, rolling away westwards and knew he was home. A picture of these hills had been forever in his mind whenever he thought of home a place where he had walked many times when courting, but looking at them now, the way he was feeling it might not be long before he may leave them, his family and all his friends once more for good.

Hesitating as he stepped off the bus, gathering his thoughts he walked slowly home giving himself time to get used to what he might expect. Turning the corner into his street, for a moment he half expected his father to be still waiting there to welcome him home. It was then for the first time since coming home he was struck by the truth, he will not see his father again, and a tear came into his eye.

The old front garden gate still had the same squeak and dipped when opened, nothing is changed there he mused. He had hardly entered when his mother, who had been at that time visiting their next-door neighbour, on seen him pass their window, came running out with her arms in the air calling out embarrassingly, 'Ma bairn's back hame.'

Some neighbours on hearing her, came out to join them. Dave was swamped with never ending hugs and kisses and handshakes of welcome. Standing in the garden he looked around them, some he could remember, others only kids when he left. One girl he could just remember when she went to school, called Abigale, walked over to him as her mum said, 'Watch her David, she has been asking for days when you would be home.'

Abigale blushed, going on eighteen and a free spirit, grinned at her mother and coming close to Dave planted a kiss on his lips then whispered in his ear, 'I've thought about doing that for ages,'

Surprised by her actions he stood motionless, and as she pulled away she kiss him again, and that brought a blush to his face.

Her mother made the embarrassment all the worse by revealing. 'Ever since she heard about you breaking up with your girlfriend, she has been asking how long before you came hame.'

Abigale, by this time, her embarrassment showing said, 'Oh! quiet Mum, your making me blush.'

'That will be the day.' Her mother retorted.

He spent the rest of the afternoon alone with his mum talking over all that had happened to the family while he had been away, and especially about his Dad. He could see his death had taken its toll on his mother. In her sadness she went on to say, 'I still miss him terribly especially when reading your letters. Dad always read them out to me as we sat by the fire.' She went on, 'and he followed all your travels as though he had been there with you.'

Since Dads death, Mum said she and some of her

neighbours had become avid bingo players, a craze that had taking over the cinemas in recent times, and coincidentally it happened to be that night. Dave told her, 'You go and enjoy yourself. After all that has happened these last few days, I would like to be on my own just to get a feel of the old house again.'

She looked so happy after tea and seemed reluctant to leave him on his own, saying, 'I don't want to leave you on your own.' And not wanting to disappoint her, he agreed when she said, 'two of the girls next door said they will keep you company.'

Once his mum left, it only took a few minutes before Abigale and her sister Nancy walked in. The night turned out not to bad as they sat and talked, and with a childlike attention they listened to Dave. When asked what they wanted from life, Abigale said she wanted to emigrate to America, but what she wanted to find out most of all was what he was going to do. After all their questions he was glad when his mum arrived home and the girls left,

Once all was quiet he went through to his old room, which just looked the same, but the magic he used to feel when he was there before, had gone. He had grown up and left all his childhood and youthful things behind. Lying on his old bed his mind drifted over all that had happened to him, and at times, it felt that it had just all been a dream. Having been home only a few hours he was feeling a stranger in his own home, the people looked different, and everything felt different.

He wondered what Lynne was thinking off at that moment and was he already out of her thoughts. He never thought he'd miss the comfort of Malaya and all that he had done during his time there, but as the walls seemed to close in on him, he wished he was back there, and regretted having not signed on again because fear of his future, was creeping into his head and he felt unsettled.

He had not thought much about Jennifer since arriving home except when asked how he felt about their splitting up. His indifference to all he had gone through had made him wonder, if that were how he would treat people in his life from now on. Meet someone, fall in love, then discard them. Quite different from how he thought it would be before going into the army. As he finally drifted off to sleep he rationalised, tomorrow is another day, let's see what it will bring.

Chapter 73

In Transition

The week at home past swiftly and except for meeting family members, Dave had kept to himself. Sitting on the train again, in a strange way he was glad to be on his way back down to Chester. The last week had been a very difficult time for him, he felt, he no longer belonged there at home. Mum, because Dad was no longer there by her side, quickly started to try to arrange his life, like he was her bairn again and had him doing the rounds of family and friends. The only time he had to think of himself was when he closed his bedroom door at night, even then it felt like he was in a hotel room, impersonal and just a place to put his head down. Gone, were all the safe feelings he used to have, just four walls surrounding him.

His only escape from the incessant toing and froing during the week, was to jump on a bus and travel over to his sister's home where he felt he could get the understanding he needed. On a couple of nights, she let him sleep on her settee, and they talked about all the things he was feeling. He admitted to Bill and her, his apprehension about meeting Jennifer for the first time, it was something he was not looking forward to. He also told them, deep down some feelings were stirring and he was not sure if he would be able to handle them.

Bill understanding Dave's dilemma expressed, 'What you're going through, I experienced myself, but not as badly, as Helen was waiting for me when I came home.'

Dave shook his head, 'I'm not sure what to think, even when I met up with some old mates for a drink the other night, that even went flat. It appeared their lives have moved on, as some were married with kids and have other responsibilities. I felt let down as our evening ended early, when I thought it should have been just starting.'

The Garage Dave had worked in before, had during his time in the army, moved into new and bigger premises, on the outskirts of town. That week he keep to himself and avoided going out to see what the garage was like. Deep down he knew the reasons for his reluctance, telling himself, *I will face that once I'm home for good.*

The weather during that week was also restricting him getting about. Feeling the cold, he spent a lot of time by the fire keeping warm. Abigale popped in now and again, not wanting for him sitting alone she said, and in a way, he was glad she did. Just to talk without having to think about the future, was fine by him.

Before leaving to go back down to Chester the following Monday morning, he told his mum, it would be a few days before he is demobbed. She promised during that time she would have his bedroom papered and painted for him coming home. It sounded ominous the way she said it. With those feelings in his head he was sitting on the train, taking his last journey as a soldier.

Chapter 74

Demob Happy

Midday in Chester, he met up with two of the lads who had been in the same N.S. intake, but had been posted to Germany to do their service. They sat and compared stories until more of the lads appeared, and when no transport turned up to take them to camp, they piled onto the local bus. It seemed the army had forgotten about them.

During the daytime over the next two days, they were kept busy filling in forms, having their kit checked before handing it in, and receiving their demob papers. Their last night together was spent in the NAAFI having a demob party drink. The feeling among the lads was a mixture of, it is all over, let's get on with our lives.

For some like himself, the story was the same of being unsettled and a bit lost and two lads were thinking of joining up again, but like himself they too decided to give civilian life a try again. Some though, couldn't wait to get back into civilian life, most however, were happy that they had come through their NS unscathed and glad of all the friendships they had formed over the last two years, which they thought sure, would help them in the days to come.

After seven hundred and thirty days in the service of the Queen, and country. On the seventeenth of January 1962 Dave became a civilian once more. Sitting in front of the Duty officer he was handed his final papers along with a certificate of National Service attached. On the back page written by Captain Hansen was the following statement under the heading Military Conduct. *'Very Good.'* Also, along with his documents was a testimonial that went on to say,

'A clean, smart and tidy young man who can be fully relied upon. He has been employed in a job where integrity, reliability and the prime considerations were honesty, he has given complete satisfaction. He is a good driver with a good mechanical aptitude. He is recommended to employers with confidence.'

Signed M. Hansen Captain.

As Dave stepped out of the office the sun shone brightly, looking up at the clear sky he mused, *Dad would have been proud that I had served my country and came back with a good recommendation.*

Free now of the army, Dave and his mates had a last drink together and after handshakes, they dispersed and went on their separate ways. The journey home this time for Dave, was for some reason a better one and now with no constraints holding him back, feeling a bit more confidant in himself, he knew what he wanted to aim for in life. As he walked down his home street again, it was with a confidant stride.

Once in the confines of home his mum on greeting him, handed him a letter and probed, 'From Malaya. Who could be writing to you from there?'

Dave recognized right away the writing, it was from Lynne, hurriedly he opened it even before he had taken his coat off. It read,

'*Dearest Dave.*

Even now as I write this letter, I'm missing you, and just had to write to let you know and to wish you a welcome home. I know how you will be feeling for I felt your pain, and although I tried to help you, I know that this pain can only be cured by you alone. I wish in some way even now that we might get together again, as I miss you terribly. But I think we both know that might not be what is in store for us.

What we had was beautiful, for you made me feel so special and I'll always love you for that. But I feel now that that was all we were able to give to one another. I cried that night after you left and still do when I think about you. I will always cherish all the times we spent together.' She went on to tell him about the family etc, and finish her letter by saying, '*I will always love you and will miss our moments we had together, so please, please keep in touch for I don't want to lose your friendship.*'

With dearest wishes and love, Lynne.

His mum looked at him and inquired, 'It must be from someone special by the smile on your face.'

'Yes, very special to me.' He said with a great deal of pleasure in his voice.

'Who was she,' she asked with a mother's intuition.

Having never mentioned Lynne in any of his letters to his mum, knowing she would not have approved him seeing a married woman. He just said. 'An angel I met out in Malaya, who was there for me and kept me on the straight and narrow.'

His mum never asked again who the angel was, but he had the feeling she was thankful to her. He consoled himself by thinking mum would have liked Lynne as much as he had.

That night he dreamed about Lynne and all the good times they had together.

The weather brightened up and the skies were clear the following days. When he ventured up into town, he bumped into an old school pal. Over a coffee in the local Café, they talked over old times, and how things were since he left, and then his pal mischievously said, 'That was a dirty trick Billy Jackson played on you.'

Dave unsure what he meant asked, 'What did he do to me.'

His pal, surprised by his lack of what went on, hesitated, and replied, 'You mean to tell me you didn't know it was Jackson who courted your girlfriend behind your back when you were away.'

Dave never knew, no one had ever said in their letters to him. Struggling to keep his feelings in check, he lied, 'I heard a rumour, but it doesn't bother me now.'

The subject changed, and his pal asked, fancy going out for a drink tonight. He gladly accepted.

Chapter 75

We Meet Again

One week later, Monday morning, his day of reckoning, he dressed up in the suit that he had tailored for him when in Singapore. The material was a bit thin for the weather that day, but he felt smart in it. With his best dudes on he started out on the journey back to controlling his own destiny. While on the bus out to the garage, he met and spoke to a couple of people he had known from when working on their Motorcycles.

One asked, 'Are you going back to your old job?'

Dave replied, 'Only temporarily, depends on how I get on. Or I may move on.'

Arriving at the new garage he braced himself, then boldly walked in and up to the counter and pressed firmly down on the service bell. As he stood admiring the new Hugh showroom full of new cars, and motorcycles, his resolve lessened and he thought, what do I say if it is her, and hoped that it would be someone other than Jennifer that would come out?

As Fate would have it, through a side door out stepped Jennifer. When she saw him, she stopped, her face full of surprise. She still looked the same beautiful girl she had been when he left home. Both stared at each other for what seemed an eternity, and he saw on her face puzzlement, and appeared not sure what she should do or say.

It was only when Dave said in a very casual manner, 'Hello Jennifer. How are you?' It felt good saying her name again to her.

She seemed to relax a little, but it was not until he said, 'You're looking well.' That the ice broke between them.

Still, she seemed nervous, and kept looking at him as though she had seen a ghost. Her facial expression changed, then she spoke in the voice he had been longing to hear these last twenty months,

'It's nice to see you again. I'm fine, but more importantly, how are you?' She then continued warmly, 'You look so tanned'

Looking into her eyes he thought he saw a glimmer of affection. This is not how it was supposed to be, he told himself. They were supposed to tear lumps out of each other, but instead he smiled as he said politely, 'I feel very well, thank you.'

That seemed to bring a smile back into her face and as though not sure about their meeting, her expression changed to one of uncertainty again, 'When did you get home?' she asked. By the look in her eyes and the sound of her voice, he had the feeling she was thinking of something else, or possibly what they had meant to each other before.

'I was home for a week, then had to go back down to Chester to be demobbed. I came back home again a few days ago, but this is the first day I've had a chance to come out here to the garage.'

For a moment he thought he saw a tear come into her eyes, and he was not sure if she was feeling guilty or just that she was glad to see him home. She kept her eyes focused on his as though looking for recognition of something from him of his past feelings.

All this time he was surprising himself, for although he would have loved to have taken her in his arms at that moment, he kept his emotions in check.

Seeing that their meeting was starting to unsettle her he changed the subject and asked, 'Is the boss in?'

Still keeping eye contact with him she hesitated, then pointed down to one end of the showroom as she said, 'I think,' hesitated again before continuing, 'he is in his office down there.'

'Thanks,' Dave turned away, and as he walked along to the office, at that moment he felt quite good and thought, *I handled our first meeting better than I thought I would.*

Before he had time to dwell on his own feelings, Frank, his old boss spotted him and came out of his office. Stopping in front of Dave they shook hands, as Frank said, 'Welcome Home. You are sight for sore eyes, and looking so well, must have been in the sun too much to get that tan.'

As they stood talking, He could not help but see Jennifer was looking along in their direction and trying hard to look like she was busy working, but he could see she hardly took her eyes of them.

Frank patting Dave on his back said, 'Come in, come in, and I'll introduce you to the rest of the staff.'

Entering the main office, the first person to come over to meet him was Jean, Frank's secretary for several years, and someone he remembered very well from before he had gone into the NS.

'Hello Dave, Welcome home,' she said as she gave him a hug. Jean, a well-endowed woman in her mid-thirties was smothering him. Frank interrupted her saying, 'Hey! Leave some for the others.' He then took the time to introduced Dave to the other two secretaries, both married and in their mid-twenties. He also introduced him to an attractive young nineteen-year-old trainee.

With introductions over, all sorts of questions were fired at him until Frank held his hands up as he said, 'Plenty of time to find out all about him once he starts back,' turning to Dave he continued asking 'You are coming back here to work aren't you?'

Dave was extremely glad Frank was still keen to take him back, and flippantly said, 'You know you can't get on without me.'

'Welcome back home again, you cheeky rascal. I can see you haven't changed one bit.' Frank retorted with a smile on his face.

After spending the best part of two hours talking to him and the older workmates he had worked with, he met the new lads that he would also be working with. The Foreman was new to Dave, and at their first meeting he was not sure if he would be able to get on with him. But as in the army, you learn to adapt your attitude to people and just get on with life.

On his way-out Jennifer was still at the front counter, still trying to look busy, Dave walked towards her and smiled. This time she seemed a bit more relaxed. He wasn't sure if she was disappointed, and had expected a scene from him when they first met, but by the way she kept looking at him, she could see he was a different person to the one that went away.

As he approached her, she seemed quite enthusiastic, and asked with a hint of excitement in her voice, 'How did you get on? Are you starting back?'

'Would you like me to?' He asked pointedly, and before she answered, 'I'll have another week off, then I'll start the following Monday and see if I like it.'

She smiled, and this time her smile looked like she was happy that he would be coming back there to work beside her.

He looked intently at her for a long moment before asking, 'What do you, yourself think, about me coming back.'

She gazed into his eyes, and what she was truly thinking, he could only guess, but he could see that there was still a great deal of affection there for him when she softly said, 'It will be nice to see you every day again, and I hope we can still be good friends.'

Observing her a moment, his defences went up, as he replied, 'You will find that I have changed quite a bit, and I don't trust people as easily as I did before. We will just need to wait and see if we remain friends.'

Her smile disappeared, and she bit her lower lip as though she had just suddenly realised, she had hurt him deeply.

At that he turned, and walked out the garage.

Walking away from the Garage he felt quite good at the way he had let her see that he was his own man now, and had control of his own life. He could tell that their meeting had been harder for her than it had been for him, and thought to himself, *I can thank Lynne for that, as she let me see, you can find love with another person.*

As he strode back into town, feeling more confident in himself, he knew he would be able to cope. The only thing that put him off, was that home now, without Dad being around, the house for him now, was a strange place and new territory.

As he walked on, he never thought, he might have preferred to have stayed in the army, rather than stay here. But still he wanted to give things ago, and made up his mind to forget all about signing on again for the moment, and concentrate on civilian life again.

At his meeting with Frank the boss, he was asked, 'Do you still play badminton.' When Dave said yes, Frank invited him to join his badminton club that night, telling him, 'That way you can get back into the swing of things, and will get to know some of your new workmates.'

As Jennifer didn't play badminton anymore, he decided to go along. That night at the club, he was pleasantly surprised how welcome they made him. Some worked in the garage, but most came from other occupations. Starting to organize his social life and preparing for back at work, his first week passed quickly with a little trepidation.

Chapter 76

A New Dawn
A New Day

Monday morning, gathering his tools together he set off to the garage, and arrived just before eight-o-clock. After a talk with Bill Gardner, the foreman, he was shown his workbench area. His first impression of Bill when they met the week before, proved to be wrong. Having served in the forces himself, he knew how Dave might be feeling, and a common bond grew between them from day one. Bill was also one of the members of the Badminton club, and this helped settle Dave into catching up on the new motorcycle machines he had to repair. He also helped him getting to know his other workmates, but in general, Dave kept to himself.

It was on his third day at work, when he first encountered Jennifer, and asked her jokingly, 'Are you trying to avoid me?'

She looked a little embarrassed and replied, 'No. I've been busy,' Then, as though remembering the way she used to talk when with him, she challenged, 'I was going to ask you the same question.'

He hesitated, 'I'm just trying to find my way around.'

'I did see you first morning when you came in but wasn't sure what to say.' She said her voice trailing away.

Dave seeing her discomfort, putting her at ease said, 'You know I won't bite you. I never would.'

Normally she would have had an answer for him, but she was still feeling a little strange beside him. He watched her walk away and knew it would take some time before she felt comfortable in his company again.

All the time he worked away and even though he liked his job, feelings inside still knead at him, and felt, he wanted to be somewhere else, especially if Lynne was there.

At night after work, he was finding it hard to fill his time, and apart from the badminton club, his mates only managed out on Friday nights and even then, only occasionally. One lad called Jim Coulter who worked beside Jennifer in the garage stores asked him if he fancied going on a blind date. With nothing better to do Dave jumped at the challenge, thinking, *time I got back into circulation.*

It turned out a disastrous night and let Dave see just how far out of touch he was with life as a single man. Before he had gone away, his time had been devoted to Jennifer, and they went everywhere together. But now, it was like starting all over again. After having spent time with Lynne, he found it hard not to compare the girls he met, with her, and that was the start of a spiral downwards for him.

Two months had passed by, and try as hard as he could, insecurity crept into his frame of mind, and he found it difficult to fit in with what was going on around him. His life he knew, was started to stall, and he felt like a recluse. During the daytime he worked and at nights, tried to get bye the best he could.

A few more weeks past and Frank called him into his office and asked, 'What's wrong with you these days? Bill tells me you are different from you were when you first started back.'

'I don't know! He hesitated, It's as if I don't fit in anymore. I think I may need to think about getting away.' Dave dejectedly said.

Frank, who had always treated him as though he was his own son, asked, 'Is it working here, or it being close to Jennifer that is unsettling you.'

Frank was surprised when Dave instantly said 'No it's not really Jennifer or anything here. It's just I've felt so out of touch since I came home, and to tell you the truth, I am missing someone a lot, but it's not Jennifer.'

'Oh, I see. Anyone I know?'

'No. Someone I met out in Malaya.'

'A local girl.' He teased.

'No, not a local girl. She's English, and comes from Nottingham. One big problem she's married and I'm not sure what will happen now.' Dave quietly said.

Frank sat down, surprise written all over his face, and looking at Dave, asked, 'Does Jennifer know that? For she has been acting a bit subdued recently.'

'You're the only person I've told here.'

'Can't you go down to see her?' Frank asked.

'I can't, she's still out in Malaya with her husband.' Dave sighed in resignation.

'Oh, it's like that.' Frank shaking his head said. 'I wish I could give you some advice to help you, but it's something you will need to work out for yourself.'

That night Dave sat down and wrote a letter to Lynne, telling her of all the things that were going through his head. He then tore it up and started all over again. It seemed he could not even come to terms how he felt about Lynne either.

Next day just before lunch break, he was working at his bench, Jennifer came up behind him, and with a mischievous smile, said, 'Hello, how are you today?'

Catching him in the mood he was in, he didn't really want to talk to anyone, so snapped 'Why do you ask.'

Her expression changed, and with a look of worry on her face said, 'I'm sorry for all that has happened between us since you went away. I hope you can forgive me as the only thing I have always hoped for is that we stay good friends, contrary to what you may think, I still care very much for you.'

'But not enough to wait for me,' He replied in annoyance.

Shocked, as though she had just lost a best friend, tears welled up in her eyes. Turning she ran out of the workshop, and back along to the stores.

When Dave looked around, some of the other mechanics where standing watching, and had heard everything. His relationship with some of the lads became strained for a while that day, as most liked Jennifer, and had not known how close they had been before he went in to do his national service in the army.

Life for Dave seemed too uncertain, and he was now just going through the motions when a letter from his mate out in New Zealand arrived. This started him again thinking of pastures new. His life here was going nowhere, and without the influence of Lynne, he felt the need to get away as quickly as he could.

Chapter 77

Peace Talks

Days past, then one morning his boss Frank called him over and asked him to go for a walk round the garage, for a wee chat, as he put it. It was still cold as they walked. This time before asking anything he stated, 'Remember I've known you since you were a raw lad out of school, and I'll know if you are telling me the truth or not. So, let's talk things over?'

As they walked the snow that lingered, crunched beneath their feet, and Dave reluctantly told him all that had happened to him. His reacted when his Dad died, the letter from Jennifer breaking off their engagement, and his going off the rails. He finished by telling him about Lynne, and how she had saved him from making a real mess of his life.

After he had finished they went into the workshop and sat down at the big fire in the middle. Looking him in the eyes Frank exclaimed, 'For goodness sake Dave, you and Jennifer where really good friends as well as going steady with one another, surely your friendship is more important than to just to go away and not speak to each other again.'

His words hit home, and Dave went quiet for a while thinking over what he had said. He knew he made sense, like his father, the advice Frank had given him before had always been honest and to the point. Frank put his arm round Dave's shoulders and asked, 'What's it to be then?'

Dave looking at him, and knowing that it was over between Jennifer and him, he supposed, *we had been good friends, and she had been a big part of my life. He also knew deep down he would be happy for her if she was happy herself.*

'Your right, I know your right. I will speak to her and, settle everything. But I have to tell you now, I think I will have to leave and start somewhere else.'

'Ok but let us talk about it some other day, but for now I'd like to see you both make you peace and get on with your lives.' With that they both got up and he went to his office and Dave got on with his work.

Later that day he made a point of catching Jennifer by herself and asked her to come into the quiet canteen, to talk things over. She was a bit apprehensive at first, but he could see she like him, was still hurting, and wanted to draw a line so they could get on with their lives.

Sitting in the corner, Dave started by saying, 'I'm sorry for the way I've been acting recently and being so abrupt with you the other day. I think deep down I wanted to hurt you for not waiting, but I know now that it was myself that I wanted to hurt.'

With a sincere look she said, 'I'm sorry too, I didn't want to hurt you being so far away, but everything changed when you went away. I was lost and lonely without you. I wanted you by his side, but you weren't.'

He gently laid his hand on her shoulder and said, 'I know, I know, I felt the same. There were times when all I had to keep me going was the thought of you, especially when dad died.'

Tears came into her eye as she replied, 'I cried for three days after he died, for I knew how close he was to you. All I thought about at the time was wanting to be with you, but that was the problem, I couldn't.' She hesitated, 'You were so far away, and when I needed you, you weren't there for me.'

Dave quietly said, 'I know by your letter at that time, I felt your distress and it help me a little to know you felt as I did. All went fine after that until I got your letter breaking it off, I'm afraid I couldn't handle it and I went to pieces for a time, until my mates wife Lynne help me.'

'Was that Lynne you mentioned in your letters, Mikes wife?'

'Yes.' He replied.

Now a little more relaxed She asked. 'The way you spoke of her name in your letters, was there more to it than just helping you.'

'Lynne was a good friend, and the one who made me see that there was more left for me in life.' He looked at her and could see surprise in her eyes. Continuing he said, 'It was months later after we broke off, I ended up having an affair with her.' He then said quietly, 'We still keep in touch with each other.'

He took out the photo of Lynne and himself and showed it to her. By her expression she now realized that it was not her that he was pining for. 'She looks beautiful.' She whispered.

Still looking at the photo she listened to him quietly, how they parted.

Jennifer appeared to be saddened with his revelations and without looking at him asked, 'Are you going to see her again?'

Dave had the feeling by the way she asked, that she was disappointed that he had found someone to take her place in his heart. 'I don't know. She said they may be divorcing, and that she wanted to see me again, so there is a possibility we will get together once things are settled, but I'm not sure what will happen.'

Still holding the photo, her voice wavering as she said again, 'I'm sorry for hurting you, I desperately wanted to wait for you, but the way things happened while you were away, I felt I needed to get out, that's when I met Bill.' She went on to explain the anguish she went through until she finally succumbed to Bill and eventually went out on a date with him. She shook her head saying once more, 'I'm sorry I couldn't wait, and for the hurt I caused you, and that it didn't work out the way we thought it would.'

They held hands and looking into her eyes he could see there was still a deep fondness for him. He smiled and said, 'It's all right now, as long as your happy, I am happy for you, and in the end, it may be all for the best.'

Dave knew then from that moment they would stay more than simply good friends, no matter what or where life took them. Before parting he gave her a hug and she responded. She felt so good in his arms, and it brought back good memories, and by her own response she felt the same. He then gently kiss her on her lips and felt her respond. He smiled as they broke away, and said, 'For old time's sake.'

She surprised him with a smile, and her next comment as they broke away, 'I'll remember for the rest of my life all the times we shared together, and I hope we will stay friends for ever?' for a moment he saw a tinge of sadness in her eyes that they were not meant to be for each other.

Before parting he said more for his own benefit, than Jennefer's 'Any way, you and Bill won't have me in the way, for I may be out of your life for good soon.'

Jennifer looking surprised by his comment, asked, 'Why! Where are you going?'

'I'm thinking seriously about going out to New Zealand. I have a job and a place to stay waiting for me out there.' He responded

'After all this time, you still have that ambition. That was all we talked about when we were together.' She said with a little regret in her voice.

He replied with a little irony, 'Some parts of our dreams still have meaning for me.'

They parted that day good friends, and from then on would stop to speak to each other no matter who saw them. So comfortable were they in each another's company, everyone sensed they would stay friends.

Three months passed and his feet where still itching to move to pasture new. He was still writing to his friend Walt out in New Zealand, and in Walt's letters, he was always asking, 'When are you coming here, Mate.'

Dave started proceedings with the Embassy and filled in the papers, but sat on them for a week before sending them off. His mum, when he told her wasn't too pleased, as she said to him, 'You are hardly home, and you haven't given yourself a chance to settle down. I blame Jennifer for all of this.'

His whole family had, apparently turned against Jennifer, and it was only made worse when he said, 'I have spoken to Jennifer, and we remained good friends.' Dave felt that each time her name was mentioned, it was as though it was his family, she had turned her back on and not him.

With the papers away he became impatient to hear if he had been accepted. He wrote to Lynne and told her of his plans,. She wrote back saying if she was free she wished he would take her with him. His mind made up he was now anxious to be on his way even if it meant breaking all ties with the people he knew at home.

All this time, his Mum was going on about him not going to Mass, and how he had always been a regular churchgoer.

She declared, 'You never know, you might meet someone that you might like.'

'It won't change my way of thinking,' He stubbornly stated, 'I've made up my mind, I'm going out to New Zealand.' He had not said to his mum or anyone else, except his sister, that he was contemplating asking Lynne to join him, as in her letters she always said, she wished she could be with him. With still a little while till everything was arranged, he would hold back, and wait until Lynne was free.

To please his mum, he finally gave into her wishes and decided to go along to the next Sunday morning mass, just to put in an appearance, and maybe see some old school friends. Then he thought that after having fulfilled his duty to his mother, he could leave, then get on and make a new life for himself.

Chapter 78

Another Door Opens

Sunday morning, Dave woke with a sense of foreboding and unable to throw of the feelings he had, he was not looking forward to going through with this Mass caper. The night before, he had been out on another disasters blind date and even though the girl was quite pleasant, he could not get into the swing of things, as he felt a misfit. But off to mass he went, feeling like in his old school days when his mum took all the family to mass every Sunday morning.

During his time in the army, a new bigger church had been built and it was a surprise to him when stepping inside, and saw the interior, and the altar. His mum made sure the priest spoke to him before ushering him into a seat near the back. He sat quiet not wanting to draw attention to himself, but a few old friends came over and welcomed him home.

He was starting to feel uncomfortable and guilty, then as fate would have it, ten minutes before mass started down the Centre aisle walked a vision of a young woman dressed in a pale-yellow coat with a white fur collar and on top of the most beautiful golden yellow hair he had ever seen, she wore a black fur hat. As she glided down the aisle there appeared to him, an aura around her that was so strong he could not take his eyes of her.

His mum noticing he was looking at her, leaned forward, and whispered, 'That's Kay! Don't you remember her? She was in your class at school.' Then still whispering, 'There has hardly been a week gone by all the time you were away that she didn't ask me how you were getting on.'

Kay sat down, and he tried to see what she looked like, but she never turned round. From that moment, his mind was not on the Mass; it was on this girl, and all he could think of was meeting her, to see if she were as wonderful looking from the front as she was from the back.

After Mass, outside surrounded by old friends, he did not notice Kay coming out of the chapel. For some strange reason he was wishing all these people talking to him would go away so he could meet her, but instead he was being polite to those around him, and all the time trying to get away.

Suddenly he felt the gentle touch of a hand on his shoulder, and turning round quickly, he was looking into the eyes of this beautiful girl standing before him, dress in yellow with beautiful blond hair. He was stunned and tongue-tied. She spoke in a very gentle soft polite voice, 'Welcome home David. How are you? Are you glad to be home?'

So simple a meeting he expected a fanfare, but as the saying goes, Beauty is in the eye of the beholder, and he was in awe by her beauty, so much so he could not get his brain or mouth into gear. For the first time in his life, he was stuck for something to say. Unable to take his eyes of her, he only managed to stammer, 'Yes! I am now,' His words were out before he realised what or how he had.

She smiled, and her expression changed as though she too was nervous, and went to say something, but, she then looked carefully at him before blurted out, 'Have to go, I'm in a hurry,

Dad takes me to the Motorcycle scrambling today.' She turned to walk away a few feet, then looked back and asked, 'Will I see you again?' she hesitated, 'At Mass next week?'

He watched her walk away and something in him said, don't let this girl slip through your fingers. He wanted to run after her and speak to her some more, but just then a few of his old friends from school came over and when he looked round again, Kay had disappeared round the corner. As his mates talked, his mind was wondering when he would see Kay again.

One of his friends said, 'You look like you have been struck down with something or someone. I saw how you looked at Kay, was it her.'

Dave looked at him, 'You know, I can't remember Kay in our class at school.'

Pat, one of his oldest school friends, casually said, 'remember the girl you got the belt for throwing water at in the playground because she wouldn't give us our ball back. Dave thought, but could not remember.

His friend continued, 'Well that was Kay.'

He looked at them dumfounded, shook his head, and said, 'I still can't remember her.'

Another friend gave him a playful nudge and said, you wouldn't for Kay has turned into a very gorgeous young woman, hasn't she.'

The rest of the day he could not take his mind of Kay and all else was pushed out of his mind. For the first time in a while, he did not feel the need to go out that night, his thoughts were all on, when he would see her again.

He asked his mum where Kay worked and was told she worked in the Ice cream parlour in the main street in town. She then said something that made him think of the old saying, Mum knows best! 'I always hoped you would meet Kay before you did something you might have regretted.'

That Sunday he felt strangely content.

Next day at work he was whistling away when he was surprised by Jennifer sneaked up on him, and chirps, 'You sound happy today. won the pools?'

He looked at her and was sure she would have seen in his eyes that the light was back in them.

'You do look as though something has happened to you. Is it you have got the go ahead, to go out to New Zealand?' She asked.

'Nop!' he said. 'Not that, I think I have meet someone that just might make me change my mind.'

Since making their peace with each other, their friendship had strengthened again allowing them to act how they used to before and to be more relaxed in each other's company when speaking to each other.

She gave him a poke in the ribs and said, 'Come on, out with it. Who is it?'

'I don't know if you know her, I only met her yesterday at Mass, and apparently she was in my class at school, but can't remember her from then,' he said.

'You only met her yesterday and you feel like this,' then jokingly she went on 'Tell me who she is, so I can find out what her magic is,' then before he said her name, Jennifer said, 'I bet I know who this sorceress is, and if it is who I think she is, I'm really happy for you, for she is a beautiful smashing girl, and she's also a good friend of mine.'

'Who is it then?' he asked teasing her.

'I bet its Kay Drummond!' She said as a matter of factually

'How do you know her name?' He queried.

'Because!' she hesitated, 'I worked beside her for a while before I left school, and we became good friends.' She hesitated again before continuing, 'When you were away, she asked about you a lot, and how you were getting on.' She smiled him,

'I even confided to her when I was having trouble on how to tell you about how I felt.

He sat on his work stool, 'Well, I'll be blown.' And shaking his head then continued, 'I don't believe this.'

Jennifer smiled and confessed, 'I often wondered after we broke up if you two would get together.' Then as thought remembering something. 'She always seemed keen to know all about you.'

Not able to contact Kay, the rest of that week seemed to drag and all he could think about was next Sunday, and Mass. This time he thought, *I will make sure she knows I'm smitten.*

Sitting in the same seat as last Sunday, he saw Kay walk in and as she passed their eyes caught each other and she smiled. She then sat in the same place as the week before and again as before he couldn't take his eyes of her. The more he looked at her the more he thought *you are the girl I will marry.*

After Mass, outside he waited for her to come out, and he spoke to Kay for a while, and the longer he was in her company he realized, that he would not be satisfied until he knew everything about her. They parted again that morning without him asking her out on a date. All the way home, he felt stupid and couldn't take his mind of Kay. His army training kicked in and he made up his mind to take some action.

After lunch, having decided his course of action, he walked to her home, and confidently rang the doorbell. Long moments later, it was her sister who opened the door. 'Can I speak to Kay if she is still in?' he stammered.

Her sister giggled, and disappeared inside, two minutes later Kay stood before him smiling. He blurted out before he lost his nerve. 'Would you like to go out with me to the cinema?' To his delight she said yes without hesitation, and seemed genuinely happy that he had asked her.

When they meet that evening, he felt like a young teenager

out on his first ever date, a bit shy and felt that he was saying all the wrong things. They giggled at the silliest things they said to each another, but when he looked into her eyes there was a depth of love shining out that he had never felt before. He knew all the things he wanted to say but couldn't find the proper words. He was under her spell and glad to be.

Their first date felt never ending, and he learned that she too was feeling the same way as him. Stopping at her front door that first night he was still feeling nervous and like a young awkward teenager leaned over to kiss her goodnight and when she did not pull away, he kissed her on the lips. It was only a peck but in that one instance the world exploded in his head and all the feelings he had had for Jennifer and Lynne just flew away. Dave knew then, this time he had found a girl that would never ever let him down.

Over the next few weeks, they went out as often as they could, he bought his first car, and they travelled about the countryside. For the first time in her life, she decided not to go with her father whom she adored, but to go with Dave to the Motorcycle races. This was the start when they got to know one another better, and the more he spoke to her the deeper he fell in love with her but this time, his love was not like he had felt with Jennifer or Lynne, this love lifted him above everything and everyone. No jealousy, no uncertainty. For the first time in a long time, he felt contented. It was then he felt sure, this was the only girl he wanted to spend the rest of his days with.

Chapter 79

Settling Down

During this period, he received word from the New Zealand Embassy telling him he had clearance to enter New Zealand as an immigrant and to contact them about his passage. He did not say anything to Kay at the time, thinking, I will tell her later.

Over the weeks, they grew closer learning more about each other. Kay, now feeling more comfortable in his company, told him, 'During the time you were away, I also become engaged, but the relationship I realized would not work, and stopped seeing him.' She went on to tell Dave, 'I often saw you and Jennifer together before you went into the army, and while you were away I thought about you often and wondered how you were getting on. I even asked your mum and Jennifer how you were. At one time,' she said, 'I was going to write to you after your breakup with Jennifer but felt it better to wait till you came home.'

It seemed Fate was at work even before he knew what was in store for him.

Kay, he was becoming aware of, was a girl who although quiet in manners, was still confidant in what direction her life was going, and the more they were in each other's company, the more he adored her. A woman who had great poise and looked every inch a lady and yet was so down to earth, and very playful with her words. She was well content within herself and always seemed at ease in his company. The old saying fits like a glove was perfect for both.

He had said in the past to two other women in his life that he had loved them, and supposed, he had at the time. But with Kay, the first time he uttered the words, *I love you*, it felt it was the first time he had ever said them to anyone, and this time, it was really true. The first time Kay said she loved him, he knew when looking into her eyes there was happiness he had never seen before in a person and thought, '*God! you are beautiful, and have been placed on earth for me alone.*'

After they had been going out a few more months they started to talk about marriage and it seemed so natural to decided that they would set a date, they decided on a date in 1964 to get married, this was to give them some time to save some money up, but as she said to Dave, 'If we have to wait till we have enough money saved up, then we will never get married. Let us fix the date and that will be it,' then she said cheekily, 'But first. you will need to ask my Dad.'

It took two weeks before he had worked up the courage to speak to her dad. It turned out the most nerve-racking experience he had ever been through, even worse than that infamous day in the station in Butterworth, out in Malaya, when he had to disarm his Courier mate. Even though her dad knew what he was going to ask, Dave still stammered out 'I want to have Kay's hand in marriage, with your permission.'

In the end all he said was, 'You have my permission for that's what Kay wants, and I wish you both all the happiness.'

A monumental thing for him, that was over in the blink

of an eye. At that moment there was not anyone prouder than him.

The next day they went along to a beach at Port Seaton and as they walked along the sand, Kay kicked of her shoes, and like a happy school kid on her first holiday from classes, ran alone the beach with her arms held out letting her blond hair and her red dress blow about in the wind, she looked so happy,

He wished at that moment that he had met her earlier and had paid more attention to her when she was at school. They spent the best time they had had together that day, and all the cobwebs that had cluttered up his life blew away with the wind. From then on, their times together were spent thinking about building a home together.

One day she asked Dave, 'What about your ambitions to go out to New Zealand your Mum told me about.'

'Oh! You found out about that. Well, all I can say to that is, my home is where you are.' he said with sincerity.

He wrote a letter to Walt explaining everything, telling him for the moment he would need to postpone going to New Zealand.

Word spread around the garage quickly that he was to be married. Jennifer who had already announced a month earlier that she was to be married to Bill Jackson in the spring of 1963. It was a week after Jennifer had announced their plans, when one morning, Jennifer's fiancé Bill, came in to speak to Dave. and Dave thinking, as this was the first time they had met since before him going away, it would be to congratulate each other on their weddings.

To Dave's surprise, Bill accused him of trying to split Jennifer and him up. Standing in the middle of the workshop, in a very agitated voice, he shouted, 'Jennifer tells me you don't believe she will marry me? Well, she is!'

Dave surprised with his manner, as most of the lads standing near heard everything, and wondered at that moment, who is playing games with whom. As Bill was turning to walk away Dave said angrily, 'Look Bill, Jennifer made her decision. As far as I am concerned that ends the matter. If you have a chip on your shoulder because I was first to go out with her then that is your problem.' Bill turned and walked out of Dave's life that day for the last time.

Working away in the garage life was getting better for Dave, He was still on good speaking terms with Jennifer, who during their chats never mentioned about Bill coming to see him or if she even knew about it, but she never mentioned her upcoming wedding either, which he was informed had been brought forward so they could emigrate out to Australia once married.

Things were moving on smoothly and he received a letter from Lynne, in reply to what he had told her about Kay. She wished him all the best, and in the way she wrote, he felt she was genuinely pleased for him, even though in a foot note, she said, *I wished that we might have come together again, but we always knew that this might happen.* The other part of her letter thought was not so good, she informed him that she was leaving Mike and returning home to England. It seemed that their marriage had finally broken down.

At that moment, he felt he had contributed to their breakup, but Lynne always told him that their problems had started long before they met. The only guilt that he felt now was that of all the things he had spoken about with Kay, they agreed that what happened in the past should remain so, and he never told her about Lynne.

From then on communications with Lynne started to get fewer and fewer until she stopped replying to his. He felt a little sad that he could not share a part of his life with her, but as she had said many times before, they both knew that it was never to be.

As the days past his time in Malaya faded into the mist of memories and was never mentioned again in conversation with Kay. They were just looking forward to the time when they would get married and set up home together. He settled well into working and lost all his army habits.

Life in general was wonderful again and he could not think of anything that would alter that, that was until the last day before Jennifer was due to leave work to prepare for her wedding day. Dave was working at his bench when Jennifer walked into the workshop and asked him if he would go outside to speak with her. He looked at her and could see something was bothering her.

Once outside she blurted out, 'Dave I don't know how to say this, but I.' She stopped speaking

He calmly asked her, 'What is wrong. Is everything alright between Bill and you?'

She looked at him and he could see in her eyes a look of uncertainty, 'I feel so mixed up, since you came back home and we have been working close together, it's been a bit harder to know what to do,' she said.

'Jennifer, it's just pre-marriage nerves you are having.' Dave said, 'Once you get married it will all settle, and when we are old and grey haired we will look back and I hope remember all the good times we had together, but we have to move on and I wish you all the happiness in the world,' He smiled, 'just remember I will always be your best friend.'

A tear came to her eye, and she then came close and kiss him, her lips felt warm and tender, but it was a kind of kiss that was searching for an answer and not just a farewell kiss, but the answer she looked for would not now be found on his lips anymore. As they parted, he held her hand and said, 'Be happy, I genuinely mean it, for you were my first love and are special to me.'

She stepped back still firmly holding his hands, looked long at him and he could see she still had a deep affection for him that would last for a long time to come. As more tears ran down her face she then said, 'You be happy too.'

He watched her walk away that day with a little sadness in his heart and the feeling he was losing her again, but he knew also that they would remain good friends for the rest of their lives.

Two days after their meeting, Jennifer's favourite Aunt stopped him in the street and said, 'Dave why didn't you grab hold of her and tell her that she was making a mistake and.'

He raised his hand to stop her before she said more, feeling annoyed with her for not thinking he too had a life, and it was not all about Jennifer. 'Look!' He stated, 'Jennifer has made her decision and I have made mine, and there is no going back.'

She looked at him with a blank expression and trembling lip, said, 'I think you both are making a big mistake.' Without another word, she walked away.

He spent his first Christmas home, with Kay's family and his mother. During the following week they went around all his family and spent time at his sisters. It was good for him to know his sister approved of Kay, as they had spent practically the day talking about women's things and the wedding they would have.

Dave sat quietly listening and felt so good at the thought his true life really started when he met Kay. As he looked at them, Kay sensed he was and turning to look at him she smiled, in that smile he knew she too was quite contented.

Later in the day when he was alone with his Sister, she asked, 'Have you heard from Lynne again?'

He replied, 'I answered her letters, and explained everything. And now, she is just a wonderful memory.'

Chapter 80

Meeting Mike Again

1963 flew past. Jennifer married and moved away out to Australia. Life in the garage went on but he had to admit to himself, he did miss seeing Jennifer each day and hoped she was happy now that she was as far away again from him, as he had been from her. To compensate these feeling, his social life with Kay was picking up with a new circle of friends.

They both like dancing, so started to go out with friends on Saturday nights. This time though there was no jealousy on his part for unlike before with Jennifer, he had complete trust in Kay. That is what true love is all about, trusting in one another in all things.

It was a wonderful year full of pleasure and commitment, his life before meeting Kay was filed away into the past, and once again they had celebrated Christmas 1963,and the start of New Year 1964, the year when they would wed.

With their plans gather momentum, in the spring of that year Dave had a surprise visitor at his work. One day, the foreman came up to him and said, 'There's an old army mate wanting to speak to you, he's outside.'

Dave went out expecting to meet a soldier in uniform,

instead here was a man dressed in a delivery uniform that greeted him. 'Dave, how are you getting on mate?'

Dave couldn't believe his eyes, standing before him was Mike! 'You, old son of a gun. What brings you up here, and what's with the new garb?'

As they shook hands he explained, 'This is my new job. I packed in the army four months ago and have been driving lorries again since coming out.'

Dave did not notice at first, but the office girls were staring through the office window at the two of them talking, one opened the window and leaned out and whistle at them. Dave smiled, turning to Mike, whom women would consider quite handsome, said, 'You haven't lost your touch have you.'

Mike smiled and said, 'Maybe I'll have to now, for I'm getting married again soon.'

'What about Lynne and the kids?' Dave asked.

'Lynne went home with the kids nine months after you left Malaya. We talked about divorcing,' he said in a disconsolate way and continued, 'I'm sure you knew how it was with us out in Malaya. We tried again when I left the army, and got back home, but it didn't work out.'

Dave mused, *that it was around about that time I lost touch with Lynne.*

They let go of each other's hands and Dave seeing a different look about him said, 'I'm sorry to hear that, I liked you both a lot and considering all the help you both gave me out there, I always hoped that it would work out for you both.' There was silence for a moment then he asked Mike, 'What happens now to the two of you, and the kids?'

'The kids are staying with Lynne,' he said, 'she has recently been going steady with a chap the last few months now, and they seem to be getting on quite well, and I still get to see the kids when I want.'

'And what about you, what are you up to?' Dave asked.

Cheerfully he replied in a more open fashion, 'I'm back with an old girlfriend called Marian. I used to go out with her before I married Lynne, and I'm quite happy with the way things have been going since coming out of the army. Once Lynne and I divorce, I may marry Marian.'

By his demeanour he appeared to be a bit more settled. Dave perceived, maybe it was all for the good.

'What about you yourself mate? Mike asked, 'What's new?' He then asked, 'What happened with your ex, Jennifer, is everything ok with her now? Lynne tells me you have a new girlfriend, are you still courting her?'

'Yes, I am, her name's Kay and I'm still with her, in fact we are getting married in the autumn. As for Jennifer she got married last year, and now lives out in Australia. And before you ask, I haven't heard how she is getting on.'

They talked over old times for a while then Mike said, 'I must get on my way mate.'

As they shook hands again Dave said, 'Next time let me know when you're up this way again, and we can go out for a drink.' Dave gave him his phone number.

Just before he turned to go away, Mike stopped. And with a quizzical look, said something that to this day, Dave's still not sure what to think of him, when he said, 'You know mate, the way Lynne and you got on, I always thought you might get together when she left to come home.'

Stuck for a reply Dave just smiled and said a little embarrassingly, 'I did stay in contact with her up until I meet Kay.

Mike smiled at him with a knowing grin, and as he walked away, he stopped and called back. 'Oh! Bye the way Lynne sends you her love and to tell you that she will always remember! Whatever she meant by that.' At that winked.

Dave replied confidently, 'When you see her again, tell her I understand. And also tell her that I have met the special girl, she said I would meet one day.'

He wanted to have him tell her a much more personal message, that he still thought fondly about her, but with life enfolding the way it was, he then thought, it would not be appropriate at that moment, and said, 'Pass on my love and best wishes for her future life.'

That day he watched another part of his past walk away out of his life, and felt he would never hear from him or Lynne again.

He pondered on what Lynne's message was, and knew when together they brought out something in each other, that they probably would never experience with anyone else, and it was that experience that made him the man he is today, for that, Dave thought, *I will be forever grateful to her, and there will be a part of me that will love her always for those wonderful times they had together.* He also fervently hoped life will be kind to her and that she and her kids would at find lasting happiness.

Dave walked back into the garage that day, happy with the knowledge that he had met Mike again, and that there was no acrimony between them, and it had been good to hear that they both had at last found what they were searching for.

It was in that moment, he realised that the love he has with Kay transcends all the experiences he has had in the past, and has taken him to a new level of understanding how he feels today. Piece by piece his life had been taken apart during his national service out in Malaya, and now over the past two years his life has been assimilated stronger than ever. The final part will be in the next few weeks as Kay and he prepare to give their vows in marriage. And this time, he knew that they would hold.

Chapter 81

I Come Full Circle

With the preparations all complete, their big day arrived. Standing there in front of the altar, his brother as best man by his side, he waited impatiently for his bride to walk down the aisle to become his wife. Deep in thought, time stood still in that moment, and his mind travelled back to the day fate had brought them together, and he realized, life was like a maze. You drift along feeling that you are never going to find your way out, until one day you meet that one special person who opens the gate, that you have been searching for.

He was thinking of all the joy Kay has brought him, and of their future together, when at that moment, the music started to play the wedding march, the hairs on the back of his head stood up. He glanced over his shoulder and saw a vision once more walk down the aisle, but this time, all the way down to his side. When she arrived and stood beside him, they looked at each other and their smiles said it all. This was their day, this was their time, and this was the reason they were here on this earth.

He held those thoughts while sitting in the garden that day the letter arrived, and as the pain he felt at the news of

Lynne's death passed, he held onto those thought's for a little while longer, and still holding onto Victoria's letter, he felt another chapter of his life pass into history. He was happy that for a brief time, he was able to share some happy times with Lynne, and that she treasured them. He also remembered the help she gave him at a time when he was at his lowest, when events had overwhelmed him. For that he would always be forever in her debt.

Off the women who have passed through his life he now realises, there is only one person in this world who completely loves him, as much as his Mum and Dad did, was his dearest Kay, even before they had met face to face that Sunday morning, all those years ago,.

A smile grew within him when he cast his mind back to when he and Kay knelt in front of the alter on their wedding day sixty years ago. After having been pronounced husband and wife, he looked at Kay and saw the radiance of love and happiness in her eyes. It was then that he remembered what his dad had said to him all those years ago.

'Son! Whatever is meant for you, will never go by you.'

He looked over at his wife Kay, as she tended the flowers in their garden and smiled, someday I may tell my story.

Not the end, only the beginning.